The Body in Society
Second Edition

The Body in Society

An Introduction

Second Edition

Alexandra Howson

polity

First edition published in 2004 by Polity Press
This edition first published in 2013 by Polity Press

Polity Press
65 Bridge Street
Cambridge CB2 1UR, UK

Polity Press
350 Main Street
Malden, MA 02148, USA

ISBN-13: 978-0-7456-5440-9
ISBN-13: 978-0-7456-5441-6(pb)

A catalogue record for this book is available from the British Library.

Typeset in 10.5 on 12 pt Plantin
by Servis Filmsetting Ltd, Stockport, Cheshire
Printed and bound in Great Britain by the MPG Books Group

The publisher has used its best endeavours to ensure that the URLs for
external websites referred to in this book are correct and active at the time of
going to press. However, the publisher has no responsibility for the websites
and can make no guarantee that a site will remain live or that the content is or
will remain appropriate.

Every effort has been made to trace all copyright holders, but if any have been
inadvertently overlooked the publisher will be pleased to include any necessary
credits in any subsequent reprint or edition.

For further information on Polity, visit our website: www.politybooks.com

Contents

Acknowledgements

The preparation of the first edition benefited enormously from the support of the late Mike Hepworth, as it did from students at the Universities of Edinburgh, Aberdeen and Abertay Dundee. In preparing the second edition, I am still indebted to Val Sheach Leith, who was generous with ideas in chapter 6, and to Julie Brownlie, whose work and example inspired me to keep moving forward. Thanks go to Holly Howson-Watt for bibliographic support and to Phoebe Kho of Point Forward for talking with me about her research on so-called intimate hygiene products. The fruits of our conversation are referred to in chapter 3. I am especially indebted to Claire Thain, who researched and retrieved sources for me. Her meticulous work made writing much easier.

It goes without saying that any deficiencies are my responsibility and that completing a book, even a second edition, requires a great deal of domestic and emotional support. Thank you, Richard, Holly and Jodie.

Introduction

Just for a moment, think about your own body. Where do you start? With your appearance (the spot that has materialized from nowhere, the bad hair day)? With its shape and size (the diet you keep meaning to go on)? With its aches, pains and reminders of daily physical struggles? How do you feel about your own body? Are there parts you would like to change? Do you feel the need to keep in shape, or try to be healthy? Are you more aware of your body at some times rather than others, such as when you trip over your feet in a crowded room, belch unexpectedly or break wind in company? How do you feel when you become aware of your body in these circumstances?

Now think about the bodies of other people. What seems most obvious to you is probably the appearance of others – how people look – but think a little harder and soon you will find that the bodies of other people become conspicuous in other ways – smell, size and shape, personal habits. Many of us expect people to smell 'fresh' or be devoid of odour, to refrain from touching us until we feel we know them sufficiently well and to demonstrate 'good manners' in public places. When you stop to think about it, it isn't hard to become conscious of the human body, yet in much of our daily life we tend to take our own bodies and the bodies of others for granted. The intention of this book is to examine those taken-for-granted aspects of the human body and what they reveal about the social organization of everyday life.

> The intention of this book is to examine taken-for-granted aspects of the human body and what they reveal about the social organization of everyday life.

Sociology and the body

It may not seem obvious why a sociologist should be interested in the human body. After all, sociology is a social science that is interested in rational actors (Weber), collective conscience (Durkheim) and social structure (Marx). Yet sociological analysis shows how important the human body is to the establishment and maintenance of social life. First, people experience and engage with the social world and with other people from an embodied perspective. Put another way, this means that the physical characteristics of our own bodies, our mannerisms, shape, size, habits and movements, contribute to and shape our perceptions and interactions with others in everyday life. Indeed, we see the world and operate within it from the particular vantage-point of our own body, and so **embodiment*** is a critical component of social interaction. Second, in order to be competent social actors, we need to be able to conduct ourselves in particular, socially pre-scribed ways. To secure the smooth flow of social interaction we have to pay particular attention to **bodily conduct**. In Western contexts such conduct typically refers to controlling the natural rhythms and urges of our bodies. When we are unable to do so, **bodily betrayals**, such as breaking wind, belching or expressing emotion inappro-priately, break the flow of interaction, and we need to work hard to recover that flow and repair the damage to interaction.

Third, to present ourselves as competent social actors, we all engage in **body work**, activities and practices associated with grooming and hygiene, as well as forms of body maintenance such as exercise and dietary management. These activities help to maintain our bodies (according to scientific standards of nutrition, growth, development and hygiene) and, because of their aesthetic component, help us to present ourselves as particular kinds of people. Hence our partici-pation in certain kinds of body work helps us to create an identity for ourselves. But such work is also morally charged. For instance, research suggests that physical appearance, body shape and size influence entry to all kinds of occupations. Put another way, labour markets favour particular kinds of bodies and, by implication, people. Finally, the rules of bodily conduct and norms of appearance that accompany everyday life are socially shaped, have changed over time and differ from culture to culture.

---

* Items in bold appear in the glossary.

Issues, perspectives and conceptual frameworks

Although the sociology of the body is now a widely taught sub-field within the discipline, and there are many texts exclusively focused on the body in society and culture, this status is relatively recent. In the 1980s, there were very few sociological texts that focused exclusively on the human body. Yet it is not as though sociology was not interested in the human body. After all, medical sociology focused on health, illness and disease, all of which are located within and affect human bodies, and feminist sociology emphasized practices and processes that oppressed women by directly constraining or controlling aspects of embodiment (physical violence, for instance). Yet it was not the body that was the focus of this work, rather medical expertise or gender relations. So, this introduction sets out to do three things. First, it explains the relative neglect of the body in sociology (and other social science disciplines); second, it develops some of the reasons for this disregard; and third, the chapter provides a brief outline of the field of the body in sociology, including key issues, established perspectives and emerging conceptual frameworks.

The Cartesian body

Though sociology is supposed to be a discipline concerned with living, breathing human beings, at first glance sociological writing has rarely acknowledged the significance of the human body in explanations of the emergence of modernity (Freund 1988). Like other disciplines emerging in the nineteenth century, the historical and conceptual development of sociology has in large part been premised on the **Cartesian** legacy, which claims an ontological distinction between mind and body and privileges the former over the latter (Turner 1984). René Descartes developed what is regarded as a classic statement concerning the relationship between mind and body – a statement that reflected a widening belief – that personhood must be seen as distinct from the human body (see Hollis 1997 for an excellent and accessible philosophical introduction to Descartes). Descartes argued that, if we stop and reflect on ourselves, we cannot reduce our sense of who we are (or identity) to our bodies or to parts of our bodies. If our bodies were to be altered or damaged in some way, our sense of who we are would not disappear. This understanding of the self has three aspects. First, mind and body are considered distinct from each other; second, body is subordinate to mind, where the former resembles a machine or an object in which the self is located;

and third, the mind is considered the source of thought through which the self is produced via cognitive rationalization and through which we view the world as external to us. In a Cartesian view of the world, though vision is privileged as the sense that connects the self to the physical and material environment in which the self is located, bodily sensation is not seen to influence or contaminate perception.

> In a Cartesian view of the world, though vision is privileged as the sense that connects the self to the physical and material environment in which the self is located, bodily sensation is not seen to influence or contaminate perception.

This philosophical dualism between mind and body, between an isolated, rational self and a world external to that self, forms the basis of Western epistemology and has informed the development of scientific rationality. This is especially marked in the example of the emergence and consolidation of modern medicine, which succeeded in claiming the human body as an object amenable to scientific observation and manipulation. Similarly, the autonomy of sociology was initially dependent on this distinction between mind and body, as it sought to distance itself intellectually from psychology and anthropology (Freund 1988). Indeed, the subject of sociology, the rational actor, was disembodied in the sense that rational thought was located in a mind already disconnected from the body (Morgan 1993; Burkitt 1999). This meant that the body was neither perceived as a source of personal knowledge or understanding, nor deemed relevant to the production of sociological knowledge. Finally, the body's association with nature and, concomitantly, with femininity (Sydie 1987) further distanced it from sociological analysis.

However, this Cartesian perspective, while subject to criticism in most of the perspectives included in this book, is difficult to renounce completely. A rich and diverse Asian literature on the sociology of the body calls attention to the persistent ethnocentrism of Western body sociology, that continues to be informed by the legacy of Cartesian dualism (Ozawa de-Silva 2002). In this way, while sociologists are critical of Cartesian dualism, nonetheless, Cartesianism continues to exist as a conceptual grid and produces 'blind spots' that present some serious limitations as a framework for a sociological analysis of the body (Ozawa de-Silva 2002). A particular blind spot is race, ethnicity and the 'whiteness' that informs much theory and many early studies on the body. Although there are examples of ways in which the body is racialized in this book, clearly there is a need for collating material for an undergraduate audience that focuses specifically on the body, race and identity.

Emerging body consciousness

Although not an explicit, tangible presence, the body ghosts through classical sociological texts. We depend on our bodies to engage in productive and reproductive work labour (Marx); the body is central to religious ritual and social classification (Durkheim) and is regulated and rationalized in modern life (Weber). In the last quarter of the twentieth century, the body acquired greater significance within sociology. In 1990 Arthur Frank noted that bodies are 'in' and provided a valuable overview of the body in sociology. There are now numerous new journals and conferences dedicated to sociological study of the body, and there has been a rapid growth in books that provide sociological treatments of the body in one way or another. As many commentators have noted (Turner 1984; Shilling 1993; Williams and Bendelow 1998), there are many factors, external and internal to sociology, that help to explain this interest. Sociology is a discipline that is uniquely responsive to social change, and the body has become more interesting to sociologists because of social developments that force us to think about it.

First, demographic changes (such as increased life expectancy) mean that a greater proportion of the population live for a longer period of time; however, they do so in circumstances of poorer health and in the likelihood of disability. This kind of change raises important questions about the life course and how it is changing, and about how Western societies ought to respond to and manage the ageing body. It also raises questions about the care and management of ageing bodies, as physical competencies are potentially transformed over the life course and bodily betrayals increase. However, processes and experiences of ageing also raise questions about the significance of the physical appearance and capacities of the body for maintaining self and social identity.

Second, late modern – or postmodern – societies are characterized by their consciousness of and anxieties about the human body. Because bodily conduct has become an important way of socially classifying and categorizing people in Western societies, we spend a lot of time, effort and money on maintaining our bodies. The presentation of the body is an important part of social life, and we may often feel that we can exert control over our own bodies in ways that we cannot over other aspects of life. For instance, we might not be able to control our personal relationships but we can control how and what we eat. We might not be able to influence global politics but we can exercise hard and show our friends how disciplined we are. And we can influence the response of others to us by manipulating how we look, perhaps even by modifying our features to conform to current ideals of beauty or exaggerating our features to sharpen the contrast between our own looks and those of fashion norms.

The body, technology and social change

Third, the expansion and availability of new technologies such as gene therapy or xenotransplantation mean that we can manipulate bodies in unprecedented ways, but these technologies also challenge key assumptions about the human body, such as what is possible and ethically justified in terms of intervention. We can manipulate genes (this causes considerable anxiety); we can replace body parts (with parts from other humans or even animals); we can reshape our faces, tighten skin, build limbs. We live longer and there are more of us on the planet. These new developments influence the meanings people attach to their own and others' bodies. What will it mean if I have someone else's heart? Will I still be the same person? If I have plastic surgery, am I merely pandering to the beauty myth or taking control of my own life? Is it demeaning or empowering? The reactions of some people in terms of disgust or disbelief to practices such as xenotransplantation (animal organs in humans) suggest that we have developed boundaries between humans and animal bodies – but what are these boundaries and where do they come from? What purpose do they serve? Hence technological developments, such as organ transplantation and cosmetic surgery, offer the potential to transform and redefine the physical body, and in doing so raise questions about the boundaries between nature and culture.

Fourth, the publication in English of the work of the French philosopher-historian Michel Foucault has directly influenced a largely Anglo-American audience and made the body more amenable to sociological analysis. His analysis of the relation between body and society has shown that we can take nothing for granted about the body, even though we live in ways that take it for granted. Finally, the women's movement and feminist thought has made visible the significance of the body in the oppression of women. Feminists have drawn attention to the ways in which the female body is objectified through medical, legal and representational practices. In some cases, the objectification of the female body has led to unnecessary surgical treatment or supported its commercial use (such as in pornography).

The body in postmodernity

However, sociological interest in the human body is also in part a reflection of the development of the discipline itself and its openness to influence from a range of perspectives. Intellectual currents associated with cultural anthropology, social psychology, psychoanalysis, continental philosophy and contemporary feminist theory influence many practitioners of sociology. These twin forces of responsiveness to social change and sensitivity to intellectual change mean that the body has become what Frank refers to as a 'reference point in a world of flux and the epitome of that same flux' (Frank 1991: 40). To put it another way, in the context of contrasting forces between modernity and postmodernity, the body provides a physical and conceptual space in which the recurring issues and tensions of sociology are revisited and reworked. On the one hand, the impulses of modernity to control and contain have reduced the body to a knowable, anatomical object (Morgan and Scott 1993), which is amenable to sociological scrutiny in terms of how society acts upon the body. On the other, the impulses of postmodernity render the body unstable and establish an explicit challenge to the dualisms inherent in Cartesian thinking. This tension between the body as a known and knowable material object and the body as discursively constituted has led some commentators to question 'what the body is' (see Shilling 1993). Is it a particular kind of object that can be known and understood or a socially constructed entity, the meaning of which changes over historical and biographical time and which is, therefore, less fixed and stable?

This uncertainty about 'what the body is' is reflected in current sociological approaches to the body. On a very broad level, these diverge between naturalistic and socially constructed approaches. The former explores how social and political contexts impinge on the body, retains an ontological distinction between mind and body and tacitly accepts the body as a primarily biological entity. The latter explores how the body itself (shape, size, movement, action and experience) is socially constructed. In practice, the latter approach often means that the focus of study is on how ideas about the body are socially constructed, and, as we shall see, there is much evidence that ideas about the human body and its significance change over time and vary from culture to culture.

The taken-for-granted body

Howson and Inglis (2001) identify many broad approaches in the conceptual development of the body in sociology and attempt to 'bring the body in' to the sociological frame. The process of 'bringing sociology in' has worked productively at the margins of other disciplines, such as anthropology, and has developed a range of perspectives such as **phenomenology**. Sociological studies of the body have centred on the social and cultural meanings conferred on the body, the body's symbolic relation to the social world and the body as a 'lived' entity. Social constructionism and symbolic interactionism highlight the importance of the human body for social expression and interaction, for making and remaking social life. Such approaches concentrate on the surfaces of the body as an interface between the physical body and the social world and often focus on body images. These approaches, which examine the social conditions in which ideas about the body develop, typically do not question the organic basis of the body and tend to take the biomedical model of the body for granted.

This model emerged in the eighteenth century and monopolizes Western understandings of the body (Illich 1986). The emergence and consolidation of modern medicine as a scientifically based occupation was enabled via a range of practices that contributed to the mapping, measurement and reduction of the human body to object status. This model of the human body is characterized by the following (Freund and McGuire 1999). The **mind–body dualism** associated with a Cartesian view of the world detaches mind from body and views the latter as an object which can be manipulated, handled and treated in various ways in isolation from the self. The biomedical model has increasingly assumed that illness is largely a consequence of biological disorder. This **physical reductionism** locates disease within individual bodies often to the exclusion of the wider environment and social contexts in which disease develops. The development of germ theory in the nineteenth century further contributed to the biomedical belief that disease was caused by a specific agent. Though modern medical practice is based on more complex and sophisticated theories of disease causation, nonetheless the development of the empirical method to isolate specific diseases underpins the modern Western reliance on and support for 'magic bullets' such as antibiotics and other pharmaceuticals. Related to the mind–body dualism associated with the biomedical model of the human body is the assumption of its machine-like status. In contrast to the metaphors in which the body is understood in non-Western cultures, mechanistic metaphors pepper Western understandings of the body (Scheper-Hughes and Lock 1987), such as 'running like clockwork' or 'feeling run down'. As many commentators observe, the machine metaphor assumes not only that the body can be repaired and its 'parts' replaced as in any other machine, but also that it can be standardized and regulated through diet, hygiene and exercise regimes.

The relational body

In contrast to the biomedical model, anthropological traditions have more explicitly questioned the perception of the human body as a physiological and anatomical object and accentuate embodiment as a *relation* between the physical body and the social and moral world. In particular, the scholarship of Norbert Elias emphasizes that the body needs to be approached not only as a biological entity but also as an organism that changes across both historical and biographical time in response to social and cultural processes. In doing so, these examples of scholarship challenge the specialist boundaries that divide the human body and social life into discrete and compartmentalized areas for examination and study. Furthermore, recent developments within sociology emphasize the instability of the body as a biological and anatomical phenomenon and question the facticity of the body itself. Post-structuralist approaches have been more influential in the arts and humanities than within the social sciences, though even this broad division of interests is under scrutiny. Such approaches highlight the importance of discourses that constitute the social world. The human body is not regarded as a natural and thus immutable entity that exists outside the language in which it is described or the historical context in which it resides (Benoist and Catheras 1993). Post-structuralist thinking poses the possibility of the body as a text and invites us to consider decoding its many inscriptions (Grosz 1994). The human body in this view or the body we know and understand collectively as a universal category is a product of particular historical contexts and social relations (Laqueur 1990). The human body has also been identified as the focus of rationalization processes, regulatory strategies and technologies of control. The work of Michel Foucault in particular has opened up new means of exploring the ways particular discourses have actively produced bodies and ideas about bodies. The development of new environments and experiences, such as cyberculture, imaging technologies and the evolution of the posthuman body, similarly challenges our thinking about what

the body is and the significance of 'boundedness' for the development and experience of self and others.

The uncertain body

In the last two decades, sociological approaches to the body have
multiplied and fragmented, and overviews of the body identify
many different kinds of body. These include the 'discursive' body,
the 'material' body, the 'medicalized' body and the 'talking' body
(Turner 1984, 1992); the 'individual/social' body, the 'physical'
body, the 'communicative' body, the 'consumer' body and the
'medical' body (O'Neill 1985); the 'sexual' body, the 'disciplined'
body, the 'somatic' body and the 'corporeal' body (Frank 1990); the
'uncertain' body, the 'naturalistic' body and the 'socially constructed'
body (Shilling 1993); and the 'commodified' body and the 'regulated'
body (Lupton 1994). Such an elaborate list of bodies underscores
Shilling's observation about the 'uncertainty that sociologists have in
identifying what the substance of the body is' (1993: 39). Moreover,
the list points to a recurring tension within the sociology of the body
over the existence of the body as an entity independent of processes
of social constitution, or whether bodies exist only in relation to the
practices and processes that produce them.

This distinction is posed as one between foundationalism and anti-
foundationalism (Nettleton 1992) and refers to tensions between
the real or apparent body. The tension itself is a product of historical and social change. In late modernity, it is difficult to define the
body (Shilling 1993) such that its 'beingness' disappears. Though
the human body has been produced as a universal category, as 'the'
body, this is now under question. In contrast, an embodied sociology
begins from a sensitivity to the relation between 'being' and 'having'
a body, in which embodiment not only serves as a bridge between
action and biology but also alerts us to 'the practices that concep-
tualise it, represent it and respond to it' (Crimp 1988; also cited in
Frank 1990: 135). Of particular importance to the emerging field of
the sociology of the body is feminism as both a social movement and
an academic field. Indeed, feminism has forced body politics onto
sociological and other disciplinary agendas. The raising of body consciousness and the reclamation of the body as central to self and identity mark a historical turn in the relationship of sociology to the body.

Sociological approaches to the body also seek to rediscover the
body in the work of classical theorists or, as Williams and Bendelow
(1998: 9) put it, to re-read the classics in a 'new, more corporeal

light'. This approach has some parallels with the diffusion of gender and the retrieval of 'herstory' from the vaults of the founding fathers (for instance, see Sydie 1987 or Bologh 1990). Moreover, it challenges the view that sociology has 'neglected' the body. A key claim associated with this approach is that corporeal concerns underlie the writings of the 'founding fathers' and, moreover, lie at the heart of traditional sociological concerns (Williams and Bendelow 1998; Morgan and Scott 1993). Goffman, for instance, is identified by many scholars as a key proponent of the corporeality of social interaction and order, and of the fundamental importance of the body in establishing society (e.g., Crossley 1995a).

Binary oppositions

Of particular significance to sociological approaches to the human body are such binary oppositions as mind/body, subject/object, self/other, and so on. Hence sociologists may pull together a range of perspectives in order to address conceptual dualisms that place limits on establishing adequate accounts of the relationship between not only body and society, but body and self. This framework requires an analytic focus on 'lived experience' as a contrast to what some view as abstract and overly theoretical accounts of the body, and defines the body as a site of knowledge and experience, action and intention. Moreover, this framework redirects sociological attention from the body as a reified object (of processes, forces, theory) towards the body as lived (Nettleton and Watson 1998; Williams and Bendelow 1998). This shift is described as an '*experientially* grounded view of human embodiment as the existential basis of our being-in-the-world' (Williams and Bendelow 1998: 8, emphasis in original). Among the concepts deployed in this framework are corporeality, physicality and materiality to emphasize the body as a physical place/location from and through which the person knows and speaks.

This move is one shared by a range of sociologists, including many whose work focuses on issues associated with health, illness and disease (for a range of examples, see the collection in Nettleton and Watson 1998). Williams and Bendelow's text *The Lived Body* (1998) is typical of the work identified here. It belongs to a strand of thought which seeks to challenge the dichotomous relationship that pertains between the body as a universal (material) object and the body as a variable system of, and resource for, representation. Part of their concern is to address the way in which sociological approaches to the body appear to privilege either representational/

discursive understandings or material/foundationalist understand-ings. They argue persuasively (as do Mellor and Shilling 1997) that dualist understandings of the body must be placed in their social and historical context. Cartesian concepts are neither universal nor per-sistent across time. Consequently, dualisms that are part of the con-temporary period represent an inheritance from historically specific conditions in which the body became a discrete object of the mind. This observation leads several authors to argue that the binary think-ing associated with Cartesian dualism can be transcended.

Such an approach is shared by other disciplines. In social psy-chology, for instance, Radley (1995) reformulates key themes and concepts in relation to the human body; similarly, Csordas (1994) provides extensive argument concerning the implications of reorient-ing anthropology towards embodiment as a key concept. Although this type of move is explicitly concerned with, and privileges, experi-ence, overall its concern is to develop a framework in which it might be possible to specify and delineate relations between the ways in which the human body is socially shaped in culturally and historically specific terms; the body as a site of knowledge, consciousness and experience; and the body as a condition and constituent of intention and action. In social geography too, the body has been rethought as a specific space from and through which we establish ourselves as persons or subjects (Rose 1993). The move is therefore ambitious in the way in which it seeks to accommodate an intentional actor/agent, with an emotional, sentient body, in turn shaped by social structures and made visible through the reflexivity of the embodied practitioner.

Common themes

The field of the body in sociology has grown rapidly in the last twenty years. It is no longer a topic of peripheral interest to sociologists but is now a major area of scholarship in social theory (Burkitt 1999), has its own dedicated journal (*Body & Society*), and provides the prin-cipal framework for addressing issues in health, gender, childhood, ethnicity and disability and many more substantive areas. While there is considerable variation in the methods one may adopt in order to approach the body sociologically, there are several features on which many sociologists agree. First, the body in sociology is more than a physical and material frame (Freund and McGuire 1999) and is largely understood as inseparable from culture and society. There may be several aspects of human embodiment that are taken for granted in everyday contemporary life, but these are the products of complex social and political processes and actions that are embedded within history and our social fabric, though they may be subject to change. Second, in modernity the body has increasingly become the target of political control, rationalization and discipline. States and agencies of the state (such as law, welfare and medicine) exert considerable control over the movement of populations in time and space (e.g., in hospitals, schools and prisons) and encourage individuals to discipline themselves in compliance with state objectives (such as improving the nation's health). Third, the body is not only a material object on which social and political processes operate, but also forms the basis of social experience and action. On the one hand, we attribute meaning to bodies (bodily states such as the production of tears are mediated and interpreted via social categories) and use the visual appearance of the body to mark and codify differences between people. We use the body as a physical symbol of our social worlds. For instance, the Statue of Liberty, gifted by the people of France to the people of the US in 1886, embodies the social values of liberty and freedom (Warner 2000). On the other hand, bodies create meaning by acting within and upon the physical and material environment in which they exist.

The body in this book

This book starts from the assumption that, in everyday life, many of us take our own bodies and the bodies of others for granted, yet the body is absolutely crucial to the way we engage with the world and the people around us. The body is lived, experienced, but is done so in ways which are profoundly influenced by social processes and shaped by particular social contexts. We do not simply have bodies that we do things with and to, but we *are* bodies, our sense of who we are is inseparable from our own body. Competent social interaction and the acquisition of personhood are dependent on becoming competent embodied beings. Through social practices the human body is endowed with varied forms of social significance, and it is this significance which sociology tries to address, by asking questions such as: In which circumstances and to what degree do individuals have control over their own bodies? What interest and control does the state have over the human body? How significant is the body to the development and performance of the self in everyday life? In what ways do images of the body influence people's experience of themselves and of others?

This book tries to answer some of these questions. Its principal aim is to introduce undergraduates to the social significance of the body in everyday life, and it will do this by beginning with situations or life events that readers are very familiar with (for instance, eating or sleeping). The starting point for the book is therefore empirical: 'real' issues and activities which individuals and institutions confront in everyday life rather than theoretical problems which are of interest mainly to professional sociologists. That is not to say, however, that theory is not a real problem – without it, we could not systematically make sense of the social world, and it is a critical resource in this process. Therefore, the book will also introduce readers to theoretical perspectives and conceptual frameworks that help us to understand the social significance of the human body.

In order to address the social significance of the body, the book has three objectives. First, it describes key issues concerning the body and defines what makes the body socially significant in the contemporary period, second, it outlines sociological perspectives and conceptual frameworks which address these issues and, third, it provides a sense of comparison between sociological and other social science approaches to the body. Throughout, use is made of case study material to provide the reader with examples of how to think sociologically about the body and how sociological knowledge about the human body has been generated.

The book is organized in the following way. Chapters 1 and 2 focus on the significance of the body in the development and presentation of self. Drawing largely on the perspective of social interactionism, these two chapters introduce material that focuses on felt identity, **somatic perception** and **performativity**. These chapters describe and explain how we rely upon habitual bodily conduct as the basis of communication and how we use the body as a resource for interaction with others. Such conduct occurs even though, as Mead put it, we are 'trained by society to keep our bodies out of our minds' (Mead 1949). Chapters 3–5 turn to social processes that construct the body in particular ways and encourage particular forms of bodily conduct. Hence, these three chapters deal with the civilizing process, the influence of consumer culture on bodily conduct and the regulation of the body. Themes discussed in these chapters include the construction, maintenance and significance of body boundaries and discourses such as healthism in contemporary conduct, as well as the role of the body in expressing responses to social change. The final chapter examines the vulnerability of the body and in particular the bearing of images on experiences of the changing body across the life course. Chapter 6 presents material that explores the social significance of the body in the context of childhood, ageing and death, and the significance of **intercorporeality** from birth to death.

Further Reading

For a selection of views on non-Western body concepts, try:

Kasulis, T. P., Ames, R. T. and Dissanayake, W. 1993. *Self as Body in Asian Theory and Practice*. New York: State University of New York Press.

For Descartes' discussion of mind–body dualism, see:

Descartes, R. 1980. Discourse 5. In *Discourses on Method*. Harmondsworth: Penguin.

A good discussion of mind–body dualism is:

Todes, S. 2001. The classic view of the way the human subject has his body and Descartes' rejection of it. *Body and World*. Cambridge, MA: MIT Press, pp. 10–22.

And on sociology and the body, see:

Shilling, C. (ed.) 2007. *Embodying Sociology: Retrospect, Progress and Prospects*. Oxford: Blackwell.

1
The Body in Everyday Life

Introduction: An embodied approach to self

Understanding the development and presentation of the **social self** is a central concern for the discipline of sociology, that is, 'those aspects of the personal life of each individual which have been created through social participation, which shape the way in which we come to experience the world and which contribute to a consciousness of being a member of society' (Lee and Newby 1989: 309). The purpose of this chapter is to outline the significance of the human body for developing a sense of self and presenting self in social interaction. The work of Erving Goffman is central here. First, the chapter examines the development of self and the importance of physical appearance and sensory experience in this development. Second, it looks at the presentation of self in everyday encounters and problems that arise in such encounters in circumstances where the body breaches social norms or expectations. Third, the chapter introduces a phenomenological perspective on embodiment.

Embodiment

There are two very broad approaches to the body in current sociology. The first views the body as a special kind of object that has increasingly become the target of control and discipline, and we will address this approach in chapters 3 and 5. The second approach views the body as a crucial dimension of self and, indeed, rejects the concept of the body as the focus of analysis in favour of **embodiment**. Embodiment can be used in various ways but generally places emphasis on the interaction between social and biological processes.

It is used to highlight the significance of the body as a lived aspect of human experience and as central rather than, as people in the West are encouraged to feel, peripheral to experience. The Cartesian legacy, outlined in the Introduction (see p. 3), reinforces the idea, in both everyday life and sociological analysis of the everyday, that there is a division between the body as felt and the body as an object. In contrast, the concept of embodiment alerts us to the relation between the objective, exterior and institutionalized body and the sensual, subjective, animated body (Turner 1992). In the German language, this division between the subjective and objective body is referred to in a more subtle way. *Körper* refers to the body as an object, while *Leib* refers to the felt, experienced body. Hence, the concept of embodiment signals the importance of approaching the body as a synthesis of *Körper* and *Leib*.

An embodied approach largely assumes that bodily integrity is central to self-identity and views self and society as constituted through the practical work done with and through the body in inter-action with others and with the physical environment. This notion of practical work is captured by two concepts: that of **agency** and that of **action**. First, agency is a concept derived from the **symbolic interactionist** framework associated with the Chicago School in the early part of the twentieth century, and addresses the body's role in responding to and creating social worlds by giving meaning to the intended and unintended actions of others. Second, action is developed within a **phenomenological** framework to highlight the emer-gence of self as embodied, constituted through the practical actions of the body upon the world in which it is situated. Though visual information and perception are important to both concepts for an understanding of how the self develops and enters into relations with others, the phenomenological view rejects any **ontological** separa-tion between mind and body, and therefore also places emphasis on other senses in the constitution and presentation of self.

> An embodied approach largely assumes that bodily integrity is central to self-identity and views self and society as constituted through the practical work done with and through the body in interaction with others and with the physical environment.

The body and presentation of self

Agency and embodiment

A key text concerning the self, central to many undergraduate sociology courses, is Erving Goffman's *The Presentation of Self in Everyday Life* (1959). This book is a detailed ethnography of life on a Scottish island in the 1950s and focuses on the various ways in which the self is presented and maintained in social encounters. Goffman's analysis of self-presentation draws on the work of two earlier colleagues at the University of Chicago, Charles Horton Cooley and George Herbert Mead. In 1902 Cooley published an influential book called *Human Nature and the Social Order* in which he proposed a theory for the development of self as a creative agent (Waters 1994). For Cooley, self-development emerges through interaction with others who reflect back to us an image of ourselves. Indeed, we learn who we are from others and our imagination of the way we appear to them. Correspondingly, the face and the eyes are an important focus for Cooley's analysis of the development of the self-idea. In contrast to cultures that conceal the face (especially the female face with the veil or burqa), in Western culture the face is generally visible and physically exposed. The visual appearance of the face is important to the presentation of self because, in Western culture, the face offers vital expressive information to others about who and what we are. People look into our faces, and our eyes in particular, to discover our identities, or who we 'really' are. Furthermore, four of the five sensory organs are located within the head and face, providing an interface between our bodies and the environment. However, as we saw in the Introduction, though all senses contribute to our perceptions and experiences of the physical environment (and as phenomenologists insist), in Western culture sight is the privileged sense.

The looking-glass self

Visual information and the appearance of the body is important for Cooley, and what he refers to as the self-idea develops in three key phases. The **self-idea** emerges, first, in relation to how we imagine we appear to others, second, in relation to how we imagine others judge our appearance, and, third, through the 'self-feeling' produced by our imagination of these judgements. To emphasize his point, Cooley uses the mirror as a metaphor for the development of the self as a **looking-glass self**. Mirrors provide us with visual access to the external appearance of our bodies, but the appearance of our

Plate 1   The 'looking-glass self': by about 18 months of age, humans can recognize themselves in the mirror
© Plus/iStockphoto

bodies is mediated through what we imagine others think of us. Mike Hepworth summarizes the process involved thus:

> Looking into a mirror is an interactive process through which connections are made between the personal subjective self of the viewer and the external world of other people. Because we have no direct access to the external reality of the body, even with the existence of aids such as mirrors and the wide range of technical apparatus available to us now (cameras, video cameras and the like), the act of human perception is always mediated symbolically by meaning. When we look into a mirror we are therefore engaged in an act of the imagination whereby the self is constructed symbolically as a portrait or picture. (Hepworth 2000: 46)

Somatic perception

The second body of work influencing Goffman's analysis of self-presentation belongs to George Herbert Mead, who in turn owes much of his approach to both Cooley and George Simmel. Mead, like Simmel, took the view that human beings are motivated by ideas and that society is constituted via the exchange of gestures and symbols. He placed considerable emphasis on the role of images and symbols in generating self through interaction with others. Though Mead acknowledged that 'we are trained by our society to keep our bodies out of our minds' (Mead 1949), he also argued that mind and body are ontologically interrelated, difficult to separate (Mead 1934), and constitutive of a **somatic perception** of the world through which we become objects to ourselves (Mead 1938). The self within a symbolic interactionist framework is not a discrete entity developed via rational thought alone, but is the product of an ongoing, never-ending social process characterized by constant interaction not only between self and others but also between different aspects of self.

For Mead, there is a two-part self that relates, first, to what he refers to as 'instinctual' and 'impulsive' habits ('I') or, to put this another way, to bodily expressions, feelings and conduct. The second aspect of self relates to the set of organized beliefs learned from the mirroring process described above, provided by social interaction between 'me' and members of the groups to which 'I' belong. This latter aspect of self is an objective self that expresses the gaze of others (society enters the self via 'me'), and which 'I' am capable of standing back from and reflecting upon. The relation between 'I' and 'me' is experienced as a form of dialogue, as a continual conversation (as in 'I said to myself') not only of words and thoughts, but also through the exchange of gestures and symbols. The self is developed gradually from infancy in interaction with others through play and games, through which we learn to develop an awareness of, anticipate and take on the roles of others. If you are around children of two-and-a-half or three years old you can probably observe what Mead is referring to here. Young children play games in which they physically mimic the actions of others before they have a complete grasp of language. They literally act out roles in their games. Moreover, for Mead, the self is not fixed in time but is constantly open to change and modification because its development occurs in interactions, which may change and become more complex across the life course, and because of the ever-present conversation between 'I' and 'me'. Therefore, in the work of both Cooley and Mead, the external appearance of the face and body are crucial to the development of self. Over time, through processes of interaction with others, we develop awareness of how they see us, which in turn influences how we see ourselves (Hepworth 2000).

Felt identity and the body

Goffman uses these ideas to develop his analysis of the presentation of self through social encounters. Goffman's work takes as read Simmel's (1908) observation that people are socially bound together through the various encounters, sensual experiences and glances that are exchanged in everyday life. Goffman is interested primarily in what makes it possible to enter into and participate in social encounters and in the presentation and maintenance of self in such encounters (Williams 1987). In *The Presentation of Self in Everyday Life*, Goffman develops a framework in which he casts social life as similar to theatre. His **dramaturgical model** emphasizes how individuals, social groups and institutions manage information in order to present a particular impression to those with whom they interact. His approach allows him to focus on the roles and performances given by selves, the settings in which they occur and the audiences such performances address. Performances are made possible by adopting roles, which operate as organized frameworks that allow people to make sense of encounters, experiences and the information with which they are presented in everyday life. People, or actors in Goffman's terms, seek to maximize or minimize visibility of information, depending on the impressions they seek to present, and the 'self-feeling' or 'self-image' people develop is related to both how effectively we present ourselves and whether encounters confirm or nullify our self-conception (Freund and McGuire 1999).

Self and identity are, thus, in Goffman's perspective, actively negotiated in an ongoing way via interactional work with others, and grounded in a tacit notion of self-feeling or 'felt identity' (Goffman 1968). The body is central to felt identity, a project to be worked on and with (Shilling 2003). Thus, for instance, when injuries occur to the body, self-identity can be profoundly threatened. As Collinson and Hockey (2007) argue, sporting injuries require direct renegotiation of identity by enacting similar physical rituals and engaging in body work (for the runners in Collinson and Hockey's study, this meant walking instead of running) that not only help to rehabilitate the body, but also go some way towards repairing disrupted identity.

Goffman himself did not necessarily begin his observations and analysis of the presentation of self in everyday life by observing and focusing on the body. Nonetheless, his approach has been developed to examine the presentation of self through both body work and face work (Shilling 1993; Williams and Bendelow 1998).

Methodological Note

Goffman's method depended on detailed observation and scrutiny of the rules and rituals that make encounters possible and sustain social order. In particular, he emphasized the significance of visual and expressive information in social encounters. Such information – facial expression, gestures, physical cues or mannerisms – is provided by and through the body. Other scholars have enlarged this perspective by arguing that successful passage through public life, or competence as a social actor, is dependent on following the rules of the interaction order and developing routine control over the body (Giddens 1991).

Body work

People make information available to others in both focused and unfocused interaction via the human body. For Goffman, the setting in which focused interaction takes place is deemed a front region. Here the body provides expressive equipment such as appearance, dress and demeanour in ways that help define the situation as being of a particular sort. For instance, in a teaching situation, the setting of focused interaction might be the classroom, arranged with the aid of physical props such as chairs strategically placed, technical equipment such as an overhead projector, and so on. Yet establishing and maintaining a definition of the situation as one focused on teaching also requires the performers to play the roles of students and teacher or lecturer. In order for these roles to be convincing, they need to be performed with corporeal integrity. That is, the presented self will be convincing only if accompanied by appropriate body conduct. For example, the role of attentive student might be performed by sitting up straight, making eye contact, laptop fired up, whereas the role of the bored student might be performed by avoiding eye contact and looking around the room or out of the window.

Although Goffman did not explicitly present his work as an analysis of the body in interaction, nonetheless some of his work draws explicit attention to shared patterns and ways of using the body in Western culture. In *Gender Advertisements* (1979), Goffman shows how bodily gestures that are part of images designed to sell products also convey meanings about relations between men and women. In this book, accompanied by many photographs that provide an inventory of gestures, he shows how particular gestures and positions imply relations of power between men and women. For instance, Goffman suggests that images in which women are seated and men are standing convey a sense of male authority. Add a man's hand to a woman's shoulder, and this image becomes one that is suggestive of sexual ownership. Goffman suggests that social interaction and interpretation of bodily gestures, expressions and positions depend on shared understandings of what they mean or on what he refers to as a shared vocabulary of **body idiom**.

Body idiom

Body idiom denotes the physical gestures, positions and conduct that are recognizable as conventional aspects of everyday life in Western culture, especially public life, such as handshakes, smiles, ways of walking, speech patterns, forms of dress, and so on (Goffman 1963). Anthropologists refer to body idiom as 'techniques of the body' (Mauss [1934] 1973) and have observed that body idiom varies cross-culturally. Because body idiom in self-presentation is shared, Goffman argues, it enables people to classify information about people's conduct (or, as psychologists might put it, body idiom is part of non-verbal communication or body language). In turn, knowledge and understanding of what bodily gestures mean influence how people present themselves in social encounters. However, Goffman uses the term body idiom not only to highlight bodily conduct as an important part of self-presentation, but also to draw attention to the way the body enters into and is used as a means of categorizing people and grading them according to their social position.

Pause and Reflect: What kinds of movements or practices would you identify as 'body techniques'? List as many as you can.

The body, norms and stigma

Virtual and actual social identity

Coherent self-presentation is sustained by a relation between what Goffman terms **virtual social identity** and **actual social identity**. The first concept expresses **normative** expectations of who and what a person ought to be in a given social context or encounter. For instance, we might reasonably expect a nurse to present her- or himself as courteous, friendly and matter-of-fact. The latter concept refers to the social, cultural and physical attributes actually possessed by a person. For instance, the nurse in our example may not be smiling (which might lead us to view her or him as unfriendly). Virtual and actual social identity exist in relation to each other. Goffman argues that we tend to see ourselves as others do and share an understanding of the expectations associated with a particular role or encounter. In Goffman's framework, our view of ourselves is, to a large extent, governed by a desire to present ourselves according to the expectations of the context in which we are situated. For Goffman, the physical appearance of the body is central to the relation between virtual and actual social identity, and his logic implies that the body I see in the mirror is mediated by what I imagine to be society's perception of me.

This suggests, first, that self-presentation (body position, conduct, gestures, and so on) is influenced by the social expectations associated with a given role or situation, that mark us as 'belonging' to a particular place or status and that serve to reinforce our 'proper place' in the world. In addition, our corporeal visibility is marked by biological criteria, such as **phenotype**, that separate people into distinct groups – as gendered, racialized or nationalized – in order to dominate or exploit (Inwood and Yarborough 2010; Grabham 2009). Second, the relation of physical appearance to virtual and actual social identity suggests that self-classification is developed from a shared vocabulary of body idiom and social perceptions about appropriate body conduct. The logic of this analysis is that the meanings attached to physical appearance and bodily performances become internalized by people as self-image, which exerts degrees of influence over their sense of self-worth and moral value. However, the emphasis on social perceptions and shared body idiom inevitably raises the question of how norms evolve.

Body Image and Discourses of Ethnicity

The relation between social perception, **body image** and shared body idiom is complex. Colin King (2004) traces academic work on black athletes produced by white writers that he later contrasts with work produced by black writers. He explores how sport and race have been interpreted in relation to the black body in order to develop a theoretical framework called 'racialized performance', which describes how black athletes feel pressure to perform to white masculine standards and values. King supports his claims with several case studies from the world of English soccer in which the voices of black players demonstrate the kinds of inclusion and exclusion they experience in relation to class, race, masculinity and sexuality as a result of their contact with white men (whether in the crowd, on the playing field or in the changing room). He argues there are consistent themes in 'white talk' sports academic literature that have 'pathologized' black sportsmen, and that stem from a 'biological obsession with the black male body'. Black sportsmen tend to be positioned in relation to their physical body, identified as having particular physical advantages, such as speed and strength, which are assumed to be derived from 'racial attributes'. King identifies the tensions and confusions that black players experience as they attempt to conform to, and be accepted by, the dominant white masculinity of the soccer world that constrains them, and argues that the implications of ignoring the socially constructed nature of the 'black male body' include reifying black men as culturally problematic.

Body Image and Self-Esteem

Self-presentation is linked to body image – how a person thinks and feels about her body, size and shape, as well as how others respond to and evaluate her body's appearance. Although the concept of body image is broad (and can be used to refer to size perception accuracy, appearance satisfaction, body satisfaction, appearance evaluation, appearance orientation, body concern, drive for thinness, body esteem, body schema and body percept), the overwhelming weight of research suggests that high self-esteem is linked to positive image (Grogan 2010). While connections between body image and self-esteem have been explored mostly in relation to young women, recent research also reveals that young men place great importance on their appearance and also report high levels of body dissatisfaction. In an Australian study in which 150 people completed a questionnaire about self-esteem, body dissatisfaction and other domains of life, although women expressed greater dissatisfaction with their bodies than men, men placed greater importance on their appearance than women, and also reported high levels of body dissatisfaction (Mellor et al. 2010). The authors suggest that because of the known association between body dissatisfaction and low self-esteem, and of the risk of developing body image disturbances and eating disorders, such findings imply that body image disturbances could be an issue for young Australian men.

Normative expectations

The emphasis Goffman (1968) places on the normative expectations attached to particular roles or social identities develops his observation that all societies make social distinctions between groups of people (social categorization) and establish ways of grading hierarchically. Concomitantly, all societies establish what is considered normal and natural for members of those categories. For instance, in contemporary Western contexts, scholars have argued that slenderness has emerged as a cultural norm (Bordo 1993) associated with the female body (and increasingly the male body), supported by the development of medically produced standards for normal weights. The premium placed on slenderness, underwritten by appeal to aesthetic and biomedical terms of reference, replaced an earlier post-World War II emphasis on a much curvier female figure (the 'hourglass' shape). Moreover, as chapter 4 explains, the social emphasis placed on slenderness reflects concerns not only about health but also about self-discipline and physical appearance (Lupton 1996). The existence of such a slenderness norm is difficult to ignore; we are all aware of it, though we may choose to avoid pursuing slenderness or fail to match its targets. Yet even though we ourselves may not embody the norm, we cannot avoid being aware of its existence. This knowledge and where we stand in relation to it contributes to the sense of being normal (that is, whether we conform to cultural norms) or deviant. Hence, the attributes that denote normality have the potential to exclude people from full social membership, either because they fail to match up to social norms or because they possess knowledge about themselves that prevents them from matching up to such norms.

Biophysical norms

But where do the attributes considered ordinary or normal for members of particular social categories come from and how do they develop? As chapter 4 outlines, consumer culture provides an array of stylized images that reproduce ideas about aesthetic normality. Similarly, though we may take for granted the norms associated with how bodies physically work and function, they are the product of specific social and historical circumstances and processes, in particular, the development of scientific medicine. The body as defined within the biomedical model is a relatively stable, predictable, objective entity. It is seen as a complex biochemical machine that can be fixed by medical intervention (Freund and McGuire 1999), and disease within this model is generally understood as being caused by a particular, identifiable agent (especially the germ). The body within this model is, in fact, self-evident (Seymour 1998).

The development of clinical medicine was dependent on access to and examination of the physical body, which increased from the eighteenth century as the number of hospitals expanded and provided a new space in which people were gathered and were available for examination and inspection (Turner 1987). As chapter 5 discusses in more detail, the opportunity to examine bodies provided medical practitioners with material that was interpreted, measured and assessed in ways that built up a basis for making comparisons between bodies (Nettleton 1992). Observations of and comparisons between bodies helped to establish biophysical averages and norms, such as developmental/age-linked height and weight (Armstrong 1995). We are probably all familiar with statements that draw attention to norms such as 'isn't she tall for her age?' or 'what a big boy he is'. When we make these kinds of statements, we measure what we see against an implicit assumption about the appropriate or normal height associated with a particular age; in doing so, we reinforce established biophysical norms.

Bodily betrayals

So far we have established that physical appearance is important because both the visual appearance of the body and the social values associated with and attached to appearance are incorporated into one's sense of self. Goffman's approach suggests that sustained social interaction is possible through knowledge of and adherence to social rules and rituals. As long as the self we perform and present corresponds to what is expected of us, we can expect a degree of predictability and stability in social encounters. Yet, we are not always able to control the rhythms and functions of the body. There are circumstances and events across the life course that jeopardize the dependability of our bodies and threaten the stability of an encounter. The body, via bodily betrayals, provides clues about what Goffman refers to as 'inconsistencies of character' and 'discontinuities of social interaction' (Williams and Bendelow 1998: 59), such as blushing, shaking, stuttering, dryness of mouth, and so on. Bodily betrayals such as belching, farting, dribbling and incontinence have the potential to undermine the integrity of social encounters by damaging self and social identity (Seymour 1998).

For instance, respondents in Seymour's study of men and women with degrees of paralysis highlighted the difficulties of dealing with bowel and urinary incontinence. Face-to-face interaction typically presented a relentless practical problem of managing the disruptive potential of unanticipated bowel or bladder 'leakage' in order to minimize embarrassment to self and others. These men and women reported vivid memories of 'shitting and urinating in front of people during bowel and bladder retraining' as memories of humiliation and mortification (Seymour 1998: 176). These betrayals may create a gap or discrepancy between virtual and actual social identity in ways that have the potential to stigmatize the individual. Such a discrepancy carries moral connotations for Goffman, since people may be reduced in the eyes of beholders to a social or physical attribute. The implications of such reductionism are that people may be stigmatized, that is, allocated a marginal **social status** and excluded from full social acceptance.

> Bodily betrayals such as belching, farting, dribbling and incontinence have the potential to undermine the integrity of social encounters by damaging self and social identity.

Stigma

What is stigma? The ancient Greeks used the term to refer to bodily signs, cut or burnt into the skin, designed to expose the bearer as a slave, criminal or social outcast. Its modern sense applies to a condition or attribute that symbolically marks the bearer as someone 'culturally unacceptable' or inferior (Williams 1987) in three main ways. First, bodily stigmas are 'blemishes' or 'deformities' that compromise appearance or function and may be associated with disease and decay, such as leprosy, the marks of Karposi's sarcoma or the visible loss of hair associated with chemotherapy. Second, stigmas of character refer to those aspects of someone's life that are considered socially unacceptable – having HIV/AIDS is increasingly addressed in the literature as a discrediting trait to which negative meanings are attached (Bogart et al. 2008). The final form of stigma is associated with membership of a social collective, such as race or tribe, and often signals exclusion from citizenship. A potent example of this final type of stigma concerns the way in which those consigned to the concentration camps of the Third Reich were tattooed with a series of numbers (Oetterman 1984).

All societies develop somatic norms that are considered stigmatizing, though there are no inherently stigmatizing attributes (Freund and McGuire 1999). Moreover, the norms that contribute to stigmatization are themselves subject to social and historical change (Susman 1993). Yet the key point to be taken from Goffman is that possession of certain socially constituted attributes has the potential to stigmatize because of the threat they pose to social interaction by exposing a gap between virtual and actual social identity. A discrepancy between virtual and actual identity is said to be present where there is evidence of a negatively valued attribute that signals a difference from what we expect and what actually exists or occurs. The difference that emerges has the potential to socially discredit someone and mark him or her as less than human.

Stigma and HIV

The perception and experience of stigma is complex. The HIV Stigma Scale is a measure that assesses perceived and experienced stigmatization directed towards people living with HIV/AIDS (PLWHA). Using Item Response Theory (IRT) methodologies, Rao et al.'s (2008) research examined HIV Stigma Scale responses from 224 Black and 317 White PLWHA to explore potential cross-cultural differences in stigmatization. They found that Black respondents were more likely to indicate greater stigmatization in contexts where others discriminated against them and White respondents were more likely to indicate they felt they had to keep their status a secret and held fears of interpersonal rejection. Thus, the experiences of stigmatization (and perceived stigmatization) of people living with HIV/AIDS differs in relation to ethnic/racial background. These differences could be interpreted as a consequence of cultural differences or as the result of differences in the ways participants interpreted items on the HIV Stigma Scale.

Discrepancies in biophysical normality

The likelihood of such a discrepancy between virtual and actual social identity arising is dependent on a number of factors. First, the potential for discrepancy is associated with the visibility of a stigma and the extent to which it can be concealed. For instance, it may be extremely difficult to conceal or minimize a facial birthmark or skin condition, and thus face-to-face interaction may be managed by both parties so as to avoid gazing directly at the mark or drawing attention to it. Second, the potential for discrepancy is associated with the 'known-aboutness', or the extent to which others are aware of a particular attribute. For instance, a person may stammer. If others know about this, they may take actions to avoid getting into conversation with the person who stammers. Similarly, the person who stammers may take actions to avoid having to talk at length (such as responding in monosyllables, nodding instead of saying yes, and so on) in order to conceal the stammer, if it is not common knowledge.

Third, the potential for a discrepancy arising is related to the degree of obtrusiveness of the stigma and the extent to which it impedes interaction. For instance, stammered speech may alter what people perceive to be the normal flow of conversation and reduce comprehension. Finally, the perception others have of the ability of the person with a stigmatizing attribute to function will have a bearing on whether discrepancy develops. For instance, obesity and overweight is associated with lack of self-control and laziness in Western culture, which equates fitness and leanness with discipline and moral value (Turner 1984). Therefore, because of the social conflation between body size, shape and moral worth, people who are fat may experience their obesity as a form of impairment that is stigmatized and constituted as a form of disablement (see also p. 33) (Kai-Cheong Chan and Gillick 2009).

Impression management

Goffman's logic implies that because all members of society are aware of what constitutes biophysical normality and how deviation from such norms is negatively valued, we all work hard to manage encounters in which there is the potential for a discrepancy between virtual and actual identity. Seymour's (1998) study of the experiences of men and women who had experienced bodily paralysis shows the difficulties entailed in self-presentation when the visible appearance of the body does not conform to expectations of biophysical normality. In such situations, interaction is full of tension and its outcomes are uncertain. This leads both parties to consider avoiding, rejecting or withdrawing from particular kinds of encounter. Tension is manifest in the extent to which people avoid eye contact (what Goffman refers to as 'careful disattention'), make guarded references to the stigma or avoid everyday words that suddenly become taboo. Hence, careful impression management of one's body, face and expressions is important in order to maintain the flow and integrity of social interaction and to avoid becoming discredited. However, as Kvigne and Kirkevold's study of 25 women who experienced stroke shows, impression management is not always easy or successful. They describe the 'profound, disturbing, and, in part, unintelligible changes' associated with the experience of stroke and the ways in which this condition forces people to deal with biological and social dys-appearance. A key struggle for the women in this study was to find ways to 're-own' or re-inhabit their bodies – bodies that often did not oblige (Kvigne and Kirkevold 2003).

Information management

In some cases, the difference between virtual and actual identity is not immediately apparent or known about prior to the encounter, yet has the potential to discredit the person. In such circumstances, information control is required to protect oneself from becoming discredited. For instance, though physical scars tell all kinds of biographical stories about our embodied past (Burnett and Holmes 2001), a person who has tried to harm themselves by cutting their wrists may try to conceal their scars by wearing long-sleeved clothes. In certain circumstances, such scars may not be amenable to camouflage. At such times, corporeal information may 'leak out' into an encounter and discredit the person. If this information is revealed, then the person needs to engage in face and body work to repair their status. Hence, it is necessary to make decisions about whether or not others need to know about certain attributes and to weigh up the costs that may be incurred by making certain kinds of disclosures that have the potential to discredit us. In these situations, we may experience the ever-present anxiety of '**passing**' as normal and live with the fear that the information we conceal from others may be at any moment disclosed (see also p. 82).

Challenging biophysical norms

The biophysical norms that are a fundamental part of the assumptions we make about the physical appearance of people were historically underpinned by assumptions about the physical requirements for economic productivity (Paterson and Hughes 2000). These economically derived notions of the biophysically normal body have influenced social distinctions between physical ability, impairment and disability. While **impairment** refers to some loss of physiological or anatomical capacity, the term **disability** registers the repercussions of impairment and the difficulties a person may have engaging with the physical and built environment. The term disability reflects not only the ways in which people with impairments are typically isolated and excluded from full social participation (Oliver 1996), but also that Western standards of disability are not universal. Whether impairment becomes a disability depends on the social and cultural contexts in which it occurs or is acquired. For instance, Freund and

McGuire (1999) draw attention to the example of inhabitants of Martha's Vineyard in the United States, a large proportion of whom were deaf in the 1940s. Sign language was known and used by both those who were deaf and those whose hearing was not impaired, and the former group was not viewed as separate from the community because it formed a significant part of the community. Impairments can be found in all societies, but whether the status of disability is conferred upon impairment depends on the responses and social arrangements of the communities in which they occur. Nonetheless, categorizing people on the basis of not only physical appearance but also physical function leads to social distinctions that may be stigmatizing in their consequences (Zola 1982, 1993).

Models of disability

Biomedical model

This fundamental distinction between impairment and disability has contributed to a critique of a **biomedical model of disability** and its reduction of disability to individualized, physical impairment (Paterson and Hughes 2000). A biomedical model of disability typically treats disability as bodily and personal 'tragedy' and assumes the dependency of those who experience impairment. Women with physical impairment are typically viewed within a medical model of disability as asexual, presumed to be heterosexual or unable to reproduce (Lonsdale 1990; Seymour 1998). Each form of categorization has the potential to exclude women with impairment from relationships and experiences that many without impairment take for granted. Such a model focuses on bodies that are damaged (Williams 1999) and perpetuates an understanding of people with impairment as a 'problem' for society (Morris 1993).

Social model

In contrast, a **social model of disability** has been central to an analysis of the extent to which physical and social environments are *dis-abling* rather than particular impairments themselves. Within this model, disabilities transpire when society fails to accommodate physical impairment or denotes such impairment as in need of 'special' arrangements (Nettleton 1995). The social model of disability operates with an expanded notion of impairment too, that includes, for instance, obesity, since people who are fat are increasingly subject to the socially constructed barriers of 'exclusion, blocked access and disability prejudice' (Kai-Cheong Chan and Gillick 2009). A social model of disability has developed from, and has been important to, the disability rights movement in the Anglophone world and its emphasis on the acquisition of citizenship entitlements. Though disability is not a homogeneous entity within a social model of disability, as Nettleton (1995) observes (and as Goffman outlines in *Stigma*), such categorization can be used in ways that have transformative potential. For instance, in twentieth-century American culture, the Disability Rights Movement has played a crucial role in giving voice to a diverse group of people who do not experience full citizenship. The Disability Rights Movement in the US has emphasized equality rather than 'special rights' yet also acknowledges the diversity of experiences of those associated with the movement.

Yet having a disability identity can also be a negative experience that denotes 'second-class citizenship'. Kai-Cheong Chan and Gillick (2009), writing about the experiences of fat people, note that for some of their respondents, the social model of disability underpinned the work that disabled people have done to politicize disability. Yet, they argue, this model 'establishes disabled people as the "other"' rather than serves as an inclusive model to assert the visibility of disabled people, including fat people who experience discrimination and exclusion as consequences of fatness. Indeed, as one of the participants of their study observed:

> If you begin to look at obesity [sic] as a disability, then you're joining a community that has very little voice. . . . I'm saying if you allow yourself to be called 'disabled' just because you're overweight, the stigma is the hardest part to overcome because you become labeled, you know, that stigma. (Kai-Cheong Chan and Gillick 2009: 242)

Furthermore, disability can mask or silence other forms of identity. For instance, Dossa (2009) casts light on what it is like to have a racialized body in a disabling world. Drawing on the experiences of refugee Muslim women with disabilities who migrate to Canada, a country with a supposedly open immigration policy, Dossa notes that:

> Differences such as gender, race, and social class among people who have disabilities are subsumed under the master category of disability; hence, women and racialized women who have disabilities do not appear as categories, let alone subjects. (p. 18)

In practice, this means that Muslim women who are disabled experienced double discrimination. Because they have been categorized in some way as disabled, they cannot meet the labour skills criteria of the Canadian immigration system; but because they are also 'racialized bodies', they are invisible in many areas of life such as social services, health care, academia and even in their daily interaction with society (Dossa 2009).

Disability as discourse

Thus, though social theories of disability have contributed to the political visibility of people with impairment, they may conceal the various ways in which such people are disabled by imagery and prejudice (Shakespeare 1994). The work of Michel Foucault (dealt with in more depth in chapter 5) has been pivotal in providing ways of challenging claims about the intransigence of biophysical norms. For Foucault, the human body cannot be defined as a universally understood and experienced entity but is a 'malleable phenomenon' that is not only defined through discourses and ideas about *normality*, but is also susceptible to redefinition in relation to modes of bodily being (Blaikie et al. 2003). For Foucault, discourses (or discursive regimes) actively shape and influence how the body is defined and experienced in any given epoch. Discourses, or specialist knowledges such as biomedicine, establish definitions of the body through the systematic classification of distinctions and differences between bodies. Through such processes, bodies are labelled as normal or deviant (for instance, healthy/unhealthy, abled/disabled) and social hierarchies are created in ways that make clear that not all bodies are considered equal (Blaikie et al. 2003).

This emphasis on discourse has been welcomed by scholars who have used post-structuralist approaches not only to confront the ways in which bodies are measured and defined against socially constructed and culturally specific standards of normality, but also to examine the ways in which the body is rendered invisible in approaches that emphasize physical and social environments over bodily experiences and the active constitution of the body through social interactions and exchanges. For instance, some scholars who adopt this kind of perspective argue that 'disability' can be understood only in relation to ideas about what it means to be 'able-bodied' (or adhere to biomedically defined biophysical norms). Both social perceptions and visual images have the potential to disable those who are the subjects of imagery (Shakespeare 1994) in ways that accentuate the 'otherness' through which disability is defined. This approach helps to conceptualize disability as an ongoing process of negotiation and interaction with others, which emphasizes how personal experiences of disability and what it means to be designated 'disabled' may differ according to gender (Thomas 1999) and other sources of social identity. For instance, a qualitative study of men with violently acquired spinal cord injury (VASCI) in the United States explored how physical disability and injury-inflicted changes in body image called their masculinity into question. The eleven study participants were former gang members whose sense of masculinity was primarily derived from physical ability – the ability to walk with a swagger, stand tall, be sexually active and engage in fights. They negotiated their post-injury experience by working hard to diminish the impact of impairment and its violation of the social understandings of what it means to be a man in a gang environment (Ostrander 2008).

Constructing Disability

In nineteenth-century America, freak shows offered a paying public 'opportunities' to view a range of 'bodily otherness' made anomalous by virtue of their visual difference (Thomson 1996). In the contemporary period, makers of visual images such as photographers similarly use their craft to create images that accentuate the physical and mental impairment of their subjects in order to draw attention to their 'freakishness' and 'otherness' (see Hevey 1992 for a critique of the ethics concerned here). Advertising images produced by commercial advertising agencies for disability campaigns or for health promotion purposes may also draw on and create iconography that reinforces the stigma associated with physical impairment. Wang (1992) observes how accident and injury prevention campaigns in the US foster the notion that physical impairment through accident is intolerable, and similar criticisms have been made of campaigns to promote social awareness of multiple sclerosis in the UK (BBC/OU 1991).

The persistence of the binary

The very notion of disability is problematic for some scholars in the sense that its use perpetuates a binary opposition between normal and deviant (Fox 1993). Disability rights activists depend on the category of disability to highlight the exclusions of a (disparate) group of people and establish an appreciation of their needs in the interests of equality. However, post-structuralist approaches suggest that the processes of normalization and, by association, stigmatization that construct the binary opposites of abled/dis-abled may only be surmounted when society is able to consider all bodily abilities and visual appearances as part of a continuum (Annandale 1998).

At the very least, these kinds of examples and interventions highlight how central are physical norms and notions of bodily perfection to the visible appearance of the body and people's responses to it in everyday social interactions. However, an important implication of Goffman's analysis of the significance of the body in self-presentation is that the dividing line between normality and deviancy is not clear-cut, and stigmatization is a process that occurs wherever there are identity and somatic norms. The general claim Goffman makes is that all societies establish ways of making social categorizations that are based on the social construction of norms, many of which are connected to the physical appearance of the body. For Goffman, there are always deviations from norms that have to be managed, and, because social encounters vary in their focus and intention, we all participate, at some time or another, as both 'normals' and deviants.

The communicative body

The body in the contemporary period is a 'communicative body' (Falk 1994), in which emotions are the expression of relations between people, rather than expressions of inner feeling and turmoil (Burkitt 1999). Emotions are experienced in and through our bodies; they 'do not come from outside relations and impact upon them, they are constituted by the relations that compose social life' (1999: 115). Emotions involve sensations (which may change across time and be subject to cultural modification) that incorporate interaction between physiology, social practice and culture. Moreover, bodily techniques (Mauss [1934] 1973) such as the smile (Elias 1991) do not simply express emotion but literally embody the emotion. That is, the smile does not express emotion as an inner state of being but is a culturally specific technique that signals the potential for a particular kind of relationship, such as friendliness. These techniques are instilled as dispositions (for instance, children are instructed by parents, carers and teachers to smile in order to 'look' friendly). Indeed, the face in Western culture is central to building up a picture of who someone is, and it is through expressive features of the face that we gain access to a perception of who someone 'really' is.

That is, the smile does not express emotion as an inner state of being but is a culturally specific technique that signals the potential for a particular kind of relationship, such as friendliness.

Masks and masquerade

Elias suggests that the human face works, or has evolved, as a kind of 'signalling board' (1991: 121). Face work is important to role perfor- mance as the principal means through which we are able to manage the impressions we give. In both focused and unfocused encounters, we immediately make information available to others with our bodies and faces. The availability of this information is a contemporary form of cultural currency, to which self-help guides contribute and on which advertising images draw. Indeed, increasingly it seems, we are encouraged to become connoisseurs of masks, manipulating facial expressions and bodily gestures to create a certain kind of impression. As we shall see in chapter 3, the contemporary period demands vigi- lance of bodily conduct and highly refined skills in the interpretation of the conduct of others (Burkitt 1999).

Expertise in the manipulation of masks is perhaps more pertinent for women in Western culture, for whom explicit mask application is both permitted and encouraged (Tseelon 1995). Making up one's face can be seen as an explicit form of face work that enables the bearer to present a particular sort of self in different situations. For instance, some women will not appear in public – at work or in the street – without making up on the grounds that the application of cosmetics provides a mask behind which to hide and so present a more confident self. The idea of make-up as a kind of mask implies artifice and the existence of something or somebody more substan- tial beneath the surface appearance created by the mask, which can be revealed if taken away (Brook 1999). Therefore it alludes to the idea of masquerade, of performing in a particular way that requires deliberate manipulation.

Body and Face Work

Body and face work can refer to not only work performed on oneself but also work performed on others, or as Gimlin (2007) calls it, body labour. Body work or labour involves a range of appearance-related practices, and, as Kwan and Trautner (2009) argue, body work 'occurs within a social system that distributes rewards and sanctions based partially on appearance'. In Western societies, physical appearance is homogenized around fairly narrow stereotypes of male and female beauty that contribute to body dissatisfaction that is also experienced in racially and ethnically distinct ways. Furthermore, physical appearance that conforms to prevailing standards of beauty, if possessed or cultivated, can result in social and economic rewards, status and power. Hence, there is a significant amount of energy and work directed towards the cultivation and maintenance of beauty, such as applying make-up, removing body hair and pursuing the slender ideal.

Furthermore, such body labour is infused with – and reinforces – meanings about race and class meanings. A study of Korean immigrant women's performances of body labour in nail salons explored three different patterns of service provision that are shaped by racial and class inequalities between women (Kang 2003). Gendered forms of labour include high service body labour, expressive body labour and routinized body labour, and Asian women in particular have been positioned as productive and docile workers who are easily exploitable in an increasingly feminized and unprotected labour force. These forms of labour are significant because they reinforce wider structures of inequality and ideologies of difference between women, including those of class and race. Physical appearance and its role in securing access to status and power is further discussed in chapters 2 and 4.

Face work and sensations

The face can be seen as a kind of mask that reveals and conceals what we are thinking and feeling. Arlie Hochschild (1983) develops this idea in her research on emotions, from which, she argues, we are alienated through the commercialization of labour and which we are expected, and indeed required, to manage or control. Hochschild's approach to the analysis of emotions uses two broad frameworks. First, the dominant model in which emotions are defined, the organismic model, emphasizes that feelings are common to all and their expression is understood as a surface signal of physiological and bio-chemical changes in response to certain kinds of stimuli. Within this model, emotions are viewed as essentially biological responses that are universal and instinctive. Yet, the emotions we feel in everyday situations – love, joy, pain, sadness – are not necessarily expressed in a straightforward way.

In contrast, Hochschild observes that, indeed, while sensations occur within the body, they have to be acknowledged and interpreted in order to have meaning as feelings. For example, we may be aware of our hearts beating faster, or experience a sensation of having a 'knot' in our stomachs, but these sensations derive meaning from the social context and relations in which they arise. Moreover, the same sensation may be given different meanings, depending on social and cultural context. We are able to interpret the sensations we experience because of a shared cultural vocabulary of emotion, or repertoire of emotional language (Harré 1991), which acts as a guide, prompting us to label a sensation in a particular way and act it out appropriately. Hence, Hochschild draws explicitly on a symbolic interactionist approach and develops Goffman's insights on the presentation of self in everyday life to analyse the relation between the body, self and society. Emotions in this framework are analysed as emergent properties of interaction between the body, its environment and social relations. We depend on awareness of social and cultural context to recognize and label a sensation as a particular kind of feeling.

Second, Hochschild locates emotions – feelings and their expression – within a materialist framework that highlights how modern market relations shape human feelings and incorporate them into the service of capital. This is especially apparent in the example of service industries. Occupational restructuring and the expansion of the service sector have increased market demand for personal relations skills (Adkins 1995), particularly those oriented towards ensuring the physical and emotional comfort of clients. The demand for such skills is especially apparent in the example of flight attendants and, moreover, is associated with femininity. Therefore Hochschild's research was designed to examine how flight attendants are trained to deploy what are regarded as feminine feelings (and therefore natural).

Face work and emotional labour

The focus of Hochschild's study was on the content and context of airline provision and the work of flight attendants. Her fieldwork focused on the recruitment, training and supervision of flight attendants, though she also undertook a number of semi-structured interviews with a range of airline personnel, advertising agencies and supervisors and observed induction and training classes. She noticed the emphasis within the work of flight attendants on making people relax and the techniques they employed. In particular, Hochschild noted the face work they undertook and the significance of smiling. In order to 'look friendly' and, in doing so, put people at their ease, flight attendants were subject to two forms of emotional control. First, company documentation and training processes stipulated the necessity and emphasized ways of displaying 'niceness'. Second, Hochschild found that flight attendants had constantly to monitor their feelings in order to ensure a fit between company norms and external expression. This form of monitoring contributed to what Hochschild refers to as an 'emotion system', of which there are several components.

First, she highlights the **feeling rules** in modern societies that reflect norms about what we should feel in a given situation. Feeling rules govern the sorts of emotions we are expected to display and how we might display them. While there were specific codes laid down for flight attendants, these codes were largely in tune with a Western cultural 'lexicon of feelings' (Hochschild 1998). Second, feelings are expressed through what Hochschild refers to as **techniques of interpersonal exchange** such as smiles, tears, trembling or touch.

Face work as techniques of interpersonal exchange

Techniques of interpersonal exchange involve two forms of acting. **Surface acting** entails changing our external appearance or adopting a strategy of pretence in order to give the impression of a particular feeling. For instance, in service occupations, a client may give an employee a hard time (making unreasonable demands or expecting more from the service than is possible). Yet, the employee may be bound by company code and culturally acceptable codes of conduct to smile, speak politely and courteously, and so on. Though the employee may be feeling hassled, they have to give the impression of professionalism. This form of surface acting is often referred to in guidance and advice books on modern parenting. For instance, such books typically suggest that, when disciplining children and telling them off when they have done something wrong, it is important to 'keep a poker face' or 'keep a neutral face' on the grounds that faces 'give away' internal states of being.

In contrast, **deep acting** involves working on the feeling in order to alter it or exchange it for another feeling. An example Hochschild provides is that, when one flight attendant experienced feelings of anger in exchanges with a client, she tried instead to 'feel sorry' for him. There are costs in these forms of acting. On the one hand, surface acting made some flight attendants feel insincere and contributed to what they felt was a 'lack of authenticity' or phoniness in their relations with clients. Experienced flight attendants were more likely to try to establish congruence between what they felt and their facial expressions or bodily techniques, at the cost of emotional 'burnout'. On the other hand, the face work flight attendants undertook contributed to external signs of ageing (or 'the look of age'; see chapter 6) such as lines and wrinkles.

The Health Consequences of Face Work

The manipulation of external appearance concealed health problems associated with the work of flight attendants such as varicose veins, loss of sleep and eating disorders. Moreover, the constant process of exchanging one feeling for another made it difficult for some flight attendants accurately to interpret bodily signals and in some cases led to depression. The emotion work involved in self-presentation, role performance and the manipulation of external appearance through face work and bodily expression can lead to dramaturgical stress (Freund 1998; Elias [1978, 1982] 1994). Or, to put this another way, the commercialization of feeling embedded within the work of flight attendants, and the ways in which this work requires that feeling be bought and sold in the marketplace, is inherently stressful.

Hochschild included a comparative study of debt collectors in her overall project, which strengthened some of the claims she makes about feelings, gender and the body. For instance, though she noted that debt collectors, predominantly men, were also required to participate in various forms of face work, they were less likely to be oriented towards making people 'feel better'. Moreover, they were more likely to be able to protect their sense of self. People in subordinate social positions may lack 'status shields' and be vulnerable to damage by those with access to social power (Williams and Bendelow 1996).

Face work and occupations

Though the flight attendants in Hochschild's study provide a particular example of women in a subordinate position, analysis of service occupations reveals that employees are predominantly female. Further, though Hochschild's analysis has been subject to criticism, its focus on emotional labour has been central to the development of studies in a range of feminized workplace settings, such as nursing (James 1989), sex work (Sanders 2004) and professional beauty therapy (Toerien and Kitzinger 2007). Not only is the expressiveness culturally associated with femininity and the female body commercialized by the marketplace, but also women are charged with managing their own feelings and the feelings of others. Women typically enter into occupations that demand emotion work such as nursing and teaching and are oriented towards affirming the well-being and status of others (James 1989). Yet the emotion work that women undertake is typically concealed as work because emotionality and expressiveness are associated with femininity and the female body. Therefore the manipulation of facial expression and bodily expression required to display the impression of particular feelings and to undertake emotion work is seen as a natural aspect of femininity.

Yet emotional labour takes skill, as suggested by Toerien and Kitzinger's (2007) study of emotional labour in the beauty salon. Using conversational analysis, the authors were able to detail the interactional skills involved in the performance of the tasks associated with emotional labour – and so make it much more visible. By taking a distinct methodological strategy, the authors are able to delineate the work it takes to *do* every day, routine interaction. Further, the management strategies deployed by particular industries serve to 'shape the surface acting of employees' (Taylor and Tyler 2000: 90), and, consequently, has spawned image consultancy as a new service profession to support the projection of an appropriate body idiom in the context of face-to-face corporate workplace interaction (Wellington and Bryson 2001).

Escaping Embarrassment: Face Work in the Rap Cipher

The somatic evidence of embarrassment features prominently in Goffman's dramaturgical framework. Signs of embarrassment, including blushing, changes in voice tone and tremors, signal that people have violated a situated code of conduct (Goffman 1956). Accordingly, Jooyoung Lee's (2008) ethnographic research explores the techniques rappers use to deal with embarrassing moments during rap ciphers. The research involved ethnographic fieldwork, in-depth interviews and video recordings of street corner ciphers (impromptu rap sessions which involve 'freestyling', where rappers make up spontaneous rap lyrics). Lee draws on Goffman's insights concerning defensive and protective face work, and explores situations where rappers 'fall off' (a local term for stuttering and stopping abruptly during an improvised performance) and how they use prescribed 'canned resources' to deal with these embarrassing social gaffes when they occur during their social interactions in rap ciphers. For example, rappers will use 'writtens' (pre-written rhymes) when they are close to falling off. There are also instances of shared face-saving resources, such as when other rappers step in and take over the rap when 'falling off' occurs, allowing the rapper who has 'messed up' to save face. Lee suggests 'canned resources' are like 'interactional life vests which keep people from drowning during embarrassing moments' (p. 321).

Somatic work

We might add to insights on body and face work the notion of **somatic work**, an original concept that denotes sensing as a social and symbolic practice, and that speaks to the issue of how it feels to be and have a body – that is, to hear, feel, see, taste and move through everyday life (Hockey 2009). Waskul and Vannini (2008) argue that somatic work points to the intersection of action (e.g., the act of smelling) and a condition (for instance, odour). As the authors observe, somatic work involves being 'dramaturgically aware' of the significance of odour and depends on drawing on an indexical order that enables us to attribute meaning to smells. Such work, note Waskul and Vannini, requires somatic rules or norms that are negotiated and, though stringently enforced via discourses of health and cleanliness, nonetheless vary according to context.

Somatic work can be challenging, nonetheless, because in contemporary culture, the mental is elevated over the visceral, and sensory knowledge is largely secondary to visual knowledge (Edvardsson and Street 2007). An obvious example in Western contexts is the interpersonal work people do in public bathrooms (or as they are euphemistically termed in the United States, restrooms), in which, as designated spaces of 'creature releases' (Goffman 1963: 69), odours of urine, flatulence and faeces are expected and common. Drawing on Goffman, Waskul and Vannini write that in the context of the public bathroom, on the one hand, those encountering the odours of others generally practise 'tactful blindness', while those creating the odours typically attempt to hide or control them (e.g., using air sprays or perfume). Thus somatic work – managing our own conditions of odour and our habitual attitudes to the odours of others – is an intimate aspect of body and face work that requires interpretation and moral evaluation.

Corporeal management and the limits of social interactionism

These forms of corporeal management, involving body, face and olfactory response, can be viewed as central to social interaction, as components of social interaction and constituents of social order. Each enactment of bodily gesture and facial expression reinforces cultural ideas about appropriate conduct for given situations. However, in order for body and face work to contribute to social interaction and to self-presentation, we need to know what they mean. We need either to share or at least to have access to knowledge about vocabularies of body idiom that provide classification frameworks, which in turn allow us to interpret the meanings behind gestures and expressions.

This raises a perennial problem associated with Goffman's work and the symbolic interactionist framework developed by others, which is where do meanings come from? From what are our preconceived assumptions about body idiom derived? For some commentators this poses something of a conundrum. On the one hand, the work of Goffman provides a robust framework for examining the significance of the body in social interaction. We can see that how we use and interpret the human body in social encounters is crucial to maintaining their flow and integrity and to the presentation of self. On the other hand, the emphasis on interpretation and meaning underpinning this framework detracts from the significance of the body as a material object in the way it reinforces the importance of image and symbol. Indeed, the emphasis on image and interpretation reproduces a division between mind and body that Goffman's predecessor Mead was at pains to eradicate, in the sense that body idiom, though perhaps habitual in some circumstances, also seems to be highly subject to rational control. So we are left with a chicken and egg situation: does the human body actually generate meanings through the range of gestures and expressions we deploy, or is the body a kind of *tabula rasa* on which we inscribe meaning and significance? This question has not been fully answered, though many sociologists are now engaged in ways of identifying how relations between the material body and the social body are constituted through a dialectical process.

Phenomenology of embodiment

The legacy of both Cooley and Mead on the development of self and the implicit significance of the body in that development, combined with Goffman's work, provide sociological insights about the role of the body in the presentation of self in social interaction. However, there are other perspectives that allow us to think about the relation of body to self. If, for Goffman, the body mediates between self and other, for phenomenologists such as Maurice Merleau-Ponty the body provides an ontological basis for self. Phenomenology in general focuses on the ways in which people 'sense and make sense of reality' (Waters 1994). Our immediate experience of the social and physical world is via continuous sense data that we 'make sense' of by ordering and allocating to discrete categories or phenomena (Waters 1994). Phenomenological sociology focuses on the social processes people depend on to categorize sense data as phenomena and examines the extent to which these phenomena are shared.

Alfred Schütz is the foremost phenomenological sociologist, and his work has been developed to examine the categorizing and indexing processes in which people participate to construct and make sense of the social world. However, because this body of work focuses primarily on language and text in order to demonstrate the sense-making processes in which people are engaged, it is to the work of the French philosopher Maurice Merleau-Ponty that sociologists have more readily turned for tools to examine the 'lived body' as a phenomenological reality.

Being-in-the-world

Merleau-Ponty begins by questioning the presumption of correspondence between external stimuli and sensory apparatus within processes of perception (Csordas 1990). Perception for Merleau-Ponty is not primarily visual and does not see us as spectators on the world, looking out onto it from a self-enclosed entity (Burkitt 1999). Rather than examine perception from the object that is being perceived, and working from there back to the perceiving subject, Merleau-Ponty asks that analysis begin from the body. In contrast to Cartesian ways of understanding the relation between body and mind, Merleau-Ponty does not view the body as a special kind of physical object separate from the mind that can be comprehended only via rational thought. Rather, he views the body as the basis of 'being-in-the-world' in the sense that embodiment precedes and grounds reflective thought.

Furthermore, we do not observe our bodies directly as we move and act in the world; we can move and act only through and with our bodies. Put another way, this implies that there is no philosophical division between object and subject, nor do objects exist prior to our perception of them. The implications of this claim for examining the relation between body, self and society are that we are not outside the world but in the world. Concomitantly, perception of the world begins from the body (Merleau-Ponty [1962] 2001).

Embodied perception

In order to pursue his analysis of perception as embodied, Merleau-Ponty suggests that the social is embodied and the body is social (Crossley 1995b). Rather than view the body as an object among other objects (Csordas 1990), Merleau-Ponty argues that the physical body and the senses associated with embodiment provide what he calls an 'opening-out' onto the world, such that we develop a sense of self and comprehend the world via physical action. For instance, reaching out to grasp a material object, such as a pen with which to write a letter, does not require cognitive reflection (as in 'I am reaching out') but occurs simultaneously with comprehension (Crossley 1995b). Similarly, we learn to ride a bike or drive a car by developing a 'feel' for it, based on experience and practice. Hence, perception itself is active, based in habits and conduct such as looking, listening or writing (Merleau-Ponty [1962] 2001), and we develop a sense of self via actions towards others and to the environments in which we are situated.

Inter-corporeality

This process of action in relation to others is referred to as **inter-corporeality**. As we act upon the world and respond to sense data we also apprehend the world. We cannot apprehend the world without the body, its actions and senses. Not only do actions make thought possible in the philosophy of embodiment, but also our sense of self develops from 'the feel we have of our body and the way it connects us to the world' (Burkitt 1999). Therefore, our bodies are not objects to us, though it is possible to think about our bodies as objects. Rather, we *are* our bodies, and engage with the world through the body, which provides 'the link between a here and a yonder, a now and a future' (Merleau-Ponty [1962] 2001: 140). Thus, a phenomenological view of embodiment stresses the body's capacity to establish both spatial and temporal unity through action. For phenomenologists, the self changes as the body changes, and in certain conditions or circumstances, such as pregnancy, surgery or organ transplantation, the unity between mind and body implied in the philosophy of embodiment may be disrupted, causing a person to become focused on bodily sensations and experiences (Leder 1990).

Limits to phenomenology

However, although many writers are enthusiastic about the insights of the phenomenology of embodiment, there are some unresolved problems for the sociologist of the body. First, where Goffman and others emphasize the importance of interpretation and meaning in relation to the body, it is not clear how symbols inform a phenomenological perspective on embodiment (Burkitt 1999). Second, though Goffman's work has been criticized for the relative absence of attention to power relations (though, as Williams and Bendelow 1998 note, this is unfounded), phenomenological perspectives on embodiment have very little to say about power. Third, relatedly, and as we shall see in the following chapter, the 'opening-out' onto the world described by Merleau-Ponty appears to be undifferentiated (Young 1990). However, there is evidence from sociology, social psychology and psychoanalytic theories that there are gender issues to consider in the relation between body and self. The following chapter, which focuses on the body, gender and sex, examines a key feminist critique of Merleau-Ponty in the work of Iris Young and her perception about differentiated embodiment (see pp. 71–3).

Summary

The emergence and development of the self and its relation to society is a central problem for the discipline of sociology. Though there is a rich tradition within sociology of examining and explaining the self through social interaction, it typically focuses on the mind and on rational thought and action in ways that effectively conceal the significance of the body. In contrast, there are approaches that seek to highlight the significance of the human body in the development and presentation of self. Two such approaches have been outlined in this chapter. First, symbolic interactionism, and in particular the legacy of Erving Goffman, shows how bodily control and knowledge of somatic norms is crucial to the competent presentation of self.

Successful interaction with others depends on impression management and information control, both of which may be achieved through managing and controlling one's body. However, such management is not always possible, and bodily disruptions and differences present interactional and political challenges. Second, a phenomenological approach to embodiment shows how important sensory experiences are to the development of a sense of self and to relations with others, even though Western culture encourages us to deny the significance of such experiences and to privilege rational thought as the basis of self.

Further Reading

The following provide detailed observations about social interaction and offer a starting point for thinking about the significance of the body:

Goffman, E. 1972. *Interaction Ritual: Essays on Face-to-Face Behaviour.* London: Allen Lane.

Goffman, E. [1959] 1971. *The Presentation of Self in Everyday Life.* Harmondsworth: Penguin.

For a symbolic interactionist approach to the body in sociology:

Waskul, D. and Vannini, P. (eds) 2006. *Body/Embodiment: Symbolic Interaction and the Sociology of the Body.* Burlington, VT: Ashgate Publishing.

Try these for discussion of the importance of the face:

Lee, J. 2009. Escaping embarrassment: Face-work in the rap cipher. *Social Psychology Quarterly*, 72 (4), 306–24.

Simmel, G. 1959. The aesthetic significance of the face. In H. Wolff (ed.) *Essays on Sociology, Philosophy and Aesthetics.* New York: Harper & Row, pp. 276–81.

See Kitzinger and Toerian for a study on emotional labour:

Kitzinger, C. and Toerian, M. 2007. Emotional labour in action: Navigating multiple involvements in the beauty salon. *Sociology*, 41 (4), 645–62.

Material on physical impairment, self-presentation and stigma:

Charmaz, K. and Rosenfeld, D. 2006. Reflections of the body, images of self: Visibility and invisibility in chronic illness and disability. In D. D. Waskul and P. Vannini (eds) *Body/Embodiment: Symbolic Interaction and the Sociology of the Body.* Aldershot: Ashgate.

Hughes, B. 2009a. Wounded/monstrous/abject: A critique of the disabled body in the sociological imaginary. *Disability & Society*, 24 (4), 399–410.

Hughes, B. 2009b. Disability activisms: Social model stalwarts and biological citizens. *Disability & Society*, 24 (6), 677–88.

Rao, D., Pryor, J. B., Gaddist, B. W. and Myer, R. 2008. Stigma, secrecy, and discrimination: Ethnic/racial differences in the concerns of people living with HIV/AIDS. *AIDS Behavior*, 12, 265–71.

Seymour, W. 1998. *Remaking the Body.* London: Routledge.

And on the sensorial body:
Low, K. E. 2006. Presenting the self, the social body, and the olfactory: Managing smells in everyday life experiences. *Sociological Perspectives*, 49 (4), 607–31.

Discussion Questions

What are the 'interactional life vests that keep you from drowning during embarrassing moments'?
To what extent do all members of society share ideas about what constitutes biophysical normality, as Goffman's work implies, and how, in your view, do such norms change?

2
The Body, Gender and Sex

Introduction: Sex and gender

When we look at other people we discern their sex from appearance. Hairstyle, body shape and size, clothes, posture, stance, facial characteristics, expression and muscular tone all tell a story about sex, about whether a person is male or female. In addition, we assume a corresponding set of capacities, behaviours and characteristics associated with gender, or masculinity or femininity. Sometimes these assumptions will be rewarded, yet at others they will be challenged by some feature or other that appears to disrupt that anticipated congruence between sex and gender. This chapter focuses on the relationship between sex, gender and bodily conduct. First, it examines the distinction between sex and gender introduced by Ann Oakley (1972) and the assumptions on which this distinction is based. The chapter will address the terms **gender** and **sex** and outline how they are used as terms of description in Western culture, or as social categories that create and sustain *differences* between people. In defining these terms, we should be able to discern the role the body plays in creating these differences. Second, the chapter introduces sociohistorical material that traces the emergence of practices and ideas that have aligned women with nature and the body and established a dichotomy between masculinity and femininity. These practices and discourses construct the female body as not only different, but also deviant, though this alignment has been challenged by second-wave feminism. Third, the chapter looks more closely at gender and the kinds of work we do with and on our bodies to present ourselves as masculine *or* feminine. As we shall see, ambiguity about gender presentation can be socially problematic, and the final focus of the chapter is on incidences such as cross-dressing and female body-building in which the social boundaries between what are considered male/female bodies are challenged.

Feminism, sociology and conceptual distinctions

The women's movement of the 1960s and 1970s and the subsequent development of feminist academic thought has had an important influence on the subjects considered suitable for academic consideration. In the 1970s, many disciplines in the humanities and social sciences began to consider gender issues. Sociology was no exception. An important early focus for feminist sociologists was to challenge the implicit conflation in sociological research between sex and gender. While there may be observed biological differences between males and females – though such differences are ordinal rather than dichotomous – they are insufficient to explain the sexual division of labour and a range of observed social differences between men and women. Feminists argued that classical sociology – and therefore the development of the discipline – tended to assume that social differentiation was an elaboration of biological differentiation (Sydie 1987). A great deal of initial feminist scholarship was concerned with demonstrating variations across time and place in gender arrangements and the sexual division of labour.

In particular, this work sought to establish a conceptual distinction between **sex** and **gender** (Oakley [1972] 1985), between differences based on biology (chromosomes, secondary sexual characteristics and hormones) and differences based on social arrangements (such as differential access to material resources or differences in bodily conduct). Sex, in this thinking, is physical, stable, natural and immutable. It refers to the body we can see, feel and touch and to the body defined in scientific and medical terms (through biology, for instance). Sex, understood in terms of the anatomical and biological body, is a primary categorical device, which we use to classify people into one of two possible types: male or female.

In contrast to sex, gender refers to the established psychological, social and representational differences between men and women, which are socially determined and culturally variable (Oakley [1972] 1985). This conceptualization of gender has underpinned many studies that aim to demonstrate how many of the actions and practices (or behaviours and traits, as psychologists might put it) we associate with masculinity and femininity are learned rather than inherent. Moreover, it allows us to explore the relationship between

contemporary understandings of the anatomical body – a body categorized primarily as either male or female – and the lived experience
of gendered embodiment. However, the categorization of the human
body into mutually exclusive groupings of either male or female is
problematic. Harold Garfinkel (1967) noted that Western societies
operate on the basis of binary opposites, or rely on a **dimorphic
model** of sex. What Garfinkel terms the 'natural attitude' towards
sex and gender has three main characteristics.

Sex and Gender

Sex is the bodily based categorization of people into one of two
possible types: male or female. Gender refers to the socially
determined psychological, social and representational differences
between men and women.

Distinctly sexed bodies

First, the human body is categorized into two *distinct, mutually exclusive* sexes. For instance, when a baby is born, its genitals are checked
and what is observed becomes the basis of initial sex categorization, though there is considerable overlap in terms of chromosomal
make-up, hormone production and genitalia. Moreover, in Western
societies, the sex that is attributed to us (male or female) implicitly
assumes a corresponding set of behaviours, traits or social practices
that are linked to or indicative of gender (masculinity or femininity). However, miscategorization based on observation alone sometimes occurs, and there are many instances (noted by Oakley 1985;
Connell 1995) in which corrective surgery or other forms of medical
intervention are requested or authorized in order to realign the physical body with the gender behaviour or conduct later exhibited. Where
there are discrepancies between the sex initially assigned to a person's
body and subsequent physical or behavioural observations that call
that assignation into question, the typical response of medical science
is to advocate corrective interventions in order to eradicate ambiguity
and ensure a fit between visible, physical characteristics and gender.
These instances of ambiguity are construed by ethnomethodologists
as an indication that neither sex nor gender are inherent properties
of individuals, but are social categories shaped by practices of social
interpretation (Kessler and McKenna 1978).

Second, the contemporary dimorphic model of sex is *invariant*, in
that sex is assigned according to a fixed set of scientifically derived
criteria, which we assume will be constant across the life course.

Western societies do not on the whole accommodate individuals whose sex is either ambiguous or altered, yet for many people such ambiguity is part and parcel of their identity. Third, sex in this model is *complementary*, and there is an assumed equivalence between the sex that is attributed to people (male or female) and their sexuality. That is, attraction to the opposite sex (heterosexuality) is the default sexuality attributed to people, although there is no necessary empirical equivalence between sex and sexuality. The 'natural attitude' towards sex and gender in the West assumes that people belong to one of two possible distinct categories determined on the basis of given biological and anatomical characteristics (that is, *either* male *or* female, *either* masculine *or* feminine).

Naturalizing difference

The distinction between sex – or the anatomical, biological body – and gender has been important in sociology and in society for at least three reasons. It provided a means for examining the social determination of gender at different levels of experience. First, for instance, many studies in sociology have demonstrated marked variations in the relative experience of boys and girls in relation to levels of educational achievement. These variations are said to be the result of differences in the ways teachers treat boys and girls or the ways in which boys and girls make subject choices, or linked to girls' and boys' perceptions of employment opportunities when they leave school. Second, when sex and gender are conflated or said to be the same thing, it is easier to argue that certain experiences are an inevitable consequence of being a woman or a man (although such an argument is usually made in relation to women rather than men) or to assume that certain social circumstances are the consequence of being a woman. For instance, it has been argued in many contexts and by many people over the decades that women who are mothers should not engage in paid work because their role is to care for children. The conflation here between sex and gender is used not only to naturalize differences between men and women but also to substantiate a moral judgement about 'women's place'. Third, therefore, the sociological insistence on a distinction between sex and gender was important for feminists and other researchers in political terms because it signalled the possibility of social and political change. Gender was developed as a sociological concept in order to emphasize that not only are traits and characteristics at a psychological level socially shaped and produced, but also the social, economic and political inequalities that can be observed between women and men are an extension not of biological differences but of particular social relations and contexts.

However, some commentators (e.g., Hood-Williams 1996) have noted that, where gender is now understood as a social construct, sex continues to be understood as natural and therefore inaccessible to sociological examination. Indeed, a now significant consequence of the feminist and sociological insistence on gender as a *social* concept has been that it reinforces the idea of the body as a stable biological foundation across time and place (Nicolson 1994). However, as historians have demonstrated, contemporary ideas about sex (or of the anatomical, biological body) as polarized opposites (male *or* female) may themselves be contingent on socio-historical processes and circumstances. Yet there is evidence that the dimorphic model of sex that shapes contemporary understandings of sex – the anatomical, biological body defined as either male or female – was preceded by a different model in which sex was viewed in terms not of binary opposites but of similarities. Moreover, the association between femininity and the body (which itself is perceived as part of nature) is relatively recent in Western culture and a product of the Cartesian dualism bequeathed by the Enlightenment (see Introduction, p. 4). This dualism, in which the mind was defined as the source both of rationality and of the self, aligned the body with nature, with the non-rational and with emotion. Feminist scholars have highlighted how the female body was increasingly viewed in the nineteenth century as troubling – as a threat to the moral order and to social stability (Canto 1985) or as unstable and as a source of sexual pollution (Walkowitz 1980). These ideas about the female body and femininity have been used to exclude women from social and political participation on the grounds of what is perceived as their natural inferiority.

Gendering the body

The body in science

There is evidence that the ways in which scientists think about the human body as distinctly male or female is relatively new and that until the eighteenth century, scientists viewed male and female as different expressions of one human body (Holmes 2009). Historians have examined scientific practices and ideas informing the production of anatomical and biological knowledge that contributed to the alignment of femininity with nature and the body (e.g., Jordanova 1989; Oudshoorn 1994; Schiebinger 1993). The consolidation of

mind–body dualism in the late eighteenth century was accompanied by the emergence of other dualisms in the nineteenth century.
Historical scholarship shows that images and ideas in the worlds
of scientific medicine and law contributed to the development of a
range of dichotomies that associated the female body with nature.
For instance, studies of the cultural production of anatomical illustrations (Laqueur 1990; Jordanova 1989) show how the work of
early anatomists (such as Galen, the best known of second-century
anatomists) was represented in ways that suggest either that male
and female reproductive organs were perceived as similar versions
of the same organ or that the female body was viewed as a continuation of the male body rather than as completely distinct (Laqueur
1990). This seems to be clearest in the representation of reproductive
anatomy, from which it is difficult for the modern, unpractised eye
to distinguish male from female. Analysis of anatomical illustrations
suggests that female reproductive organs were routinely represented
as interior versions of male organs (Shildrick and Price 1994). The
vagina was depicted as an interior penis, the uterus as scrotum and
the ovaries as testes. It is suggested that women's reproductive organs
were seen as homologous to male organs, not as particularly distinct
or inferior (Lupton 1994).

Therefore, there appears to be evidence that, before the
Enlightenment, medical practitioners did not view the female body
as radically different from the male body, nor was the female body
evaluated in the negative terms associated with later nineteenth-
century views. However, the emerging practices of both pathology
and anatomy helped to forge perceptions of difference between the
bodies of men and women. The Enlightenment was a period in which
the mind became increasingly celebrated and knowledge became
associated with empirical – visual – observation, and both pathology
and anatomy were practices that relied heavily on visual observation. On the one hand, pathology was based on the idea that the
body could be made legible through clinical examination or that the
truth of the body's interior was revealed through signs evident and
available to scrutiny on its surface (Armstrong 1983). On the other,
anatomy developed as a practice associated with dissecting the many
surfaces and layers of the body, for the purpose of 'revealing' nature.

Scientific understandings of the differences between male and
female bodies were accompanied by an increasing emphasis on
oppositional difference. The hierarchical ordering between male and
female bodies is most apparent when we look, as Jordanova does
(1989), at the use of wax models for the purpose of teaching anatomy

to medical students in the nineteenth century. These models became increasingly differentiated in terms of gender and scientific knowledge described through sexual metaphors. For instance, the female models (called 'Venuses') were often displayed on velvet cushions, decorated with jewellery and hair, and arranged in positions that might be read as provocative.

Representation and gender differentiation

Thomas Laqueur (1990) notes that differentiation in the representation of the body and of reproductive anatomy in particular became marked after 1800, when illustrations began to highlight differences between bodies. Illustrations were accompanied by an increasing insistence in texts of the oppositional difference between the male and female body. Similarly, though anatomists were aware of the existence of the ovaries from the late seventeenth century, when they were referred to by the word also used for testes (Morgan and Scott 1993), Oudshoorn (1994) observes that their role in hormone production was not fully understood until much later. Ovaries were later described as control centres in which hormones were especially important signallers and seen as the essence of femininity.

There are other examples from the world of anatomy that reveal how social and political changes shaped the production of knowledge about the body and how the body was increasingly used as evidence to establish moral and social differences between men and women. For instance, Londa Schiebinger (1993) observes that, while illustrations of the human skull were relatively undifferentiated before the Enlightenment, by 1750 visual representations depicted differences in size between the male and female skull. Schiebinger attributes this to the responsiveness of anatomists and their illustrators to emerging anxieties about population growth in a context of demographic decline and a concern to promote reproduction as the proper role for women. Moreover, analysis of nineteenth-century anatomy texts reveals that the language used to describe the relation of science to the body is a language of exploration and colonialism. For instance, Jordanova (1989) notes how such texts viewed the female body as a territory to be mapped and revealed and how it was viewed as a secret to be unveiled. Indeed, Jordanova draws attention to a sculpture in Paris titled *Nature revealing herself before Science* as characteristic of the mastery over nature pursued by science. There is evidence from research undertaken in the late twentieth century that contemporary anatomy texts continue to represent the female body as distinctly different from the male body, as feeble, inferior and designed for the purpose of reproduction (Lawrence and Bendixen 1992; Scully and Bart 1978; Martin 1989). In this way, the male body is constituted as a standard from which the female body deviates, and the female body is defined as primarily reproductive.

Hood-Williams (1996) suggests two possible explanations for the shift from a non-hierarchical, non-dichotomous representation of female anatomy to one that emphasized difference. First, it may be the case that the practice of anatomy in the eighteenth and nineteenth centuries led to the identification of new parts of the human body (such as the ovaries) in ways that challenged early anatomical knowledge. This would not, however, explain why female and male anatomy in the nineteenth century was increasingly represented in terms of contrast and opposition. Therefore, second, we need to consider shifts in the interpretative framework in which anatomy and medical illustrations were produced. Significantly, from the late eighteenth to the early nineteenth century, middle-class women experienced rapid changes in their social, economic and political position. Where until the late eighteenth century such women had experienced a degree of public participation, the emergence of a bourgeois, domestic ideology contributed to their exclusion from public life. Concomitantly, the female body was interpreted increasingly in terms of its contrast to the male body, as a 'dark continent' to be explored by the developing profession of scientific medicine (Jordanova 1989). Hence, this new perception of the female body (as natural, or weak, or troublesome) was a product of social and political impulses that sought to exclude women from entry into the new public world of the bourgeoisie.

The examples of scholarship outlined here rebut claims about the natural inferiority of the material female body. Moreover, they demonstrate how practitioners located within social relations and contexts that are already gendered interpret the body. In particular, Thomas Laqueur suggests that, as political and social changes increasingly raised questions about women's place in the world, anatomists focused on body parts that differentiated the female body from the male body. In turn these body parts came to stand for difference and to be used as the basis on which to make claims about female inferiority; in other words, understandings about the human body have become part of the way that gender is understood as part of a binary system, in which 'men' and 'women' are naturally and socially different (Van Doorn et al. 2008).

The female body as an object of expert scrutiny
Examining the female body

Feminists have argued that the practices of scientific rationality (inspection, examination and visualization) render the female body as an object of expert scrutiny. This was the result of the development of medicine as a profession and the concomitant specialization within medicine that enhanced the emphasis placed on the female body as distinct from the male body. For instance, the proliferation of women-only hospitals in the nineteenth century helped to consolidate gynaecology as a specialism within medicine oriented towards female reproductive organs (Moscucci 1990). The emerging speciality of gynaecology was viewed as the 'science of woman', and, as Moscucci notes, there is no equivalent speciality oriented towards male reproductive organs. The development of gynaecology and its concentration within hospital space reinforced reproduction as central to femininity in ways that further separate the female body as conceptually distinct from the male body. The expansion of new spaces of observation also provided new communities for the profession of medicine to observe. Women-only hospitals improved the degree of access that practitioners had to the bodies of women, and this in turn provided new opportunities for intervention and indeed, in some cases, experimentation (Corea 1985; Dally 1991; Oakley 1998).

As women-only hospitals expanded in number, so too did the techniques of inspection available to practitioners. The development of the speculum in particular enabled clearer visualization of the internal spaces of the female body – the vagina, the cervix – but was controversial. The speculum was associated with sexual penetration (Poovey 1987) by non-gynaecological practitioners within medicine and by other middle- and upper-class men, and was seen as especially problematic in cases involving young, unmarried (and, therefore, sexually inexperienced) women. Such debates involved men as fathers and practitioners with an interest in discrediting gynaecology as the self-appointed custodian of female honour.

New images and metaphors concerning the body contributed to the development of a biomedical view of the body that emphasized the body as a machine that can be broken into parts and repaired (Martin 1989). This view of the body as amenable to visual scrutiny and technological intervention underpinned other ways in which medical discourses regarded the female body as deviant. For instance, there are a number of conditions and/or syndromes experienced by women that not only function in ways that reinforce the idea of the female body as inferior but also are exploited as grounds on which to exclude women from social and political participation. In the nineteenth century, hysteria was one such condition.

The hysterical body

Known as 'wandering womb' since the medieval period, hysteria appeared to increase as a female complaint in the nineteenth century as a condition peculiar to middle- and upper-class women (Ehrenreich and English 1974). Its symptoms included fainting, weeping, loss of voice and appetite, excessive screaming and laughing, collectively defined in terms of uterine malfunction. The uterus, in particular, was seen through the medical gaze as the seat of mysticism and as a symbol of femininity. Medical and legal discourse associated a cluster of symptoms with a dysfunctional uterus in ways that highlighted the irrationality and lack of control embodied by the hysterical woman. However, the distribution of hysteria was largely among single, divorced or widowed women. As women in the nineteenth century began to identify possible routes of entry into professional and political space, the female body was increasingly defined in terms of pathology, as a body in need of containment and control (Sachs and Wilson 1978).

Though these symptoms were defined in pathological terms, feminists have suggested that they functioned as a response from certain groups of women to their lack of social position or failure to meet the expectations of middle-class femininity during a period in which the 'cult of domesticity' was developing. Medical practitioners regarded the expression of these symptoms as evidence of pathology, which in turn was defined as a disease of modern womanhood that required specific treatments (ranging from inactivity and isolation for a period of time to hysterectomy and later radium implantation). Yet these symptoms were also an acceptable way for women to react to the constraints of middle-class femininity at a time of narrow role confinement (Ehrenreich and English 1974). Professional debates within medicine upheld middle-class notions of femininity and were deployed to legitimize the exclusion of middle-class women from the public sphere (Turner 1984). Moreover, because such symptoms invited medical surveillance, Ehrenreich and English argue that all acts of rebellion were subject to definition as hysteria in a way that ensured the social control of deviance (Zola 1972).

Ehrenreich and English (1979) further argued that modern

medicine adopted the patriarchal mantle previously worn by religious institutions and targeted the female body as an object for expert scrutiny. In addition, professional specialization within medicine supported the organization of the female body into compartments concerned with diseases defined by their location within particular parts of the female body. Hence, particular aspects of female embodiment have been medicalized, for instance, menstruation.

Medicalization and the Female Body

The concept of **medicalization** has proved invaluable to feminist analyses of the female body. The idea of medicine as an institution of social control is central to sociological scrutiny of health, illness and disease, which are seen as forms of deviance that must be regulated through specified and sanctioned agencies (Zola 1982). Medicalization is a concept that expresses the processes through which medical culture encroaches on various aspects of social life and to a degree wins social consent for doing so (de Swaan 1990). In the context of capitalist processes of specialization and differentiation, medicine deliberately seeks to expand its boundaries and 'colonize' new areas of the body and mind (Illich 1976).

Bleeding women

Feminist research has demonstrated how menstruation is viewed within a biomedical framework as a biological deviation, and this deviation provides the basis for intervention and treatment. Hormonal therapy and surgical practice are just two of the ways that menstruation is treated within medical discourse (Dally 1991; Lewis 1993). In her study of menstruation, *Issues of Blood*, Sophie Laws (1990) uses this insight to illustrate how the creation of new medical categories in relation to female embodiment should be understood as a strategy through which the female body is socially shaped as a deviant body. For instance, 'pre-menstrual syndrome' (PMS) is a conceptual umbrella under which a variety of embodied experiences are addressed within gynaecology and general practice (Rodin 1992). PMS is used as a diagnostic category that focuses on hormonal imbalance. However, it also reflects views about femininity and the female body, and about women's place in society as carers. Rodin argues that, just as hysteria was defined in the nineteenth century in terms of its unpredictability (and marriage offered as a solution), the category of PMS was sometimes used in the twentieth century to legitimate claims that women ought not to be given positions of responsibility.

However, while medical terms such as PMS can sometimes be used against women, they have also been employed to women's advantage. For instance, the legal category of 'diminished responsibility' due to PMS has increasingly been used as a defence for women charged with crimes of violence (Atkins and Hoggett 1984). Moreover, anthropologists have suggested that the cluster of symptoms women experience that are grouped under the category PMS may be culturally specific. Johnson (1987) notes that PMS might be seen as a 'symbolic safety valve' through which women give expression to the social contradictions that accompany expectations around production and reproduction. As Martin (1989) observes in her book *The Woman in the Body*, women experience material and bodily disruptions that are not accommodated by Western culture in ways that make it difficult to carry on the diverse burdens that accompany their social position.

Hence, though the female body may be the target of expert scrutiny, and women's distinct embodied experiences may be defined as pathological, it is not inevitable that processes of medicalization will be used against women. As Riessman (1992) points out, women themselves have at times participated in the construction of medical categories as ways of finding solutions to the embodied experiences that pose disruptions to their lives. The medicalization of symptoms associated with PMS may invite further medical intervention and treatment, but they also provide a mechanism through which women have been able to find legitimization and authoritative support for symptoms associated with pain and discomfort. Hence, women in such circumstances are not necessarily the victims of medicalization but participants in the construction of discourses that define female embodiment.

The power of culture

Although the female body is understood as naturally different from the male body, it has been made so via the development of scientific rationality and in particular the practices of pathology and anatomy. As Gatens observes, culture constructs the body so that it is understood as a biological given (1988: 62), an immutable fact that cannot be altered. The 'givenness' of the female body as naturally weaker, more inferior, less stable than the male body – as different and deviant – has been used in the recent past, and continues to be used in the present, as evidence of women's moral and intellectual inferiority. Yet historical and cultural analysis paints quite a different picture of the givenness of the female body as naturally deviant. These analyses submit that the emergence in the nineteenth century of expert knowledges about the female body was shaped by social, economic and demographic changes that sharpened perceptions of biological or anatomical difference. Moreover, as a consequence of increased accessibility to the bodies of women, the female body has been constituted as a 'repository for ideas' (de Beauvoir [1949] 1972) – a pathological body in need of surveillance and intervention. Second-wave feminism has challenged these constructions of the female body, and feminist sociologists have argued that women's embodied experiences need to be taken more seriously by experts and professionals.

The Enlightenment produced new ways of thinking about the human body and introduced a conceptual separation between the matter of the body and mind. Concomitantly, the body gradually became associated with nature and femininity whereas the mind became identified with masculinity and culture. As the research of feminist cultural historians demonstrates, the meaning of the human body, including the sex we assign to it – oppositional and distinct – is heavily determined by the interpretations placed on it (Hood-Williams 1996). Contemporary understandings of the human body have inherited these contrasts. The female body continues to be viewed as an object amenable to medical examination and observation, but also as one that can be commodified (through the pornography industry and prostitution), contained (for instance, metaphorically through the concealment of menstruation) and controlled (for instance, through violence). Men are rarely associated with or reduced to the body (Morgan 1993) except in relation to sport and other activities that emphasize physical activity and strength (though this is perhaps changing for reasons we will examine later). Indeed, the male body tends to be disguised by the forms of dress that have accompanied the emergence of modernity: the suit of the bureaucrat or the uniform of the military.

Moreover, either the study of women has not been deemed an appropriate focus for disciplines such as sociology because of women's association with nature (Durkheim, for instance, viewed women in terms of their aesthetic and moral function) or women's social position in the division of labour has been explained in terms of their relationship to nature (via reproduction especially). However, the second wave of feminism in the twentieth century challenged these associations by establishing an important distinction between the physical body, or sex, and gender, a socially and culturally defined phenomenon. Rather than gender being viewed as the external and inevitable display of innate differences, the body is seen as a medium for the display or performance of gender, and it is to these ideas that the chapter now turns.

The interpretative shift framing knowledge production in relation to the female body, defining it as qualitatively distinct from the male body in terms not only of anatomy but also of physiology and psychology, had profound implications for women's social and political participation. The medical management of hysteria reinforced this notion of the female body as weak: hysteria was seen as a condition in which women were controlled by the fluctuations of the uterus, and women were therefore seen as unpredictable, as a threat to the social order that needed to be controlled and contained (Turner 1987; Ehrenreich and English 1979). Pathological definitions of the female body underpinned surgical interventions and examinations into the female body (Dally 1991) and were used to discredit women. For instance, in the late nineteenth century women were believed to be physically frail and delicate and to have smaller brains than men. This medically endorsed view was used to exclude women from entering the academy on the grounds that they were unsuited to the pursuits of scientific rationality, and hence pathological definitions of the female body contributed to a form of social closure. As other historical studies of scientific research and medical practice (for instance, in relation to hormones and skeletons) in the nineteenth century reveal, the male body was increasingly valorized as standard and the female body devalorized as deviant and pathological.

Cultural variability

In the mid-twentieth century, it was commonplace in both popular and academic discourse to explain observable social differences between men and women, such as acute differences in the kinds of work done by men and women, by reference to sex. Social differentiation was understood as stemming from biological differentiation, and thus social and cultural differences between men and women were naturalized. Ann Oakley (1972) was one of the first sociologists to challenge this link by establishing a conceptual distinction *between* sex and gender. Oakley argued that, while sex refers to physical, genital differentiation as the primary means of categorizing people, gender refers to established differences between men and women in psychological, social and representational terms.

Gender in this view is both socially determined and culturally variable, and feminist research has demonstrated that the social cannot be directly read off from the biological by reference to cross-cultural, temporal and internal variability. Gender, or masculinity and femininity, is expressed and arranged in different ways at different points in time and in different social spaces, and there is anthropological evidence of cultural variation in concepts of gender and sex. Of particular note are the cross-gender opportunities for men and women in certain Native American tribes in pre-industrial America (Blackwood 2002). For instance, in the 1800s the social organization of some tribes included an institutionalized system referred to as **berdache**. This system allowed persons who were anatomically of one sex to dress, act and talk like those of the other sex and undertake work and activities associated with the gender roles associated with the other sex (Whitehead 1981). This system of berdache allowed men to exist socially as women, but also women to exist socially as men, though this latter group was fewer in number. Moreover, cross-gender persons engaged in sexual relationships with those of the same sex. That is, cross-gender women entered into sexual relationships with anatomical women (Blackwood 2002).

Confounding categories

Though the berdache and cross-gender roles in Native American tribes were gradually replaced by Western cultural ideals of sex and gender, they confound the dichotomized relation between sex and gender and illustrate the variability of the relation between sex and gender. Categorization as a particular sex (that is, as either male or female) need not lead to the roles and practices associated with gender in Western cultures. Hence, as a sociological concept, gender provides a means of examining the social production of differences between men and women and challenges these differences as natural, inevitable and immutable. However, as Hood-Williams (1996) has pointed out, while gender has received considerable attention from social scientists, who emphasize that gender arrangements are socially constructed rather than emerge as a biological inevitability, there has been very little application of this argument to the human body itself. That is, if gender is amenable to social and cultural variation and manipulation, then what role does the body play in the social construction of gender and, in particular, in the disruption and/or maintenance of boundaries between masculinity and femininity?

As the previous section on the historical construction of the female body as frail and distinctly different suggests, gender arrangements and cultural assumptions about gender may shape contemporary assumptions about and understandings of the human body. One implication of this claim is that bodily conduct may not necessarily be genetically programmed or inherent. Rather, the various gestures and movements that people make as they move through physical space and that contribute to meaningful interaction are shaped or socially constructed by assumptions about and images of gender. Hence, gender becomes an everyday practice in which people are engaged, and assumptions about gender involve us in 'doing gender', which has the effect of reinforcing assumptions about gender differences (Morgan 1986; West and Zimmerman 1987).

Masculinity, physicality and space

Hegemonic masculinity

Connell (1987, 1995) makes the point that the particular ways in which any one individual displays masculinity and femininity will vary and points to the considerable range of gender displays discernible in Western culture. Like Morgan, Connell suggests that the term gender is not a description of attributes or traits possessed by individuals but is indicative of social relations and cultural norms that shape processes of interaction and bodily conduct. The body is, in this view, a cultural artefact shaped by ideas (Adams 2005). Hence, it is perhaps more helpful to think of masculinities and femininities in the plural, rather than the singular masculinity and femininity. Nonetheless, Connell identifies dominant versions of masculinity and femininity that inform how people 'do' gender. Hegemonic masculinity is the dominant version of masculinity in Western culture and is associated with three main characteristics. First, hegemonic masculinity emphasizes heterosexuality and subordinates homosexuality. As many commentators have observed (e.g., Weeks 1986), though homosexuality has existed across historical time, those who identify themselves as homosexuals may experience discrimination. Second, hegemonic masculinity is constructed and exists in relation to emphasized femininity, such that femininity can be defined only in relation to hegemonic masculinity. Third, hegemonic masculinity privileges a particular kind of male body, a muscular body. Analysis of visual culture demonstrates the prevalence of hegemonic masculinity as a cultural norm, but the point made by Connell is that such images influence self-identity and shape bodily conduct.

For instance, the cultural emphasis on muscular masculinity may influence boys' use of space and interaction with others. Connell observes that: 'To be an adult male is distinctly to occupy space, to have a physical presence in the world' (1995: 57). For Connell, inhabiting a male body provides one with a distinct perspective on the world that cannot be explained exclusively by references to genes, hormones and chromosomes, but has more to do with how boys learn the social significance of size, gesture and an active orientation to the world. There is evidence, for instance, that boys are more regularly exposed to certain kinds of physical contact that encourage bodily awareness. It has been documented how parents and primary carers, even with the best of intentions, are more likely to play rough-and-tumble games with boys than with girls. Such games help to develop motor skills, coordination and physical confidence in ways that promote what phenomenologists refer to as an active sense of being-in-the-world, a sense of oneself as an active subject (see chapter 1).

Connell suggests that these differences are not incidental, nor can they be wholly explained by reference to anatomical or physiologi-cal features. Rather, the emphasis on a particular form of physicality (institutionalized in the education curriculum) has a direct bearing on and contributes to the development of bodily conduct. Indeed, physical activity – especially sport – forms the basis for how boys learn to be adult men, and 'to be in possession of themselves' (Brace-Govan 2010). Physicality is thus an important feature of **hegemonic masculinity**, the prevailing set of cultural norms that actively shapes the presentation of self and the bodily conduct necessary to such presentation.

Hegemonic masculinity and race

Hegemonic masculinity is also a specific contemporary Western response to perceived cultural threats from the demands of feminism and the challenges to white privilege from non-white groups (e.g., the civil rights movement in the US) (Oates and Durham 2004). In particular, the extensive use of space that accompanies hegemonic masculinity serves to symbolize the social power of men and rein-force relations of domination and subordination not only between women and men, but also between different groups of men. For instance, professional American football players epitomize the ideal of hegemonic masculinity. The bodies of these players are continu-ally measured and quantified in preparation for the National Football League (NFL) Draft, a process of selection through which the bodies of players (who are predominantly African American) are scrutinized

– indeed, commodified (see chapter 4) – by largely white men. As Oates and Durham (2004) put it in their study of the male racialized body in American football, in the Draft, black, male athletes 'are the objects of the gaze of wealthy white men'. This scrutiny normalizes 'a conception of masculinity that reasserts class dominance while controlling and managing the labour potential for the hyper-masculine physique' (p. 320).

Doing Gender – Masculinity and Space

The ways in which men occupy public space illustrate Connell's point. Observe men in public transport, for instance, or in a lecture theatre, and note the amount of physical space they claim by sitting with their legs wide apart or reaching out into the space of others by stretching an arm across the adjacent seat. Note styles of walking: are there differences between men and women? Are there struts and swaggers in comparison to walks with shorter strides? Are there differences in who monopolizes other forms of public space such as football terraces or street corners? This active subjectivity is formalized through what Jan Brace-Govan terms *ritualized visibility*. For instance, male participation in sport receives extensive media and marketing coverage in ways that 'mobilize bias' and therefore symbolically reinforce the social significance of male physicality (Brace-Govan 2010).

Physicality and embodied subjectivity

Empirical studies suggest that young men do things to, and talk about, their bodies in ways that construct and police appropriate masculine behaviours – in effect, self-regulating normative masculinity (Brace-Govan 2010). That is, as Connell points out, 'gender is a social practice that constantly refers to bodies and what bodies do . . . it is not social practice reduced to the body' (2005: 71). Recent empirical research involving interviews with firefighters, male hairdressers and estate agents lends weight to this suggestion that men's experiences of their bodies figure in their embodied notions of who they are. However, as Hall, Hockey and Robinson point out in their study, Connell's 'structures of practice' intersect with local realities and relations that modify and complicate stereotypes and dominant discourses of masculinity, replacing, for instance, the stereotype of the 'camp' male hairdresser with a home-handyman hairdresser (Hall et al. 2007).

You may wish to argue that not all men take up space in such an overtly physical way. Nor are all men exposed to the kinds of physical contact encouraged by certain sports, and many indeed may even reject the kinds of physical display and contact generated by sports and other physical activities. Moreover, even men who do engage in practices that require a high degree of physicality – such as dance – may find that their particular form of physicality is culturally marginalized. In Western culture, although dance is now considered 'a legitimately masculine practice', male dancers 'challenge expectations of how men should use their bodies' and are still often associated with effeminacy (Adams 2005). While dance requires power, muscle and strength, the culture of dance continues to be represented as a feminized culture, in which male physicality is subsumed. As Adams puts it, 'while hard bodies epitomize contemporary North American masculine ideals, dancers' bodies, chiseled and taut as they are, don't seem quite hard enough' (p. 82).

In a similar way, women who develop physical power and strength may find that, despite their keenly developed physicality, nonetheless they continue to be culturally marginalized. Women who lift weights are a case in point. Such women appreciate the sense of mastery and empowerment provided by weightlifting (Brace-Govan 2004). Furthermore, women who are physically active, such as women who lift weights, are role models of 'desirable femininity', at least in terms of marketing and advertising (Brace-Govan 2010), and 'challenge the social power that derives from muscularity' (Brace-Govan 2004). However, while some women viewed the development of physical strength as an opportunity for insight into the experience of male physicality, women who lift weights are typically perceived as *different from* other women in a way that reinforces a gender order (Brace-Govan 2004).

Physicality and the looking-glass self

Such examples do not necessarily negate the way that hegemonic masculinity reinforces an emphasis on physicality, which in turn contributes to the bodily conduct of men. Indeed, it underscores how the social meanings attached to the human body – meanings that are already gendered – become internalized in ways that influence not only conduct but also our sense of self. Here the concept of the **looking-glass self** (see p. 18) may again be helpful. Charles Horton Cooley (1902) developed this concept to highlight the importance of visual information and perception in social life. Connell draws on the example of ball-throwing to illustrate this point. The boy who is

Plate 2 'Throwing like a girl'? Hank Greenberg, of the Detroit Tigers, shows Miss Marta Barnett how a ball should be thrown!
© Bettmann/CORBIS

unable to throw a ball 'like a man', and who knows this, must already understand what it means to throw a ball like a man and, moreover, that his bodily conduct does not conform to this norm. He is, therefore, in the process of throwing the ball, using his body but standing outside his conduct, observing and judging on the basis of a dominant image of how a ball is 'properly' thrown.

Femininity and objectification

The objectified body

Where hegemonic masculinity emphasizes a physical sense of self and of being-in-the-world, which is presented and communicated to others by taking up and using physical space in particular ways, inhabiting a female body presents a different order. Adrienne Rich, a feminist writing in the 1970s, remarked:

I know no woman – virgin, mother, lesbian, married, celibate – whether she earns her keep as a housewife, a cocktail waitress, or a scanner of brain waves – for whom her body is not a fundamental problem: its

clouded meaning, its fertility, its desire, its so-called frigidity, its bloody
speech, its silence, its changes and mutilations, its rapes and ripenings.
(Rich 1977: 284)

As Simone de Beauvoir ([1949] 1972) observed, the female body
is considered an object that is looked into and examined. As the
previous section describes, scientific imagery and the medicalization
of women's embodied experiences have objectified the female body.
Similarly, a range of practices from foot-binding to corseting to rape
contribute to cultural definitions of the female body as an object. As
the art critic John Berger has observed: 'men act and women appear.
Men look at women. Women watch themselves being looked at'
(1972: 48). Berger made this observation in the context of examining
the specific position that the female body occupies in the history of
art. Its representation has been largely the province of male artists,
whose practice has tended to objectify women for a male audience
(Mulvey 1975), render the female nude in idealized terms (Williams
and Bendelow 1998), and represent woman as alien Other and as
'uncharted and peripheral wildness' (McRobbie 1990: 12). Yet the
representation of the female body as 'other' is not confined to visual
art but, it is argued, is indicative of a more banal relation to women
in Western culture, in which the female body is made invisible by
representational strategies that are distorting and silencing (Budgeon
2003).

Pause and Reflect: What do you think Adrienne Rich meant by
her statement that the body for women is a problem? In what ways
do women challenge this claim in everyday life?

The troubled body

The female body is also viewed as a 'troubled body' (Hughes and Witz
1997) that is often perceived as a spectacle or fantasy and fetishized
within popular culture. The female body is a body that is encouraged
to be on show, and women are obliged to produce their bodies as
adequate and acceptable spectacle, as objects external to self (Doane
1982). In this view, girls grow into women aware of being watched
or objectified, and this profoundly influences their interactions with
themselves and with others. This is especially so for black women,
whose bodies have been objectified, sexualized and turned into spectacle for the white male gaze (Hill-Collins 1990). Hill-Collins argues
that the image of black women was historically one that emphasized

them as breeders, as sexual objects and as sexually promiscuous. These images helped shape and justify the exploitation and rape of black women. Black women were historically subject to the voyeuristic gaze of white men on the auction block in early nineteenth-century Europe (Gilman 2002). The story of Saarbjiie Baartman (Sarah Bartman), a slave from Africa who died in 1815, exemplifies this experience. Saarbjiie's body was dissected, her buttocks and genitalia were preserved and a plaster cast was made of her body. This was subsequently displayed at fashionable parties in Paris until it was finally exhibited at the Musée de l'Homme. The appearance of her body, especially her enlarged genitalia, fed a European obsession with physiognomy, which was seen as the foundation of racial difference and sexual deviance. Though physiognomy is now a discredited practice, its legacy and that of white hegemony continues to inform representations and experiences of black femininity. Moreover, even visual representations of black women by black men tend to serve white stereotypes. hooks (1992) draws attention to Spike Lee's Nora Darling in *She's Gotta Have It* as a stereotype of a sexually voracious black woman that is close to white assumptions about black female sexual promiscuity. Moreover, the self-presentation of black women in the public eye typically engages in the eradication of physiognomic difference in the pursuit of white ideals of femininity. For instance, Cher's cosmetic surgery has erased features that draw attention to her Native American ethnicity (Franckenstein 1997).

However, the female body is also the object of the male gaze in more mundane aspects of everyday life, and feminist research demonstrates how the experience of being watched encourages women to be conscious of themselves and invest in their bodies as the expression of self. This concern with the body is a relatively modern phenomenon (Brumberg 1997) and consumes a great deal of time and energy. Moreover, though the contemporary period has gradually fostered new body freedoms (such as baring arms and legs and wearing swimsuits and bikinis in public; see Lawler 1991), the acquisition of these freedoms entails a high degree of internal control and discipline (Bordo 1989), an idea that will be examined further in chapter 4.

Embodiment and gendered modalities

Iris Young draws on Merleau-Ponty's rebuttal of a Cartesian conceptualization of the relationship between mind and body and its concomitant understanding of perception as an 'inner representation

of an outer world of given objects' (Crossley 1995b: 46). As the
previous chapter described, in contrast to the Cartesian view of self,
Merleau-Ponty asserts that mind and body are not separate entities,
and that their articulation is fundamental as a state of being that
precedes objectivity (Diprose 1994). Perception is always located
in and through the space of the lived body, and the material body
is an integral dimension of the perceiving subject (Csordas 1990).
Following this argument, we do not reflect on our own bodies or
the bodies of others as objects a priori, but live our bodies as our
selves. However, the lived body/self can become an object for self
and others (Crossley 1995b) through various processes and events
that create phenomenological disruption, such as injury or sickness
(Leder 1990). Hence, Merleau-Ponty's philosophy of embodiment
asserts, first, that self is projected in and through action and, second,
that awareness of one's own body as an object emerges as a form of
alienation.

However, Young challenges the universal account of the neutral
body suggested by Merleau-Ponty, and asserts that gendered modali-
ties are partial, inhibited and ambiguous, reactive rather than proac-
tive, and discontinuous in their engagement with the world around
them rather than continuous. The female body is not necessarily
experienced as in direct communication with self, as an active expression of self, but as an object, a thing. Young (1990) notes that studies
in the use of space demonstrate differences between men and women
and suggest a distinctly feminine style of comportment and movement. On average, women walk with a shorter stride than men; hold
their arms close to their bodies; avoid meeting the gaze of others (particularly men) in public spaces; use their arms to shield themselves
and protect themselves; and draw back from objects thrown to them
rather than reach out to receive them. For Young there are two possible explanations for this 'feminine modality'.

First, drawing on de Beauvoir, women are not born but are taught
to become feminine in ways that emphasize containment and control.
Young suggests that women are inhibited by lack of confidence about
their bodies which comes from under-use, restricted access to opportunities for physical engagement and differences in the relative exposure of boys and girls to physical play and activity. She theorizes that
the restricted space in which women operate and the **closed body**
characteristic of feminine comportment and movement signifies an
imaginary space that confines women.

Second, women are encouraged to become more aware of themselves as 'objects' of others' scrutiny. In public spaces where the

female body is potentially transgressive, the 'male gaze' (Mulvey 1975) operates as a disciplining mechanism that encourages docility. Awareness of being watched and of seeing oneself as an object has the potential to shape how women move through and engage with the physical environment. The point to note here is that the sense of physical space and body use that accompanies 'being a man' or 'being a woman' represents a *shared vocabulary of* **body idiom** (see chapter 1), that influences how men and women use and present their bodies. These uses and presentations are consolidated as habits or bodily conduct, and reinforce gender distinctions.

At the same time, Young suggests there are aspects to female embodiment that are pleasurable and premised on 'movement and energy' rather than on 'thingness'. For instance, transforming the body according to gender norms takes time, resources and thought (Smith 1990). Indeed, the production of the gendered body is itself a form of skilled work from which woman may derive pleasure. Similarly, phenomenological accounts of the experience of and assumptions surrounding pregnancy challenge philosophical claims concerning the way the body impinges on self only in contexts of pain and 'dysruption' (Leder 1990). In contrast, such accounts suggest that self-awareness of the pregnant body is not necessarily an awareness of the body as an uncomfortable object from which one is alienated, but an awareness of continuity with life and change, pleasure and growth (B. Marshall 1994).

Women, Physicality and Sport

Differences in the relative exposure of boys and girls to physical play are something that the corporate giant Nike has incorporated into advertising campaigns. One advert presents the face of a young girl, looking at us through the chains of a swing. The caption reads:

> If you let me play: I will like myself more, I will have more self-confidence, I will suffer less depression, I will be 60% less likely to get breast cancer, I will be more likely to leave a man who beats me, I will be less likely to get pregnant before I want to, I will learn what it means to be strong. If you let me play sports.

The advert reinforces the idea that there is a connection between physical play and contact and the degree of confidence and awareness that young people, and girls in particular, possess. However, there has been dramatic growth in women's athleticism and involvement in sport in the last two decades, which *has*, as Molly George notes, 'allowed women to gain control over their bodies, develop autonomy and self definition, as well as given many athletes confidence and opportunities in other areas of life' (George 2005). Nonetheless, women's sport continues to be marginalized by male sports in terms of marketing, promotion, media coverage and sponsorship (Brace-Govan 2010), and there continues to operate a subtle boundary around acceptable musculature for women in sports, as well as a persistent calling into question of women athletes' femininity and sexuality (George 2005).

At the same time, McGrath and Chananie-Hill (2009) note that female bodybuilding can be considered subversive and empowering, as well as colluding and reinforcing of the normative gender order. While women may feel personally empowered in their development of musculature and strength, cultural and institutional forces 'function to nullify or reduce bodybuilding's subversive potential and recuperate transgressive bodily displays through constraint and reinscription' (p. 236). In addition, too much bulk on the body of female bodybuilders crosses a gender border and can be interpreted negatively in ways that undermine female empowerment by signalling what is culturally viewed as 'freakishness'.

Challenging gender boundaries

Crossing gender borders

The previous section emphasized, first, that gender (masculinity and femininity) is socially constructed and, second, that cultural assumptions about and the social relations that shape gender influence bodily conduct. Using the work of R. W. Connell, the section suggested that hegemonic masculinity and emphasized femininity refer to dominant cultural norms and social arrangements that shape how we see ourselves and influence our interaction with others. In this line of thinking, gender is considered not as an innate, fixed element of the self, but as something that is developed through interaction with others in ways that reinforce boundaries between masculinity and femininity. In social interaction, we interpret certain forms of bodily conduct as indicative of either masculinity or femininity. One's phenomenological experience and awareness of self, as male or female, is informed and reinforced through bodily conduct – certain ways of moving, gesturing, using space – which may develop through social interaction across the life course rather than emerge as the outcome of anatomical form and physiological features.

This raises the possibility that, if gender is embodied according to prevailing cultural norms, gender (that is, masculinity and femininity) could be viewed as a kind of performance. Certainly, when we look at examples where normative conceptions of masculinity and femininity are challenged or disrupted in some way, we can see more clearly how everyday bodily conduct reinforces a dichotomized view of gender. Three examples illustrate this idea. First, history is littered with examples of people who 'do gender' (that is, as West and Zimmerman 1987 describe, accomplish gendered difference through everyday interaction) in ways that cut against expectations, typically to gain access to some kind of occupation or activity from which they have been restricted or excluded. For instance, in the nineteenth century, there are examples of women who wished to travel unencumbered by the conventions of femininity (such as decorum, modesty, and so on). These women explorers dressed in order to 'pass' as men and developed masculine ways of walking and talking in order to achieve their goals.

Second, there are many documented examples of male cross-gender practice. Though transvestism is the term most often used to describe male to female cross-dressing, Ekins and King suggest the term 'transgendering' to refer to the various ways in which people assigned one sex adopt the 'behaviors, emotions and cognitions' that are socially and culturally associated with another (2001: 363). Cross-gender practices vary, but typically involve careful attention to detail, such as concealing body parts that will be construed as signs of the gender the cross-gender person seeks to elude. Cross-gender practices may, for the 'male femaler', involve over-emphasizing characteristics associated with the presentation of femininity, focusing on clothes, hair, jewellery and make-up (often reminiscent of 'golden ages' of femininity such as the 1930s or the 1950s). This level of detail is important, for instance, to men who cross-dress in order to produce feelings of femininity and to 'pass' as a woman (Garber 1992). Cross-gendering requires hard work to achieve a competent and credible performance in displaying the background routines associated with masculinity or femininity, or what are recognized and acknowledged as gendered styles of dress, language, gesture and movement. Failure to pass, by inappropriate and/or inadequate display of such background routines, will result in **spoiled identity** (Goffman 1968).

Gender and performativity

The bodies and experiences of transgender and transsexual people explicitly draw attention to the artifice involved in 'doing gender' and challenge the social construction of the categories 'sex' and 'gender'. Judith Butler (1993), a feminist philosopher, suggests that the performance of drag within gay culture takes the form of a self-consciously exaggerated performance and parade of femininity that depends on a distinction between 'the anatomy of the performer and the gender that is being performed' (1993: 137). Butler argues that the pleasure and delight of drag is that the audience is never in doubt that the queen is a man (in anatomical terms at the very least). This observation leads Butler to question the sex/gender distinction so valuable to sociologists of gender and to suggest there is nothing self-evidently gendered about either bodily conduct or the sexed body. Gender is not only influenced by ideas, assumptions and stereotypes (or discourses, as she prefers) but is actively produced or materialized through a 'stylized repetition of acts' that come to be understood as natural – as sex – over time. In the example of drag, the exaggeration of what are recognized as conventional displays of femininity encourages the audience to consider all gender displays as a kind of performance.

Butler uses the concept of performativity to side-step biologically reductionist models of the body and the pathologizing of women's position they reinforce. She reworks the sex/gender distinction in order to make gender visible as:

> a *stylized repetition of acts* . . . understood as the mundane way in which bodily gestures, movements, and styles of various kinds constitute the illusion of an abiding gendered self. (Butler 1990: 140, emphasis in original)

However, sex, in the earlier sense of the term (as the assignation of male/female based on possession of particular characteristics), is not matter, in the sense of being a final foundation for identity or conduct. Rather, the 'materiality of the sexed body is discursively constituted' through the regulatory frame of reproductive heterosexuality, or, in other words, the norms to which Garfinkel referred (see above). Neither is gender separate from sex; rather, it is implicated in the frame of reproductive heterosexuality, and the sense of gender as a fixed reality is produced through repetitions and enactments that *make it seem* as though gender (as identity) is fixed and attached to sex (as in the 'sexed body'). Hence, for Butler, materiality is defined as 'matter' shaped by a 'process of materialization that stabilizes over time to produce the effect of boundary, fixing and surface' (Alcoff 2000: 858).

Ethnicity, Dance and Femininity

Matthew Atencio's (2008) ethnographic research suggests different ways that young women from culturally and ethnically diverse backgrounds use performativity as a resource to create multiple, coexisting femininities. He interviewed young women involved in dance cultures that are underpinned by dance forms that reproduce specific versions of 'normalized' femininity. Nonetheless, the young women in the study construct multiple and shifting minority ethnic subjectivities through their negotiation of their dance cultures. One of the girls, Carrie, uses high school dance spaces, festival and club dance spaces to construct fluid white, black and 'mixed' subjectivities. Another girl, Jenny, who identified as both black and Haitian, constructed a diasporic identity through her salsa dance space in which she re-enacted various other subjectivities. Atencio uses his observations to argue that complex psychic and embodied processes are involved in creating subjectivities that are, in practice, more fluid and multiple than Butler's work implies. He argues that young women are able to take up multiple versions of femininity through their leisure participation, including versions that resist and conform to dominant discourses.

Virtual worlds and performativity

There are examples in everyday life that are amenable to analysis in terms of Butler's concept of performativity. For instance, research on people's use of social network spaces suggests that networked interaction provides a context in which gender binaries are constantly transgressed via text, image and video (Van Doorn 2010). Indeed, scholars argue that computer-mediated communication in general mobilizes a space in which gender can be enacted and performed in new ways. Bloggers, for instance, create identities that explicitly perform gender via language choices and content focus, and may be especially significant as sources of gender performance for women in countries that limit freedoms for women (Hans et al. 2011). Another form of virtual performativity lies in the example of 'gender-bending' through gaming, for instance, or online chat rooms, in which participants may mask their gender identity and bend stereotypes in ways that challenge rigid notions of gender and, in the long term, may destabilize how society constructs gender (Hans et al. 2011). Through online performativity and interaction with others, participants may 'try on' different gendered identities.

However, scholars have also observed that while the anonymity of the Internet promises the potential for disembodied performance and identity construction, it may be that users cannot really escape the body after all. For instance, research on Internet dating sites suggests that virtual relationships are no substitute for 'meeting in the flesh' (Hardey 2002) and the disembodied performance that is encouraged may in fact negatively affect well-being (Kang 2007). Indeed, as Sondheim (2007) puts it, virtual subjects (on the Internet) inevitably have real bodies '*elsewhere*' (p. 201).

These tensions have been explored by an English photographer, Della Grace, who manipulates the images of herself and her subjects to create 'drag kings' as a way of challenging a 'femme' style of lesbian performance. Her 'fem drag' depends on appropriating the dress codes of straight men in order to challenge what she views as a tacit social acceptance of male to female cross-dressing on the grounds that 'masculinity that expresses itself on a female body is still considered abject and is universally ridiculed'.[1] Grace's interpretation of the negative value people attribute to lesbian bodies that are presented and performed in ways that evoke heterosexual masculinity suggests that the physical body continues to place material limits on the extent to which performances may subvert any relationship between the 'imitation' and the 'original', as Butler puts it (1990: 137). The implication of this kind of example is that perceptions of the human body as a fixed and stable entity may be less amenable to subversion in the contexts of everyday lives than we might like to think.

Pause and Reflect: To what extent do you think virtual communities like Facebook allow people to transcend – or perform – gender in the way they create an online presence and identity?

---

[1] <http://www.bothways.com/splash/absdella.htm#della>. Della Grace has now (1999) developed into Del LaGrace Volcano, a self-styled gender variant (or transgendered person) who challenges the 'binary imperative' associated with a dimorphic model of sex and gender.

Marginalizing embodied experience

To reiterate then, in Butler's work, sex and gender are not separate, and indeed both are implicated in the other in a discursive loop. Social perceptions of the materiality of the sexed body (as a foundation for gender) are indissoluble from its signification in language, through which the body becomes fixed as matter over time (Hughes and Witz 1997). Butler's work has prompted considerable debate within academic feminist communities not only in philosophy, her own discipline, but also within sociology. Her texts are set reading for undergraduate courses in women's studies, gender studies, feminist theory, and so on. Moreover, perhaps it is important to remember that Butler's work is located within a wider feminist philosophical project that seeks to disclose the culturally mediated character of what has been naturalized within the philosophical frame (i.e., gender). However, her work has been criticized for marginalizing the study of embodied experience in the performance of gender. Butler's attempts to renegotiate the sex/gender distinction valorize the body but 'devalorize gender' and the sociality of women that the concept of gender pulled into the sociological imagination (Witz 2000). In doing so, Butler's approach leaves aside sociologically inflected understandings of the social. And the problem with this devalorization, accompanied by the conflation of materiality and a linguistic understanding of discourse, is that it encourages a view of the body detached from experiences, and collaterally from material, flesh and blood bodies. Though she is engaged in a project of trying to discern ways for bodies to matter in philosophical discourse, her resolutely post-structuralist stance insists on the indissolubility of materiality and representation (and language in particular). This has the effect of reducing the material body to discourse and privileges deconstruction (Alcoff 2000) as the principal methodological strategy in ways that efface the experiences and perspectives of subjects themselves. Indeed, as Butler herself acknowledges, habit, routine, and unconscious behaviours are part of performativity, as is the 'accumulating and dissimulating historicity of force' over which individuals have little control (Butler 1993: 226).

Cyber Culture

Although the highly visual environment of online culture (e.g., MySpace, YouTube, Facebook) acts as an extension of everyday life, text is central to how people use these technologies and present themselves (Van Doorn et al. 2008). Van Doorn et al.'s research on Internet relay chat in the context of queer cyber culture examines how gender is performed, or rather, how people 'do' gender, in online spaces. The research suggests that even in such a highly visual space, people draw on the physical body as a common point of reference that informs their online talk and draw on physical classification schemes (see discussion of Goffman in chapter 1) to mediate online relations. Even though gender and sexuality is performative in this environment, argue Van Doorn et al., the body (physical and discursively enacted) not only plays an instrumental role in performing gender, but does so in a way that reinforces the norms of a binary gender system by maintaining a 'natural' connection between gender and sex (Van Doorn et al. 2008).

Changing bodies – changing sex: Garfinkel and Agnes

A different kind of social practice – sex changing – moves beyond the concealment and surface modification of the body towards physical reconfiguration of body parts. Sex changing or transsexualism, a predominantly medical term, is often associated with people who feel they inhabit the 'wrong body'. Sex changing or 'transgendering' (Ekins and King 2001) involves a number of strategies. For instance, 'substituting' involves replacing given body parts associated with one gender with those of another gender. For those Ekins and King refer to as 'male femalers', this may involve replacing the penis with a vagina, constructing breasts where none previously existed, and so on. A classic documented case of sex changing is Harold Garfinkel's study of 'Agnes' (1967). When Garfinkel met Agnes, she had female body contours, breasts and hair, but no uterus or ovaries. In addition, Agnes had male chromosomes accompanied by high oestrogen activity. At birth, Agnes had been categorized as male on the basis of genitalia that had the appearance of a penis. She was subsequently raised as a boy. However, Agnes documented her difficulties growing up and referred to her dislike of boys' games but having to participate in them in order to avoid being labelled as a 'sissy'. At puberty, female breasts and body hair developed, and Agnes later had reconstructive surgery to fashion external female genitalia from male genitalia.

Garfinkel documents the process of Agnes's journey from male to female and from masculinity to femininity, and the highly complex business of sorting out the relationship between the body Agnes

inhabited (which possessed both male and female physical and physiological attributes) and the self she believed herself to be. Despite
the presence of male primary sexual characteristics, Agnes grew up
believing herself to be a woman, and, moreover, she considered the
development of secondary female sex characteristics as vindication
of her belief. According to Garfinkel, much of her development
was devoted to achieving the display and performance of femininity, which was independent of the sex she was assigned. She had to
work hard at appearance, to learn to act as a woman in order to be
taken for granted as a woman (including the construction of a biog-
raphy that described the life story of a girl, rather than that of a boy
growing up as a girl) and to comply with what she believed would be
recognized as a legitimate gender performance. Agnes had to ensure
that she passed as a woman in order to secure the entitlements that
accompany her elected gender, but this was also accompanied by an
ever-present awareness of the potential for discovery.

Garfinkel's interpretation of Agnes's account of her experience
tells us that competent gender performance is crucial in order to
avoid the threat of exposure. However, the performances associated with transvestism, inter-sexed persons or transsexualism differ.
For instance, transvestism concentrates on gender display through
surface modifications, whereas transsexualism requires competent
performances as a basis for transition from assigned sex to surgically
reconstructed sex. Gender transgression involves not only surgery
and hormone therapy to reconfigure the physical body (and cannot
be achieved solely through these means) but also a gradual transition
from one gender to the other. This transition requires various measures of modification concerning dress, gesture, voice tone and register, movement, posture and language. For transsexual men, it entails
living as though one were a woman, imagining what this requires and
adapting oneself in accordance with perceptions of femininity and
modifying one's body to become visibly female.

See Jeffery Eugenides's *Middlesex* for a fictional account of
hermaphroditism.

Passing/trans borders

There are circumstances such as cross-dressing and transsexualism in
which people categorized as being of one sex (usually male) present
themselves according to the norms and expectations associated with
the opposite gender. Achieving a competent performance, however,

requires careful attention to detail and to the background routines associated with masculinity and femininity. Garfinkel's study of Agnes demonstrates how crucial the development of such competence (or **passing**, see p. 31) can be, because when one is engaged in the display of characteristics that one believes to be, and will be recognized by others as, masculine or feminine, one also lives with the threat of exposure. Performance in this case is not, therefore, a surface modification (of dress, voice tone and register, gesture) but a crucial modification, which is necessary to accomplish a polished and convincing presentation of gender.

Transgender issues are now finding their way more firmly into undergraduate sociology courses (Wrentling et al. 2010), and scholarship has argued that a binary model of gender identity (masculinity/femininity) is limited for understanding transgender identities and lived experiences (Hines 2007). For instance, the concept of 'passing' reinforces the notion of 'being born into the wrong body' on which a medical model of Gender Identity Disorder is premised (Iantaffi and Bockting 2011). Indeed, many people who identify themselves as transgender refer to themselves in different ways, such as 'dynamically gendered' or transmasculine, suggesting a more complex relation between gender and sexuality than is implied in a binary model of gender. Transgender identities and experiences call for deeper exploration of the intersections between gender, sexuality and heteronormativity (Iantaffi and Bockting 2011), and the transgressive possibilities that queer theory, for instance, has emphasized are embodied in transgenderism (Hines 2007).

Yet living as a transgender person is not all about gender transgression. While scholarship has shown how some societies (e.g., in Southeast Asia) historically provided greater legitimacy and acceptance for transgenderism than multicultural democracies, at least until Southeast Asia began to have greater contact with globalization (Peletz 2009), persons of colour still experience marginalization within the transgender movement. Sabrina Alimahomed's (2010) interviews with 25 queer identified women show that women of colour, while not explicitly excluded from the lesbian, gay, bisexual and transgender (LGBT) movement, as scholars have shown was the case for women of colour in the feminist movement (hooks 1981), nonetheless experience forms of marginalization from within the LGBT movement. She argues that the racial/ethnic positions of Latina and Asian/Pacific women she interviewed render them invisible within LGBT communities, which, among other disadvantages, limits their options for political organization, and throws into stark relief the 'white racial frame' that the LGBT movement embodies (Alimahomed 2010). Nonetheless, queer theory has taken an approach to exploring transgender lives that emphasizes its transgressive possibilities, through, for instance, performativity.

Heteronormativity refers to the formal institutional and informal relational practices that legitimize certain kinds of sexualities, for instance via marriage, tax rules and legislation (Warner 1993).

Summary

The relationship between the human body, sex and gender is complex and not easily disentangled because of the way in which each is naturalized. That is, each appears to be beyond social influence. However, this chapter suggests that, though we experience the body, sex and gender as natural and immutable, careful analysis demonstrates that each part of the whole is shaped by social action and interaction. The focus of the chapter has been on three key issues. First, the human body is perceived and understood through a set of ideas and frameworks that are themselves the product of particular social and historical contexts. For instance, biomedical and psychoanalytic practices have shaped contemporary Western understandings of sex as anatomical, biological, dichotomous and implicitly stable. Second, although the anatomy and biology of the human body is an important means of categorizing people as either male or female, these physical differences have been made or constructed as socially meaningful because they are visible or have been made amenable to visual observation. Third, although the sex/gender distinction has been an important conceptual and political development within sociological analysis, until recently there has been very little focus on the relation between contemporary understandings and experiences of gender and human embodiment. New approaches to distinctions between, and understandings of, the relation between the body, sex and gender not only emphasize gender as a range of social capacities that could be associated with either sex, but also that sex, and the bodies to which sex is assigned, is the product of processes of social classification.

Further Reading

For material on gendered embodiment see:

Evaldsson, A. C. 2003. Throwing like a girl? Situating gender differences in physicality across game contexts. *Childhood*, 10 (4), 475–97.

Inckle, K. 2007. *Writing on the Body? Thinking through Gendered Embodiment and Marked Flesh*. Cambridge: Cambridge Scholars Publishing.

And for material on gender identity and body image, see:

Algars, M., Santtila, P. and Sandnabba, N. K. 2010. Conflicted gender identity, body dissatisfaction, and disordered eating in adult men and women. *Sex Roles*, 63 (1–2), 118–25.

Brown, J. and Graham, D. 2008. Body satisfaction in gym-active males: An exploration of sexuality, gender, and narcissism. *Sex Roles*, 59 (1–2), 94–106.

Finley, N. J. 2010. Skating femininity: Gender maneuvering in women's roller derby. *Journal of Contemporary Ethnography*, 39 (4), 359–87.

Gallagher, A. and Pecot-Herbert, L. 2007. 'You need a makeover!': The social construction of female body image in 'A Makeover Story', 'What Not to Wear', and 'Extreme Makeover'. *Popular Communication*, 5 (1), 57–79.

For discussion of bodily conduct, performativity and gender transgression, see:

McGrath, S. A. and Chananie-Hill, R. A. 2009. 'Big freaky-looking women': Normalizing gender transgression through bodybuilding. *Sociology of Sport Journal*, 26 (2), 235–54.

Trautner, M. N. 2005. Doing gender, doing class: The performance of sexuality in exotic dance clubs. *Gender & Society*, 19 (6), 771–88.

van Doorn, N., Wyatt, S. and van Zoonen, L. 2008. A body of text: Revisiting textual performances of gender and sexuality on the internet. *Feminist Media Studies*, 8 (4), 357–74.

Weber, B. R. 2006. What makes the man? Television makeovers, made-over masculinity, and male body image. *Men's Studies Press*, 5 (3), 287–306.

For a recent perspective on Butler:

Chambers, S. A. 2007. 'Sex' and the problem of the body: Reconstructing Judith Butler's theory of sex/gender. *Body & Society*, 13 (4), 47–75.

Discussion Questions

How do you 'do gender'?

How do practices such as body-building challenge the social boundaries between what are considered male/female bodies?

3

The Civilized Body

Introduction

Chapter 1 introduced the significance of the body in social interaction and highlighted the importance of bodily control and manipulation in this process. In Goffman's work, central to contemporary analyses of the body in everyday life, a recurring issue is that of social and bodily breakdown and the embarrassment such breakdown is capable of producing. Goffman is concerned about the social consequences of such breakdown: how do we continue to manage interaction so as to maintain its flow and integrity? Why do our bodies and their functions embarrass us in certain situations? In order to answer these questions, we need a sociological gaze with a historical reach. We can find such a reach in the work of a German sociologist, Norbert Elias, who asks how the social standards for dealing with each other in everyday life, described by Goffman in such painstaking detail, have developed over time. Therefore, this chapter examines contemporary bodily conduct through the lens of historical sociology and will, first, outline the civilizing process according to Elias and the characteristics of the civilized body. Second, it examines the development and social management of disgust and, third, it briefly considers the civilizing process and bodily boundaries.

The civilizing process

In works such as *The Civilizing Process* (1978, 1982) and *The Court Society* (1983) Elias begins from the understanding that everyday life is a tangle of biological, psychological, social and cultural relations and processes that are difficult in practice to unravel or isolate. Society is not separate from the individual but emerges through the forces that people exert on themselves and on each other (Lee and Newby 1989). Elias tries to explain the relation between historically variable forms of social control and the way people in the contemporary West conduct themselves, express emotions and relate to bodily functions. One of the things that makes Elias's approach distinct from that of other sociologists is his endeavour to view body, self and society as intrinsically linked to each other. This is reflected in his methodology, which views the human body simultaneously as a social and biological entity, as unfinished and interdependent with its social and physical environment (Shilling 1993).

The body for Elias is amenable to change over both historical and biographical time, and his approach reveals how the body has become increasingly subject to certain forms of social control. His data allowed him to establish links between a given level of civilization and its psychological and macrosociological manifestation. Rather than use historical material to make comparisons between 'then' and 'now', Elias tried to demonstrate contemporary social, psychological and bodily conduct (including emotional and instinctive life) as socially determined across time. As commentators on his work note (Kuzmics 1988), this methodological approach is guided by the comprehension that contemporary aspects of conduct (such as 'spontaneity' or 'self-restraint'), and in particular the notion of an individual self distinct and separate from its environment (as discussed in the Introduction), are the product of specific historical processes (or social figurations, as Elias calls them). Elias views the individual self as understood in contemporary Western contexts not as an immanent or necessarily progressive evolution of the human spirit, but as the outcome of complex social processes which continue to produce change.

It is worth noting that the civilizing process has been central to processes of ethnic categorization and colonization. For instance, McVeigh and Rolston (2009) argue that the use of violence was justified by the colonizers of North America, Australia and Ireland as a way of creating a distinction between 'civilized' and 'barbaric' people.

Self-discipline

The civilizing process refers to a broad process of social and sensory change which, according to Elias, began in the eleventh century and contributed towards a more mannered, structured pattern of bodily conduct. This change accompanied shifts in the distribution of power in European society and involved an alteration in consciousness in terms of people's awareness of themselves as individuals. Elias used the concept of the civilizing process to illuminate a complex yet specific transformation of human conduct from the 'grotesque' to the 'civilized'. Where the notion of the grotesque refers to forms of embodiment and conduct associated with a pre-modern, specifically medieval, and volatile form of conduct (Bakhtin 1984), the civilized is characterized by **self-discipline** and restraint. The most important elements of civilized conduct noted by Elias are 'the degree of pacification, the refinement of customs, the degree of restraint in social interactions and the (reflexive) relationship individuals have with themselves' (Kuzmics 1988: 151).

In particular, the civilized body is one that conceals its rhythms and is highly individualized and competently managed, and the civilized person is discernible from the uncivilized person by the extent to which the former is capable of exercising emotional restraint and establishing control over bodily impulses. Furthermore, a central tenet of the civilizing process has been, as argued by figurational sociologists, to 'tame' masculinity, by transforming the aggressiveness associated with masculinity such that inner restraint came to signal social distinction rather than over-plays of physical prowess (Atkinson 2008).

Concealment and disgust

A key element of the civilizing process is its emphasis upon the control and management of body functions, rhythms, products and noises. People in Western societies have gradually but increasingly internalized **shame** and **embarrassment** (see p. 42) as the most appropriate responses to uncontrolled body functions. Thus, a significant part of child socialization is oriented towards helping children to become aware of their own body and conceal its functions and substances. In particular, Elias draws attention to the concealment of natural rhythms and functions that have been incorporated into beliefs about what constitutes 'civilized behaviour'. His analysis of guides on etiquette in Northern Europe shows evidence of the development of shame and embarrassment concerning social conduct and bodily function. He traced a broad process of social and sensory change that contributed towards more mannered, structured patterns of bodily conduct and expression. There are evident changes in the extent to which people are expected and encouraged to control bodily impulses, and Elias meticulously catalogued the processes and functions no longer considered acceptable in polite society, such as spitting, urinating, defecating, vomiting, sexual activity, birthing, dying. These changes were also linked to an intensification of distinction between private and public spaces and places. While rules to prohibit certain forms of conduct were initially imposed on people externally, it is central to Elias's argument that such rules have increasingly been internalized and, over time, have become 'bedded down' in consciousness such that they form part of the habits and customs of civilized persons. Civilized habits, or 'techniques of the body' (Mauss [1934] 1973), refer to the full range of 'manners of daily life' in contemporary Western societies. However, the acquisition of such habits is no longer governed by external restraints (such as etiquette guides) but managed through the development of internal restraint over historical and biographical time.

Pause and Reflect: There are generational and cultural differences in the significance of restraint, and in how such restraint is manifest. What are the main differences between how Gen X and Gen Y think about the body? Are the latter more relaxed? If so, why?

Internalized restraint

An important part of Elias's thesis, shared by other scholars such as Foucault (1979, 1988), is that the forms of control determining social and bodily conduct shifted from 'restraint by others to self-restraint' (Kuzmics 1988: 154). In a context in which 'growing demands from an increasingly complex social environment necessitate a more subtle tuning of behaviour' and in which social interactions take place between people in more interconnected and interdependent ways, individuals are increasingly expected and required to exhibit restraint and control bodily functions. Self-restraint is accompanied by a higher threshold of shame and embarrassment in which people not only restrain themselves from participating in certain forms of bodily conduct that have become proscribed (such as urinating in open public spaces) but also refrain from discussing them publicly.

Elias's analysis of etiquette guides shows how there was a gradual but distinct shift from explicit discussion of certain bodily functions and how to manage them (not belching or blowing one's nose without a handkerchief in front of one's superiors) to almost no reference to these functions at all.

Elias's explanation for this virtual disappearance of explicit reference to social codes over time is that people increasingly internalized self-restraint and management norms in relation to particular functions and impulses. Moreover, a failure or rejection of self-restraint is usually attended by shame, experienced by oneself, and embarrassment, experienced by others.

Restraining Sleep and Sex

Internalized restraint stems from a gradual awareness that one has to maintain an inner standard of proper conduct. Sex and sleep are two readily available examples from everyday life that have been subject to historical and cultural transformation and have shifted increasingly from activities undertaken in shared public spaces to activities undertaken in discrete, private, domestic spaces. Elias's analysis of etiquette guides reveals that, in the past, no special nightclothes were worn for sleep and individuals went to bed, often with many others in the same room, either with no clothes or fully clothed. Moreover, the development of the modern house, with its many rooms and divisions, reflects a change in consciousness about the body. Similarly, sexual activity has shifted from activity conducted in public spaces to activity conducted behind closed doors in particular parts of the house, between particular categories of persons. The middle classes in nineteenth-century Britain became especially preoccupied with defining the boundaries of sex and developing social codes that proscribed forms of sexual conduct for people of different social classes (Weeks 1985). For the middle class, sexuality was governed by codes of privacy, heterosexuality and modesty, against which there were social sanctions that gave rise to shame and embarrassment if transgressed. In contrast, working-class sexuality was defined by different parameters. Though the working classes were held to account for less constrained forms of sexual conduct, the middle classes nonetheless expected such conduct, as well as the absence of shame and embarrassment (Bland 1982).

Civilizing bodily waste

The social management and disposal of bodily waste has become increasingly accompanied by both olfactory and auditory sensitivity, and verbal reference to human waste products carefully avoids direct reference to excreta (Inglis 2000). This sensitivity was reflected in the architecture and design of mid-nineteenth-century middle-class housing, in which toilets were moved inside behind closed doors – from privies, closets and 'middens' to internal household privies with cisterns. Post-war housing design, in which toilets were located more frequently inside dwellings, reflected a heightened sense of shame and embarrassment associated with being seen to enter and leave the outside toilet (Gurney 2000). The spatial regulation of bodily elimination was influenced by changes in the architecture and design of toilets, but, in addition, the temporal regulation of bodily elimination was affected by the development of capitalism (Inglis and Holmes 2000). The factory system in particular prescribed rules and regulations that impinged on the worker's body (Freund 1982). For instance, increasingly under capitalist time (Thompson 1967) toilet visits had to be taken within official breaks. In her study of women's experiences of menstruation, Emily Martin (1989) shows how difficult it continues to be for women to take time to visit the toilet outside of official breaks. Moreover, Mayall's account of how children perceive and manage their bodies at home and at school suggests that children quickly learn that they are required to 'subordinate their bodies to the formal regime' (1998: 147). They cannot, for instance, go to the toilet as they please, as they may at home, but must ask adults in positions of authority for permission. The bodily rhythms of the child are thus subject to adult control. However, though bodily rhythms such as those associated with the elimination of waste are influenced by time and operate in accordance with rhythms imposed on them, the human body continues to breach these impositions (Inglis and Holmes 2000), reflected in the prevalence and proliferation of 'toilet humour' (Inglis 2000).

Gender and restraint

There are gender implications in the shift of bodily functions from open, visible, public spaces to the concealed, private sanctum of domestic spaces. First, the spatial reorganization of polluting activities such as elimination, accompanied by the modern obsession with the ubiquity of germs (Patton 1986), requires vigilance

in terms of domestic hygiene, and more labour for those charged
with the maintenance of hygiene standards. Data from sources such
as the *British Social Attitudes Survey* and the International Labour
Organization suggest that, despite expressions of a more egalitarian
attitude from both women and men concerning divisions of domestic
labour, women on the whole tend to continue to undertake the bulk
of domestic work. Second, women are obliged to spend more time
in the toilet than men, by virtue of anatomy, variations in clothing
management and toilet etiquette, yet there are proportionately fewer
public facilities available for women (Edwards and McKie 1996). A
third gender implication in this shift concerns the reproduction of the
civilizing process across biographical time.

While self-restraint has replaced external controls imposed by
others over historical time, such restraint still needs to be fostered
within each generation. This task falls to the parents and carers of
children, and mothers in particular. Mothers and day carers spend a
great deal of their time in the early years of a child's life encouraging
them to become aware of their own bodies and sensitive to those of
others. This awareness is accompanied by teaching the techniques
of concealing and managing bodily functions and substances, of
acquiring the inner standards of bodily conduct consistent with a
civilized, and thus controlled, life. However, toilet training may be
a fraught process and children 'may defecate at precisely the point
in time when least expected or least desired' (Inglis and Holmes
2000: 237). Finally, there is some evidence that breaching codes of
bodily conduct can be used to establish social boundaries and create
physical space in contexts where these are threatened or limited. For
instance, one study of young women's experiences of homelessness
notes that the body features as a crucial resource of survival (Costello
1993). In this study, body odour in particular became a notable and
cultivated feature of life on the street that girls used to protect themselves from unwanted sexual advances.

The bounded self and individualization

A second aspect of the civilizing process is a change in consciousness such that people have become much more aware over time
of themselves as individuals (a process called 'individualization').
Concomitantly, people become more aware of both their own and
other bodies as separate, demarcated entities. Consequently the
boundaries between my/your body and ways of maintaining them
become increasingly important. For instance, physical space provides

a mechanism that ensures individual bodies are held at a discrete distance from each other. In the contemporary West, there are social rules concerning touch, such as who can touch whom, on which part of the body and in what kind of manner. This awareness of oneself as an individual is also a sense of oneself as relatively disconnected from others, as discrete or, indeed, as a self encased in a body which has become an object for oneself (Burkitt 1999).

The process of individualization and the emotional restraint increasingly valued from the onset of the civilizing process meant that the body became a form of armour or shield which could be used to protect or expertly to express oneself (Burkitt 1999). This is evident in the proliferation of rules and codes that helped establish physical distance both between people and between the human and natural world. Moreover, the emerging sense of individualization was reflected in clothing and dress, which became increasingly elaborate at the zenith of court society.

Social distinction: table conduct

Elias also discerned a shift in the tone and form of advice concerning appetite and table manners. One study (Mennell 1991) that develops Elias's thesis focuses on the civilizing of appetite and examines how 'sumptuary laws' from the late Middle Ages were initially meant to prevent people from over-indulging in times of relative food scarcity and discourage over-eating. Gradually, these laws included more details and guidelines about foods that were considered indulgent or frugal, dishes that could be served and the ways in which they could be served. In particular, an increasing emphasis upon table manners and an emerging tendency to value foods for their delicacy and elegance (Lupton 1996) was linked to an awareness of social status in a courtly society that was hierarchical and segmented. Moreover, the way in which advice was given changed from a broad view of what was considered good and bad (vulgar) and began to describe acceptable table conduct on the basis of what those with **social status** (or power) were already doing. Therefore advice focused on instructions that essentially differentiated between not only different kinds of conduct, but also conduct associated with people of different social status. For instance, the development of culinary utensils in the nineteenth century made it possible for the emerging European bourgeoisie to eat without touching food with their hands, in the belief that such touch was undignified and unrefined.

Dining Out

The role of manners in establishing social distinction (a consequence of the civilizing process) is taken up by the French sociologist Pierre Bourdieu, who shows how the acquisition and display of manners marks differences within economically and culturally privileged groups (1984: 68). This seems evident in the practice of dining out, a social event that differs from either eating within the context of domestic space (Lupton 1996) or consuming 'fast food' on the run (Ritzer 1993). The choice of restaurant and displays of knowledge about food, wine and restaurant etiquette exemplify how manners establish social distance and distinction (Finkelstein 1989). On the one hand, restaurant conduct requires actors to engage in activities that are both stylized, such as using cutlery in particular ways and sequences, and ritualized, such as eating food prepared as a course in a particular order. On the other, according to Finkelstein, the experience of dining out stifles the expression of emotion in its emphasis on ritual and order, and this too may be seen as a product of the civilizing process.

Emotional restraint

The change in consciousness or ontology identified by Elias was associated with an emerging perception of an external world as from within a separate and distinct bodily location. Elias describes this shift in consciousness in terms of looking out onto the world as it were, as a 'thinking statue', in still and silent contemplation of a world external to us with which we have lost contact (Burkitt 1999). Therefore a third important element of the civilizing process concerns the emphasis placed increasingly on finer control over emotional expression and physical gestures towards others on two levels. First, Elias traces the diminution of displays of aggressiveness of the sort associated with the feudal anarchy of the European High Middle Ages. The emergence of nation-states broadly displaced such displays with orderly and disciplined military conduct and the power of the law. It is not so much that displays of aggressiveness are now subject to prohibition in all circumstances, but that opportunities for such display are highly regulated and spatially organized. For instance, sport provides socially approved opportunities for men in particular to engage in such displays, though there are discernible codes of conduct concerning degrees and forms of display (Shilling 1993).

Second, Elias outlines a shift in psychological attitude towards a greater concern for, and expanded ability to, discern the thoughts and feelings of persons, which are in turn increasingly hidden behind masks of politeness. Weber's ideal-type of the faceless bureaucrat (immortalized in George Orwell's *1984*) provides an illustration of the observation Elias is making. Elias observes how a premium has increasingly been placed on emotional restraint, in that people are expected to control their emotions and feelings and not allow themselves to display them indiscriminately. Emotional reserve also emerged as a consequence of urban dwelling. Because city life offers too much stimulation, it becomes more and more difficult to respond spontaneously, and instead people cultivate a 'blasé attitude' (Simmel 1971: 326) as a form of protection against the vacillations of metropolitan life. Thus, in social situations, feelings may be felt but may not always be shown (Burkitt 1999) and emotions are no longer pliable to open display. This means that people need to become more skilled in reading and interpreting the faces and gestures of others (as we have seen in the previous chapter) and work hard to avoid offence. However, opportunities for the collective display of emotional forms such as grief or joy may be increasing (Maffesoli 1995), as public responses to the death of Diana, Princess of Wales, or John Kennedy Jr. seem to suggest. Moreover, though masculinity in modernity has been associated largely with emotional control (Seidler 1994), there has been a marked shift in the public display of feeling. World leaders such as Tony Blair or Bill Clinton, for instance, have become adept at knowing when and how to display emotions and which emotions might be appropriately displayed.

The body as a natural symbol

Matter-out-of-place

Elias's analysis demonstrates how the emergence of modernity is predicated on the civilizing process. His approach is extremely valuable because it establishes a historical dimension based on empirically derived observations of textual data that are amenable to re-examination and re-analysis. However, how are control, concealment and individualization maintained in the contemporary period and what purpose does this serve? To answer this question sociologists have found the anthropological perspective of Mary Douglas useful. Douglas views the human body as a **natural symbol**, or as a classification system which is common to all human beings and which is used to express ideas about the social order. The kinds of beliefs which societies hold about the body reveal something about what is deemed important in that society, and tell us about the kinds of things which that society finds **sacred** or **profane**.

Douglas developed her approach from a close reading of the work of the French sociologist Emile Durkheim and his view that all societies differentiate between the sacred and the profane (Durkheim 1976). Durkheim observed that all societies make distinctions between objects and ideas that are special and require protection, and objects or ideas that are profane, which are categorically distinct from the sacred and must be kept at a physical distance. While for Durkheim religious ceremony establishes and maintains these distinctions, for Douglas, in a secular context, beliefs and rituals play a part in upholding this distinction. Douglas extends this to beliefs about the body, which make distinctions between the sacred and profane, or between what is clean or pure and what is considered **dirt** or **pollution** (Douglas 1970). For Douglas, what is considered **dirt** in any one society is simply that which is **matter-out-of-place**. For our purposes, following Elias, it is what Western societies consider to be 'uncivilized'.

For Douglas, the relationship between the body and society is like looking in a mirror, and in a now oft-quoted text she notes:

> The social body constrains the way in which the physical body is perceived. The physical experience of the body, always modified by the social categories through which it is known, sustains a particular view of society. There is a continual exchange of meanings between the two forms of bodily experience so that each reinforces the categories of the other. As a result of this interaction the body itself is a highly restricted medium of expression. 'The forms it adopts in movement and repose express social pressures in manifold ways . . . all the cultural categories in which it is perceived must correlate closely with the categories in which society is seen in so far as these also draw upon the same culturally processed idea of the body. (Douglas 1970: xiii)

That is, the meanings of the physical body and of the social body reinforce each other, and it is difficult to understand one without understanding the other.

Bidets and Buttocks as Matter-out-of-Place

There are cultural differences in the significance of disgust and its relation to civilizing bodily waste. For instance, in 2006, a Japanese manufacturer of bidets launched an advertising campaign in New

York to market bidets to the US. The company, Toto, launched a website titled *Clean is Happy*, featuring the image of naked buttocks with smiley faces. An accompanying billboard advertisement in Times Square featured the images of six naked people seen from behind, along with smiley faces, as on the website. However, a local church complained about the billboard advertisement (they were disgusted?) and so the billboard ran with an image of naked people from behind, their buttocks covered with a wide white bar (Terada 2007).[2]

Dirt and dirty work

In Douglas's work, the body is seen as a natural symbol which different societies use to make classifications between what they consider to be pure/polluted, clean/dirty. Orifices are especially potent because of the way that body products must cross orifices in order to enter the social world, where they may be disruptive and have to be appropriately managed. Subsequently, bodily substances are perceived largely as dirt and have designated places that are generally hidden from public view, because when such products leave the body they are considered to be on the wrong side of the boundary, as matter-out-of-place. Dirt in this framework is anything that is defined as matter-out-of-place, anything that has crossed a body boundary (usually an orifice) and is, therefore, in the wrong place. **Taboos** are beliefs and rules which societies develop (construct) to maintain dirt in its rightful place and which, in turn, represent or symbolize the social order (for instance, they often reflect the social positions of the dominant social group). Dirt is therefore a relative concept since all substances are potentially polluting.

It is sociologically interesting to ask what is considered dirty, in what set of circumstances and by whom? The work that gynaecology nurses do illustrates Douglas's distinction between clean and dirty. As Bolton (2005) observes, this work involves touching intimate places and spaces of the body that are deemed 'unmentionable' via their association with the termination of pregnancy, incontinence, infertility and sexually transmitted disease. Consequently, this 'dirty work' renders nurses morally and socially 'tainted' 'because what should remain private and invisible is made public and rendered visible' (Bolton 2005: 176).

---

[2] I am grateful to Phoebe Kho of *Point Forward* for bringing this example to my attention.

Therefore, concepts of clean and dirty are mechanisms that express what is considered the proper order of things. When we examine social taboos we are also looking at relations of power in societies and at which groups exercise power over others. Hence, distinctions between purity and pollution not only differentiate between social groups but also carry a moral load that is used to express a particular moral order.

Pause and Reflect: In 2009 Energizer Inc. introduced the *Schick Quattro Trimstyle Razor*, which includes a bikini trimmer. An advert for the product, which launched in Europe, shows women dancing to a catchy song called 'Mow the Lawn' as they trim hedges. The ad went viral online. But in the United States, a toned down version of the advert shows shrubs shrinking into various designs as women walk by them – an allusion to trimming the bikini line. What do you think these examples reveal about modern bodily taboos? What key changes do you see in the language people use to discuss the body? What do you feel about such changes?

Cleanliness and germs

The cleanliness of the body and the significance of body boundaries are central in contemporary ideas about disease. Before the identification of the germ, cleanliness was associated with hiding visible dirt (Vigarello 1988). Though contemporary understandings of cleanliness are largely predicated upon ideas about hygiene that are defined by a germ-free environment, knowledge about the germ is relatively new in historical terms and stems from scientific endeavour in the nineteenth century. The germ is of course invisible to the naked eye, and is potentially everywhere, ubiquitous and anxiety-provoking because of its hidden nature (Patton 1986). The belief that the body was a source of contamination and danger strengthened in the late nineteenth century, influenced by ideas about the ubiquity of dirt and disease. Personal cleanliness became a focus for zealous campaign and reform, not only because it was thought a clean body washed with soap would keep disease at bay, but also because of an increasing equivalence between personal cleanliness and moral purity (Lupton 1995). Beliefs about the body as the source of potential physical and symbolic pollution strengthened in the nineteenth century, as, for members of the middle classes, a clean body came increasingly to represent a clean mind.

The eradication of personal germs has become a feature of the late modern era, where a range of products is now marketed to remove visible and invisible dirt, body odours and bacteria. For instance, television advertising for anti-perspirants in the UK and the US typically allude to the invisible bacteria that exist on the surface of the skin and combine with perspiration to create odours. Products are presented to the audience as 'working' against these bacteria in ways that contribute to 'fresh'-smelling skin. Presented thus, it reinforces both the notion that the social concealment of smell is desirable and that what is perceived as clean is largely associated with a germ-free environment. Dirt is associated (though not exclusively) with the presence of germs and cleanliness is identified with the eradication of germs, of the invisible.

However, while germs are literally associated with the maintenance of cleanliness and hygiene, the germ also operates as a metaphor for social hygiene. The germ has become increasingly significant in the contemporary West as a metaphor for invasion (Sontag 1991), for things that should be in one place crossing over to another place, where they don't belong. In the late modern age, because of their ubiquity and invisibility, germs are associated with anxiety, which is highly ironic, since people in the contemporary West are exposed to relatively fewer sources of bacteria than were previous generations. Yet we fear germs: they are the bad guys. For some cultural commentators, panic is the dominant mood of the late twentieth century, reflected in concerns about the integrity of the body and an obsession about the cleanliness of body fluids, a kind of 'body McCarthyism' (e.g., Kroker and Kroker 1988). In part, cultural anxiety about germs as invisible invaders has been fuelled by the emergence of HIV and AIDS (Patton 1986) and the ways in which language and metaphor frame how disease and illness is understood (Lakoff and Johnson 1980).

Metaphors of pollution

As of the end of 2009, an estimated 33.3 million people worldwide were living with HIV/AIDS. More than 67 per cent of these people live in sub-Saharan Africa (USAID 2011). HIV is a virus that can be contracted via blood and blood products and sexual fluids. Previously known as 'HTLV' and as the 'gay plague', HIV usually leads to AIDS, which causes the immune system to collapse, and 'people with AIDS' (PWA) are prey to a whole range of problems, from thrush to pneumonia. There are few effective treatments, although some drugs may delay the progression of AIDS. Similarly, HIV-positive people may live for a long period of time before developing AIDS. HIV emerged in the early 1980s as a cluster of symptoms which were registered and tracked by the Center for Disease Control and the National Institutes of Health in the US (Shilts 1988) and the Contagious Diseases Surveillance Centres in the UK (one in Scotland, one in England). As a new infectious disease, HIV shook faith in medical progress and shattered the idea that medicine had triumphed in the eradication of infectious diseases (Fox 1986).

HIV/AIDS has been subject to demonizing metaphors not only of invasion, but also of pollution, implying invasion from outside rather than from within. Susan Sontag (1991) makes the point that it is difficult to think about AIDS beyond the metaphors that give it meaning. The body is typically viewed as a fortress or a nation-state and diseases as invaders of one kind or another (Martin 1990). Whereas tuberculosis in the nineteenth century or cancer in the twentieth century were characterized as body invaders from within, HIV is characterized as an invader from outside the body, removing its defences and allowing the opportunistic infections associated with AIDS to overwhelm the body. HIV/AIDS is often represented as a punishment for living particular kinds of **lifestyle** (such as taking health risks, excesses of diet, weaknesses of will, self-indulgence, addiction) and compared to the plague (Sontag 1991). This comparison seems particularly evident in some of the initial public health campaigns that used visual images. For instance, HIV/AIDS was associated with images of death (the grim reaper campaign in Australia and the tombstone campaign in the UK). Analysis of these images suggests they incited fears about the mysterious and inevitable spread of HIV and emphasized its potential to affect or to 'strike down' large numbers of people without warning (Lupton 1994). Hence, initial public health images associated HIV with plague and reinforced ideas about punishment and moral judgements on society.

The images and metaphors that give meaning to AIDS also shaped the responses of politicians, the voluntary sector and the public. Images of the body as a fortress invaded by germs invoke metaphorical boundaries between 'them' and 'us' in ways that reinforce ideas about clean and dirty. Such boundaries perpetuate stigmatizing attitudes and responses. Analyses of the metaphors associated with HIV suggest that they signalled a range of meanings. First, they hinted at a degree of moral panic (Weeks 1988) in the sense that they evoked social uncertainty and effectively stigmatized particular social groups (gay men, Haitians, drug users, sex workers). Second, such metaphors aroused a sense of social and moral pollution and were used by moral entrepreneurs (such as tabloid newspapers) to 'man the barricades' against such pollution (Watney 1988). For instance, parliamentary records in the UK (*Hansard*, 30 April 1986) show how the Right Honourable John McKay, then Secretary of State for Health, asserted in a parliamentary debate that AIDS was a 'punishment from God' which was 'self-inflicted' and 'morally reprehensible'. Such comment illustrates morally and politically conservative concerns about the breakdown of a post-war moral consensus (Weeks 1988) and the expansion of sexual diversity represented by HIV (Sontag 1991). Third, such metaphors contributed to both informal and formal quarantine measures, which had the effect of perpetuating metaphorical and literal boundaries between pure and polluted bodies. On the one hand, the state instigated new powers associated with quarantine measures such as compulsory blood testing of certain social groups, more stringent immigration controls and powers of detention of those considered to be in a 'dangerously infected state' (Public Health (Control of Diseases) Act 1984). On the other hand, informal 'practices of decontamination' such as excluding gay men from restaurants and clubs or refusing dental treatment to gay men perpetuated symbolic boundaries between clean and dirty bodies (Patton 1986). These solutions and images define a boundary between self and other; between clean and dirty; between pure and polluted (Crawford 1994). However, many people affected by HIV formed groups (such as ACTUP – the AIDS Coalition to Unleash Power) and staged protests and media events (Watney 1988) that challenge these boundaries and establish new images.

Pollution and contamination

Heterosexual responses to HIV were largely symbolic, and their function was to reinforce social boundaries between what was considered clean and innocent (the bodies of haemophiliacs) and dirty (the bodies of gay men and drug users). The intention of such boundary-drawing was to reduce the perceived threat of physical contamination (the blood supply) and of symbolic contamination (e.g., the idea of homosexuality). Therefore, pollution beliefs about the body can be used to make social distinctions between categories of people, and in particular these distinctions represent power differences. Douglas puts it thus:

> A polluting person is always in the wrong. He has developed some
> wrong condition or simply crossed over some line which should

not have been crossed and this displacement unleashes danger for someone. (1970: 4)

Pollution beliefs associated with sexual activity and the exchange of body fluids uphold a particular version of the moral order in which homosexuality was deemed polluted or dirty (Alcorn 1988). The way in which HIV was described and discussed (invasion, threat, alien attack) reflected not only knowledge about viruses and immune systems but also beliefs about certain practices and relationships. Therefore, analyses of the images and metaphors associated with HIV/AIDS demonstrate further that the body has a symbolic role in identifying and maintaining boundaries between different social groups and is used symbolically to express power relations. In the example of HIV in the UK, Australia and the US, those with greater access to social power have monopolized the meanings associated with the body. Similarly, the beliefs that are embedded in contemporary views of menstruation reveal something about the social position of women in contemporary Western contexts.

Body taboos

For Douglas, body orifices are especially problematic because they are points or margins over which fluids, substances and objects can cross in either direction, from the body into the social world (e.g., blood, saliva, urine, faeces, pus) or from the social world into the body. They are potentially troublesome because they disrupt bodily order, and the way in which they are dealt with by society can tell us about the nature of order in that society. Indeed, such fluids or substances are coded in terms of unclean or dirty, and 'dirt', and refer simply to anything that challenges the order of things and moves from one place to another – becoming matter-out-of-place.

A key aspect of Douglas's argument concerns the importance of sustaining boundaries between what is considered clean and dirty, or pure and polluted. Taboos – beliefs about what can be touched or talked about in any one society – in secular Western societies are often associated with the social management of bodily orifices and secretions, which are seen as having a particular, well-defined social place and space. When substances leave the body they represent the movement of the natural world into the social world, and, similarly, when substances are taken into the body they cross over from the social to the natural world. The movement of such substances reinforces the significance of the **margins** of the body, the vulnerable points of contact between the body (the natural world) and the social world. Douglas contends that, because this movement of substances from one place to another involves crossing boundaries between the social and the natural world, they have to be carefully managed. Such secretions are deemed potentially disruptive, and therefore taboos and the practices associated with them function as mechanisms that hold specified forms of conduct in place. As illustrated in the example of menstruation, taboos create social classifications between people and establish degrees of social control.

Menstruation: still taboo?

It has long been held in feminist scholarship that a taboo of silence and etiquette conceals menstruation in the contemporary West (Laws 1990). Blood carries many meanings, such as pain, death and warfare, which in turn represent disorder (Douglas 1970), and blood on the surface of the body breaches its boundaries, be it through injury or in the controlled environment of surgery (Lupton 1994). Menstrual blood in particular, as the 'living matter that helps to sustain and bring forth life' (Grosz 1990: 92), is a meaningful and potentially anxiety-provoking fluid, and many cultures have established pollution beliefs and taboos associated with menstrual blood (Buckley and Gottlieb 1988). Menstrual blood, therefore, is considered taboo in many cultures and historical eras and elicits feelings of shame and disgust when revealed or exposed (Thurren 1994). For instance, Pliny thought that menstruating women could ruin crops, kill bees and sour milk; in some contexts it is considered weakening to vitality if men have sexual relations with a menstruating woman; and in biblical times menstruating women were physically isolated from others, since they were considered impure at this time (de Beauvoir [1949] 1972). Martin (1989) notes that in 1878 the *British Medical Journal* announced as scientific fact that meat spoils if menstruating women touch it. In many cultural and historical contexts, women have been segregated physically and socially when menstruating.

Clearly women in the contemporary West are not forced into physical segregation. However, some scholars have observed that, even in the liberal and liberated West, there are beliefs and taboos associated with menstruation, which tell us something about power relations between men and women. Anthropological research undertaken by Emily Martin (1989) examined what women in the US thought and felt about reproduction, pregnancy and menstruation. She conducted interviews with a broad sample of women and asked them to talk in depth about their experiences. Once she had collected her data she began to examine the transcripts for the ways in which women described their experiences, and in particular she examined the language and metaphors they used. One of the things she found was that certain metaphors and images kept recurring as the women talked about experiences of menstruation and childbirth.

For many women in Martin's study, menstruation represented hassle. All the women recognized menstruation as something that they considered messy, gross, dirty, and all held a general awareness that anything that drew attention to menstruation was considered taboo. They acknowledged that to draw attention to menstruation was socially out of bounds, but this hidden nature of menstruation was a real, or material, problem for many women. For instance, in the context of heavily supervised paid employment or of the thoroughly timetabled education system, it often proved difficult to find space and time to change sanitary wear and it was hard to point out the discomforts of menstruation. There was a tension for many women between not attracting notice when they are menstruating, but being constrained by the demands of work or school in ways that made it difficult to hide the fact that they were menstruating. More recent research suggests that menstruation taboos may no longer be as powerful as perhaps they once were, although girls are still taught strategies of concealment, and menarche may still invoke shame and embarrassment (Lee 2008).

Constructing Menstrual Taboos

Martin also examined medical and scientific texts on reproduction, pregnancy and menstruation, and her analysis suggests that the prevailing metaphor underpinning contemporary ideas about menstruation is one of industrial production. According to Martin, twentieth-century medical texts have a tendency to describe menstruation as failed reproduction and are characteristic of industrialized societies in which production is paramount. Hence, not to be productive is to be deviant in industrialized societies, and women who are not (re)productive are considered an aberration. Moreover, because the male body is generally considered the norm in medical practice, menstruation, perceived as the failure to produce, represents decay and disorder. Martin makes the point that the language and metaphorical devices used to describe menstruation reveal something about its place in Western culture. For her, the reliance on metaphors of production suggests that menstruating women are viewed as not being productive, and menstruation is therefore seen as matter-out-of-place. She argues that, while menstruation in the contemporary West is not physically segregated, it is nonetheless concealed and not accommodated. This is especially marked in the context of paid employment. As women have increasingly moved into the workforce, often in contexts supervised by men, their embodied needs as women have been ignored because of the taboos that prevent open and specific discussion of these needs.

Menstrual etiquette as concealment

Another study on menstruation develops a distinct analysis that argues that not only does the contemporary West fail to accommodate menstruation, in fact, menstruation is culturally concealed. The approach taken by Sophie Laws (1990) differs from that taken by Martin. While still within an ethnographic tradition, Laws examined the content and imagery of medical texts and conducted interviews with men on their views and attitudes concerning menstruation. From them, she learned that menstruation was something that was talked about neither in the households in which her respondents grew up nor in their current households. Moreover, the men in her study had rarely been aware of their mothers' menstruation, and they reported that their current female partners rarely talked about menstruation, except in the context of discomfort. Indeed, women were perceived by many men as using menstruation to withdraw sexual participation, a point noted in studies of heterosexual intimacy (e.g., Duncombe and Marsden 1993). Finally, jokes and euphemisms were associated with menstruation, such as 'red flag', 'lady in red', 'jam' or 'the curse'. Therefore Laws argued that menstruation is associated with 'dirt'. It is forbidden as a subject of talk except in certain highly constrained contexts and it tends to be seen as a form of social contamination. While menstruation was clearly known about by men, they kept it at a distance and it was kept from them.

For Laws, talk about menstruation was governed by what she termed a menstrual etiquette that regulated who can say what to whom and in what circumstances. The consequences of this etiquette are that women are meant to buy, store, use and dispose of sanitary wear without anyone knowing, especially the men with whom they live. In particular for Laws, this suggests that, for many women, the shame of menstruation stems from men's attitudes. However, though similar views have been identified in other studies of menstruation, it is not necessarily the case that all women and men share a commitment to the etiquette of concealment to which Laws refers. For instance, George and Murcott (1992) interviewed men and women and found that whether men were aware of or acknowledged the menstruation of their partners and friends depended on their exposure to and awareness of their mothers' menstruation. Moreover, you may wish to argue here that menstruation in the contemporary West is no longer kept hidden. For instance, advertising for feminine hygiene products in the UK has expanded in terms of both topic and timing. The first magazine advertising for sanitary wear or feminine hygiene products appeared in 1921, when Kotex promoted its first product (Laws 1990). By 1933, advertisements for sanitary wear were a staple feature of women's magazines. When the first television advert appeared in 1979, it was governed by very strict codes in terms of what words could be used and how feminine hygiene could be presented (Treneman 1988). For instance, blood was never to be mentioned (and still isn't); odour was never to be alluded to and any upfront naming of menstruation was to be avoided. Moreover, no reference could be made to anything that might undermine women's self-confidence in hygiene (Laws 1990).

Cordon sanitaire

Newer visual formats are employed that structure the advertising of many feminine hygiene products in the UK and US. One format has women talking in a focus group about their experience of using the products (toilet paper products advertising uses this format too). Another draws on vignettes in which women are seen doing unusual or daring things or wearing white clothes; these scenarios suggest that the products themselves are so good that women need not restrict what they are doing or the kind of clothes they wear. While menstrual blood itself is not talked about, allusions are knowingly and sometimes playfully made to it (think about the blue liquid poured onto fabric as an illustration of product absorption). This advertising formula was largely followed until new codes were introduced in the late 1990s that expanded the words that can be used. The themes embedded in feminine hygiene advertising also changed to include freedom, discretion, activity, and increasingly, openness, while subtle changes in advertising emphasize the realities of women's experience and the possibilities of 'carrying on as usual'.

Yet these feminine hygiene advertisements managed to imply

freedom while at the same time laying stress on concealment and discretion (you can carry on as normal and no one need ever know – for instance, think about recent adverts that suggest feminine hygiene products can be mistaken for sweets or sugar). Hence, a boundary was drawn around menstruation. Drawing on Douglas, Laws refers to this as a *cordon sanitaire*, which allows the illusion of freedom on the one hand, but also contains the pollution threat. It does so by referring to menstruation in a discrete language which women are assumed to understand, so that men do not have to deal with the consequences of the leaky, messy female body.

Talking about Feminine Hygiene

In 2010 Kimberly-Clark launched a series of television advertisements that self-consciously deconstruct stereotypically touchy-feely feminine products. The new line of pads and tampons was packaged in bright colours, and in the commercials, a woman says (with irony), 'I want to hold really soft things, like my cat' and 'sometimes I just want to run on the beach, I like to twirl, maybe in slow motion.' The commercial then closes with the line: 'Why are tampon ads so ridiculous?' There is a series of these adverts and you can check them out on YouTube (http://www.youtube.com/watch?v=lpypeLL1dAs&feature=player_embedded).   However, it's worth reflecting that the original adverts were banned in the United States because they featured the word vagina.

Resisting taboo

The kind of analysis presented by Martin and Laws focuses on pollution beliefs and metaphors associated with menstruation and the ways in which it continues to be seen in the contemporary West as something which is shameful and must be concealed. For Martin, women internalize shame in ways that create tensions between the social requirement to conceal menstruation and the practical difficulties of doing so in environments that are often male-dominated (work) or tightly timetabled (education). For Laws, women internalize shame because pollution beliefs stem from male disgust, and hence they conceal menstruation in order to protect men from having to confront the female body. While Martin and Laws share the view that menstruation continues to be subject to concealment, they differ in their analysis of the origins of pollution beliefs. Whereas, for Laws, the symbolic segregation of menstruation is a deeply problematic indication of a patriarchal society, Martin sees some value in the

cordon sanitaire placed around menstruation. In a society characterized by bodily regulation and industrial order, taboos have the potential for rebellion. If women have to confront menstruation secretly,
they may also use this as an opportunity to discuss other hidden
aspects of female experience, as 'back regions' in which women *can*
take time out from industrial or capitalist time (work) or the scrutiny
of men (Edwards and McKie 1996).

Body boundaries

Douglas argues that the body symbolizes society (its structure and
organization, its beliefs) and society symbolizes the body. Because
the body is universal to human beings it is like a model of a system
that is bounded, which has a definite shape. Boundaries are special
entities because they are vulnerable; they can be crossed, disrupted,
challenged. Therefore, boundaries in any social system have to be
policed, guarded and monitored by gatekeepers. In the Douglas
framework, the kind and degree of care which social groups exercise
over the physical body reflect concerns and anxieties about what is
important in the social body. In these terms, the power relations
embedded within any social structure will be reproduced in terms of
how the body is regarded and dealt with. For instance, many feminist scholars note that the female body is considered uncontrollable,
wayward, leaky and uncontained. In particular, the childbearing
body is associated with a suspension of bodily control (Carter 2010),
epitomizing a 'boundary situation' (Davidson 2000c). A boundary
situation represents the potential for disruption of the boundary
between containment and leakiness, in which the unbounded body
could at any time 'release matter' (Lawton 1998). For women especially, it is argued that being embodied necessarily entails maintaining and protecting bodily boundaries.

Agora- and other phobias

Women who suffer from agoraphobia experience a cluster of symptoms that are associated with a fear of public or crowded spaces,
which may be a gender-specific expression of a boundary problem
(Davidson 2000b). The culprit is space, which, as Davidson notes,
quoting Probyn, 'presses against bodies differently' (1995: 83) as a
pathological space of consumption. In managing their fear of space,
women in Davidson's study recalled how they used strategies such as

touching or holding onto objects (e.g., keys, a bicycle), which help in a phenomenological way to control the boundaries (or the destabilization of the boundaries) between inner and outer lived space. As Davidson observes, these strategies helped women to retain a bodily sense of where they are in the taken-for-granted world of 'lived space' (Davidson 2000a, 2000b).

Boundaries and efforts to control the potential for 'matter-out-of-place' play a role in explaining other phobias too, because of the ways in which the phobic objects (e.g., spiders, feathers) threaten danger. Phobic objects contain the potential to constitute a boundary breach by the unpredictability of the noises or movement they can make (Davidson and Smith 2003). Here the culprit seems to be less space itself than anxieties about specific objects, a fear of being contaminated by the phobic object and a highly tuned disgust sensitivity. As discussed earlier, disgust is associated with the civilizing process and plays a role in creating social and moral distinction. As Kolnai puts it (2004), we register disgust as an embodied sensibility, or a 'gut' feeling, that suggests a thing or person is somehow morally contaminating (although moral contamination, as Nussbaum 2004 suggests, can be culturally variable and quite deliberately cultivated by social groups to demarcate themselves from others they deem 'disgusting').

Davidson, however, drawing on the work of Julia Kristeva, also argues that disgust functions to maintain a boundary between nature (the body, especially the skin, which acts as an outer boundary to the self) and culture, and in doing so preserves the symbolic order (Davidson 2000c). This preservation may be especially significant as boundaries between the natural and cultural are challenged by social and technological changes.

Pause and Reflect: 'Evolution ends when technology enters the body' (Stelarc 1998). To what extent do visual representations challenge so-called boundaries between the body and technology?

Body fluidity and the bounded self

The American theorist Donna Haraway, who writes across disciplinary boundaries, has commented that we live in a cyborg culture, that indeed we are all cyborgs (Haraway 1985). This observation seems especially apt if we look at medical technologies and devices that can take the place of limbs and other body parts and processes. Such devices take the form of implants, replacements (using metals such as titanium, as in hip replacements) and grafts (using not only human but also animal tissue, such as porcine skin). Organs (heart, lung, liver) can be transplanted from one body to another, often involving the prolongation of the life of one body in order to secure organic material for another (Strathern 1992). From mundane medical technologies such as cardiac pacemakers to hyper-real processes that 're-engineer' the body through, for instance, the manipulation of genetic material (Williams 1997) or the use of the human body as a source of 'spare parts' (Fox and Swazey 1992), medical and other technologies are increasingly a deeply embedded part of everyday life.

Indeed, the development of biotechnologies in particular has expanded body boundaries, such that matter or parts from one body can be installed in the bodies of others. Through biotechnological means (e.g., instruments and chemistry), many human body parts (e.g., eggs, organs, sperm, embryonic stem cells) can be donated or traded; the body is increasingly marked as a particular kind of material object that can enter into a system of exchange (Everett 2003), albeit in ways that are generally considered illegitimate (Ertman and Williams 2005). As Gupta and Richters put it, the body is capable of being transformed from a reproductive to a productive body through body parts that can be marketed and sold in a context that increasingly supports global movement and cross-border transactions (Gupta and Richters 2008). Body parts can be transformed into lucrative commodities, from essential substances (e.g., organs) to tissue transformed into patentable cell lines, genetic information or pharmaceuticals (Waldby et al. 2004).

This fluidity of body boundaries has led some scholars to refer to the body as a 'mosaic of detachable pieces', or 'organs-without-bodies' (Braidotti 1989) that are enmeshed within a continuum of technologies, from the banal to the spectacular (Kunzru 1996). This fluidity and continuity between the body and technology through practices of trade and transfer blur boundaries between a discretely intact body/self and a distributed self (Tober 2007), and challenge what it means to be an individual and destabilize the idea of selfhood (Gupta and Richters 2008). Developments in both the legal and illegitimate exchange of body parts raise legal, moral and identity questions about personhood, bioidentity and ownership, about the extent to which our bodies are ourselves, and the status of body parts once they become detached from their bodies of origin. These questions are at the heart of several legal cases in Europe, North America and Australia. For instance, while organ donation is a relatively widespread phenomenon in which a donor 'gifts' blood or a body part to another upon death (Valentine 2005; Haddow 2005), in the UK and Australia, the organs of hospitalized children who died in infancy were collected and retained without the knowledge of their parents, creating (as discussed in chapter 6) not only scandal but raising questions about the notion of bodily wholeness and its relation to personhood (Sheach Leith 2008).

Finally, not only is the body enmeshed within a continuum of technologies, but also power relations that differ by ethnicity. For instance, Kathleen Erwin et al. (2009) explore how the circulation of blood outside the individual body intersects with its circulation in the Chinese social body and how individuals frame their acts of blood donation in this process. While many of the participants who took part in ethnographic interviews viewed their blood donation as both a voluntary act and also as fulfilling a social obligation, these donations were structured by a 'social contract'. The participants' accounts reflected socialist calls for individuals to contribute to society's greater good, and the propaganda of mass education campaigns that compels citizens to do 'glorious deeds' whilst at the same time providing compensation in the form of money, goods and time off. Erwin et al. (2009) conclude that these descriptions demonstrate the complexities of socio-cultural change in a 'postsocialist' Chinese society, involving a growing consumer culture and increasing individual autonomy. While the socialist workplace continues to be an important social and economic structure in China, whereby workers' production is transformed into a social 'good', this transformation is situated within the individual bodies of workers and extracted through compelling them to contribute to a better society via the work unit and the worker's obligations to the work unit.

Pause and Reflect: Under what circumstances could your body become property that can be transferred to a different owner?

Children, Technology and Disability

A qualitative study by Susan Kirk (2010) explored the experiences of 28 children living with medical technologies such as mechanical ventilation, oxygen therapy or peritoneal dialysis. In-depth interviews yielded information about how these technologies affected their everyday lives and relationships, and in particular, their ambivalence to technology which they saw as having both enabling and disabling effects on their lives. On the one hand, these technologies, which many children viewed as an extension

of their bodies, supported their health and often kept them out
of hospital. On the other, these technologies also intruded in
their sensory lives through noise, discomfort and pain, disrupted
school, and required additional surveillance from others to ensure
the technology functioned effectively. As an 11-year-old boy, Pele,
who required overnight mechanical ventilation, observed: 'I can't
go away with just me and my Mum, I have to have somebody else,
if they starts alarming. I can't have peace with my Mum' (p. 1799).

The children in this study worked hard to reduce the intrusions
of technology into their lives, by working around constraints.
They also worked hard to incorporate the technology they lived
with into their personal and social identities at a time of profound
and intense development (adolescence), when bodily comparison
is key. In order to soften the tangible and often visible ways their
bodies were marked as different (via technologies that pose a
physical and symbolic threat to their developing identities), many
children sought to control information about the technology (see
chapter 1 on information management to reduce identity discrep
ancies). For instance, one strategy involved not revealing their
technology dependence to others if it was possible to conceal it,
in order to reduce the need to manage the emotional responses
of others. Another involved 'normalizing' the technology and presenting it to others as a 'natural' part of their bodies and everyday
lives.

Cyborg dys/utopias

Though the technical definition of cyborg highlights the fusion
between human and machine, it has taken on a wider cultural significance and raises questions about the ways that body experience and
selfhood are altered by the human–machine interface (Lupton and
Seymour 2000). Extensions to the boundaries of the body through
biotechnologies, virtual worlds and digital manipulation challenge
the location of identity and the status of what is considered human
(Toffoletti 2007). It is part of the Western imagination, from Mary
Shelley's *Frankenstein*, to space travel in the 1960s, to the 'bionic
man' of the 1970s ('we can rebuild him, we have the technology')
to the military research conducted in the Cold War era. Cyborg
refers to a hybrid entity combining some element of technology with
the organic and elicits mixed responses from people, in which, as
Haraway argues, there is no boundary between what is artificial and

Plate 3   Bioengineering: a golfer with a prosthetic leg
© Shutter | Dreamstime.com

what is real, since these boundaries, if they existed at all, are thoroughly dissolved. The human body is enhanced by a range of products, activities and technologies that call into question boundaries between nature and culture. The cyborg encourages us to ask how we define 'the human body', how it differs from 'technology' (Hogle 1995) and the extent to which technologies contribute to a sense of the permeability of boundaries between the natural and the sociocultural in ways that are suggestive of a 'post-human' body.

On the one hand, the notion of the cyborg contributes to cultural anxieties about nature – what is deemed natural – and undermines a precarious sense of what the body is and what it might become. This boundary paranoia about post-human society is reflected in popular culture through themes such as alien invasion (an *X Files* favourite), cyborgs (such as *Terminator*) or artificiality. Analysis of how Cherilyn Sarkisian LaPierre (Cher) is discussed in German media (Franckenstein 1997) suggests that, for many, cosmetic surgery and 'technological enhancement' represents the suppression of what is considered authentic or natural (see also p. 145). Moreover, the mobilization of categories such as 'natural' in discussion of cosmetic surgery is used to establish a moral boundary between the natural body and a body that is viewed as 'artificial'. Boundary anxieties are also evident in public responses to new forms of medical technology such as reproductive technologies, organ transplantation or biotechnology research.

On the other hand, the idea of the cyborg offers a utopian model that challenges dualisms and their negative consequences and raises important questions about the production of social hierarchies in relation to bodies (Blaikie et al. 2003). The motif and materiality of the cyborg troubles supposedly 'natural' hierarchies (think *Tombraider*'s Lara Croft here) and suggests that the human body can no longer be viewed as beyond social intervention and modification, but is, in fact, actively shaped by and achieved through social practices. The political implications of these empirical changes are associated with the claim that, if it is already impossible to say where the human body ends and technology begins, perhaps boundaries between other oppositions can be challenged, such as male/female, abled/disabled, queer/straight. The cyborg, then, is more than a description of social circumstances. The physical boundaries challenged by body modification techniques and practices also stand for creative possibility. As such, the boundary dissolution materialized in the cyborg functions as a motif of the possibility for political and social change.

Summary

The main focus of this chapter has been on the civilizing process and its implications for bodily conduct in modern Western contexts. The historical sociology of Norbert Elias shows how the concealment of bodily rhythms, individualization and emotional restraint characteristic of modernity are not inherent or natural characteristics but are products of social and historical change. Though there may be challenges, reversals and unevenness associated with the impact of the civilizing process, nonetheless it remains a central phenomenon in the development of modern Western societies. Responses of disgust to breaches of bodily control reveal the persistent power of the civilizing process. Moreover, anthropological research on the management of the infant body, HIV and menstruation shows how bodily control and concealment are sustained through contemporary pollution beliefs and practices. These are typically discerned in visual and textual metaphors that reveal the various ways in which social groups with access to power police and protect body boundaries and boundaries between the physical and social body. However, social and cultural phenomena are simultaneously dissolving boundaries between the physical and social body. The emergence of cyborg culture suggests that people in the contemporary West live in a post-human age in which natural and social worlds are deeply interconnected. Though such boundary dissolution gives rise to anxiety about the loss of the natural and the authentic, the cyborg motif also signals the possibility of radical change in social and political organization.

Further Reading

A good starting point in Elias's *Civilizing Process* is:
Elias, N. 1994. On blowing one's nose (part 2, section VI). *The Civilizing Process*. Oxford: Blackwell.
For material on menstruation, see:
Fingerson, L. 2006. *Girls in Power: Gender, Body and Menstruation in Adolescence*. New York: State University of New York Press.
Lee, J. 2008. Bodies at menarche: Stories of shame, concealment, and sexual maturation. *Sex Roles*, 60 (9–10), 615–27.
For material on body boundaries, see:
Draper, J. 2003. Blurring, moving and broken boundaries: Men's encounters with the pregnant body. *Sociology of Health & Illness*, 25 (7), 743–67.
Material on cyborgs and cyberbodies can be found in:
Campbell, B., O'Driscoll, A. and Saren, M. 2006. Cyborg consciousness: A visual culture approach to the technologised body. *European Advances in Consumer Research*, 7, 344–51.
Gies, L. 2008. How material are cyberbodies? Broadband internet and embodied subjectivity. *Crime Media Culture*, 4 (3), 311–30.
Haraway, D. 1985. A manifesto for cyborgs: Science, technology and socialist feminism. *Socialist Review*, 80, 65–108.

Discussion Questions

What role does popular culture play in shaping how people think and talk about the body?
Is the male body 'civilized'?

4

The Body in Consumer Culture

Introduction

A key characteristic of late capitalist society is the emphasis placed on consumption. The expansion of consumption has been accompanied by extensive changes in central areas of social experience, such as work, family and community, in ways that have profound implications for people's sense of self. The body is particularly significant in such a context, and therefore this chapter examines how consumer culture shapes embodiment. First, the chapter will outline consumer culture – what it is and how it has developed. Second, it will examine the relation between consumption and identity and the body's symbolic role in the process of shaping identity. Finally, it will look at various kinds of body work in which individuals participate in order to construct and maintain self and social identity in the late modern age.

The emergence of consumer culture

The dominant context for everyday life at the beginning of the twenty-first century is consumption rather than production (Lash and Urry 1994). This involves the purchase of goods and services not necessarily for their 'use' value, but because of their desirability and the kinds of statements they make about the consumer. The global scale of consumption is the result of particular events and processes that have had a profound impact on the self. Indeed, **consumer culture** actively creates a particular kind of self, which is oriented towards self-indulgence rather than self-denial and which regards the self as being of prime importance. Ewan (1976), for instance, argues that consumer culture motivates people to engage in indulgent or hedonistic practices and eliminates the guilt previously associated with spending money or acquiring credit. There are particular reasons for the development of consumer culture that help to explain its influence.

First, changes from the mid- to late nineteenth century in the way that goods were produced expanded the range and amount of goods available to people. The introduction of scientific management and Taylorist time-and-motion calculations improved productivity so that more goods were available in a shorter space of time (Braverman 1974). Second, the growth of advertising fuelled demand for goods through new techniques of selling that educated the social imagination and encouraged people to desire goods (Wernick 1991) and imagine their importance in everyday life. Advertising promotes desire by educating the consumer and informing them what to buy, through what routes and at what point in their lives.

Third, changes in the nature of work, through advances in technology, reduced the number of hours people were tied to paid work and increased the time available to consume. As consumption has taken on greater social and cultural significance, it requires more investment of personal time (Giddens 1991). Fourth, rising wage levels in the post-war period increased the availability of goods and services such that a greater proportion of the population have access to desirable goods. Finally, the development of the department store had a profound impact on the nature of shopping, which has been transformed, as a feature of urban life, from a necessity to a major leisure activity. Laermans (1993) argues that department stores from the 1860s encouraged customers to perceive the goods in a distinct way. Stores used particular techniques to display goods in ways that invited the customer to look closely at them and imagine how they would transform their lives (Tamari 2006 provides an overview of the rise of the department store in Japan). Customers were encouraged to walk around the store and observe the goods and experience a visual and sensual spectacle, through which shopping gradually became a predominantly visual activity that transformed the relation between consumer and goods. The latter are increasingly displayed in ways that emphasize their symbolic rather than their use value and involve a complex manipulation of visual observations and emotional investment (Bowlby 1993).

Commodity consumption involves satisfying desire rather than need (Falk 1994) and should be understood as a particular form of culturally meaningful practice rather than as a practice oriented solely to subsistence. Consumption involves the pursuit of **lifestyles** through the acquisition of desired goods that suggest shared symbolic meanings and codes of stylized conduct (Giddens 1991). This implies that people consume goods that they feel make some statement about who they are or aspire to be, and that they recognize themselves – or are encouraged to do so – in the things they consume. Therefore, consumer culture and consumption has become a significant means of making claims about who and what we are or how we would like to be seen by others. Moreover, consumer culture has played a significant role in the development of a more individualized society more oriented towards the pursuit of self and self-interest.

Modernity and reflexivity

In affluent societies, material goods and possessions (clothes, cars and other personal items) are part and parcel of everyday life. Though there are profound divisions in terms of which groups of people can afford which items, consumer culture ensures that everyone is caught up in the pursuit of desire (Giddens 1991). Indeed, the consumption of goods and services helps people construct a sense of self in an age when the sources of self-identity are otherwise unstable. Processes of **modernization** have displaced traditional sources of identity, such as work and occupation or family and community membership (Beck 1992). People are much less likely to define themselves, and to be defined exclusively, in terms of, for instance, occupation, because lack of job security and changing labour markets make it unlikely that people will stay employed in the same occupation across their life course.

These changes in the institutions of modernity (Giddens 1991) have several implications, not least of which is the repression of affective life, as theorized by Adorno and Horkheimer (1972) and as documented by, for instance, Hochschild's work on the **commodification** of emotions (see chapter 2). Such changes also encourage **reflexivity** and foster a sharp sense of awareness of the uncertainty and insecurity that characterizes the times in which people live in the West. For instance, the emergence of HIV in the 1980s created a culture of panic sex (Kroker and Kroker 1988), marked by anxieties and uncertainties about the 'reliability' of sexual partners. Similarly, the emergence of bovine spongiform encephalitis (BSE) in the US and the UK in the 1990s raised anxieties about the reliability and safety of meat, anxieties remobilized in the early years of the second millennium in relation to the reliability and quality of public water supplies in the UK and Australia.

Identity and anxiety

This uncertainty and instability contributes to how people think about themselves and leads them actively to construct identities as a way of establishing a degree of control over their lives. The risk anxiety engendered by reflexive modernization establishes a sense of personal responsibility for self and self-identity in which people use the tools of science and technology to counter the loss of traditional securities. Hence, individuals are encouraged to become agents of the self (Beck 1992), for instance, through advertising, and to use the consumption of goods and services to create a sense of self – increasingly in transgressive or erotic ways (think not only of piercing and tattooing, but low-rider jeans and labiaplasties) (Langman 2008). However, the paradox is that, in a context of uncertainty, it becomes increasingly difficult to establish a sense of coherence over self-identity (Giddens 1991), especially as the volume of consumer goods expands. The growth in the quantity of goods associated with late capitalism means that consumption choices have to become ever more finely tuned (for instance, we do not buy just shoes, but shoes for different purposes and occasions). Though identity construction in late modernity encourages consumption, identity has the potential to become increasingly unstable because we have to keep up with the expansion in goods, be knowledgeable about what to purchase and worry about making appropriate choices. Magazines contribute to this process by publishing lists of goods, services and subjects that are either 'in' or 'out' in ways that invite self-comparison.

The uncertainty that characterizes the late modern age is accompanied by a tendency for people to become ever more concerned with appearance and to view the body as a vehicle of self-expression (Lasch 1979). For Lasch, the narcissism inherent in consumer culture (or secular culture, as he puts it) means people seek salvation, meaning and a sense of self through consumption activities that are increasingly associated with the cultivation of the body. Indeed, Lasch argues that the modern self is a performing self that requires the praise and validation of others and invests time and effort in the construction and maintenance of bodily appearance. Self, or who we believe ourselves to be, is defined by the kind of appearance we can create through the consumption of particular goods and services that enable us actively to shape and modify the body (Shilling 1993).

Of course, such consumption contains the potential for repression through valorization of the image over substance and a mass culture that is disguised as erotic freedom (Langman 2008). Nonetheless, identity is embodied in the external performances people give and over which they feel they can exert varying degrees of control (Shilling 1993). Featherstone (1982) provides an explanation for the emergence of the body as a symbol of identity.

Visual appearance and imagery

Visual appearance and imagery is privileged and emphasized in modern Western societies (Pointon 1993). New technological developments from the 1840s have contributed to the production and consolidation of what Featherstone refers to as 'the look'. For instance, photography, the birth of cinema and the Hollywood studio system, which packaged and disseminated images of its stars for wide consumption, and the introduction of cosmetics advertising in women's magazines in the 1920s (Wolf 1990), underline the importance of visual image and appearance. This distinct emphasis on visual appearance, captured by the notion of the *flâneur* (Tester 1995) engaged in 'fleeting encounters and purposeless strolling', produced a new consciousness in which people were increasingly aware of being looked at by, and looking at, others. For Featherstone, this new consciousness created new points of comparison between who we are and who we might become, and not only stimulates desire but places a new emphasis on body work and body maintenance. Moreover, the imagery created and circulated in consumer culture places a premium on images of youth, beauty and health and fitness. The closer the body approximates these idealized images, the greater its exchange value, or the more likely one's body can be used as a resource on which to base employment or gain access to celebrity status. Hence, in consumer culture, the body itself can be transformed into a commodity of sorts through techniques of **body maintenance**.

Body Maintenance and the Imperative of Health

Participating in practices oriented towards body maintenance is not entirely specific to consumer culture. Turner (1984, 1996) observes how disciplinary mechanisms in pre-modern ascetic regimes, such as dietary control, served as a means of achieving spiritual goals by repressing the temptations of the flesh. However, in consumer culture, the emphasis of body maintenance is on transforming the outer appearance of the body in pursuit of the idealized forms. Featherstone suggests that this emphasis is a consequence of a conflation between the inner self and the outer body engendered by the importance placed on certain key values, and on health in particular. Though the state in industrialized, capitalist societies has stressed the importance of a healthy and fit population since the early nineteenth century (Hewitt 1983), European health policy has increasingly emphasized the need to prevent disease and promote health (Allsop and Freeman 1993). In particular, the transformation from infectious diseases (and the high mortality rates associated with diseases such as tuberculosis and diphtheria) to chronic diseases and new forms of cancer has been accompanied by a rise in life expectancy, which has contributed to an emphasis on the importance of health and fitness. Indeed, since the early 1980s there has been a greater priority given to health and fitness, from health promotion campaigns focused on raising people's awareness of the dangers of sedentary lifestyles to government policies targeting 'risky' activities such as smoking. This imperative of health (Lupton 1995) encourages individuals to become concerned and reflexive about lifestyle, and invites people to view their lives and bodies as open to transformation and modification (Glassner 1995).

Instrumental body maintenance

According to Featherstone, people living in the West have been increasingly encouraged to become conscious of the body in relation to health and fitness values in ways that highlight physical appearance. He identifies three main modes of body maintenance that are oriented towards values of health and fitness but also reflect a concern for the physical and visual appearance of the body. The first style Featherstone identifies is **instrumental**, in which maintenance activities, such as exercise and dietary control, are informed by self-preservation and emphasize appearance. In fact, recent scholarship suggests that 'looking good' is a significant, if not the most important, driver of physical and health-related activities, such as weight training or vitamin supplementation (Rysst 2010; Atkinson 2007). A potential side effect of this mode of maintenance is that, by following prescriptions for maintaining one's body, one not only 'looks good' but also 'feels great'. However, this rational approach to body maintenance and attention to surface appearance is accompanied by the pursuit of pleasure, or what Featherstone refers to as 'calculating hedonism'. In short, consumer culture, oriented to indulgence without guilt, encourages us to concern ourselves with appearance, which in turn offers others an external manifestation of the inner self. Hence, excess and indulgence in consumption may be disciplined through exercise and dietary control, and the hedonism fostered by consumer culture offset by the preservation of efficiency.

Body maintenance and healthism

A second mode of maintenance is informed by a sense of responsibility for one's body in response to health messages about disease prevention, especially cardiovascular disease and cancers. This responsibility is underpinned by the 'healthism' that pervades modern life, in which the individual, rather than the state, is considered responsible for her health, and through which people are encouraged to pay attention to how they feel and look (Rysst 2010). The underlying body image informing this mode of maintenance is that of the body as a resource that can be preserved through vigilance. Here, the pursuit of healthy regimes produces cosmetic side effects such that people not only 'feel great' but also 'look good'. Indeed, there has been 'an exponential growth in the health and fitness sector' in the UK and in the US that targets a core market of healthy and aesthetically conscious consumers (Frew and McGillivray 2005). Featherstone suggests that, in this mode of body maintenance, inner state is conflated with outward appearance such that the latter is interpreted as the external manifestation of a desired healthy state. Appearance symbolizes inner discipline and invites moral evaluation in such terms. Participation in health and fitness practices through exercise regimes or dietary control is as much oriented towards the cultivation of a particular kind of appearance (fit and healthy) as it is about achieving an inner sense of health. That is, the cultivation of a toned, fit body is also a way of expressing a particular kind of attitude. It becomes a means of expressing to others that you are the sort of person who cares for yourself and will work hard to establish and maintain a fit, healthy body. This suggests **discipline**, will-power and the ability to 'make something of oneself' (Bordo 1993). Getting in shape may promote a sense of well-being and enhance one's sense of self, but it also signals an ability to discipline oneself in accordance with dominant discourses about what it means to be healthy, as well as in ways that work to control essentially 'uncontrollable' bodies (Moore 2010).

Body maintenance and lifestyle

A final mode of maintenance is one that is more a way of life, a lifestyle, in which the pursuit of healthy living is not only accompanied by exercise and dietary regimes but also associated with a range of consumption choices. In turn, the purchase of associated products that represent and shore up the notion of health reaffirm the performance of a 'healthy self'. There is an expanding range of markets for products supporting healthy lifestyles, such as foods, vitamins, clothes, hygiene products, fitness videos and simulations of activities (Lupton 1995). Here, body maintenance is a form of leisure that is underpinned by appearance anxiety, and fine-tuning the body is pursued in ways that produce desired cosmetic effects.

The underlying image of the body in consumer culture, in which the pursuit of health through exercise and dietary regimes is central, has long been that of a machine (Shilling 1993). For instance, in Watson's study of men's health (Watson 2000), participants were asked about their images and ideas about their bodies. For many, the body was a machine that can be maintained, finely tuned and tinkered with. In health advertising too, the male body as a machine has been evoked. For instance, accompanying the launch of the government's 'Health of the Nation' strategy, the Department of Health's 1991 advertisement aimed at men depicted a male body in the pose of Auguste Rodin's *The Thinker*. Sections of skin were stripped back to reveal machinery parts, and the booklet accompanying the strategy launch was referred to in the advertisement as a 'manual' (Watson 2000). This image of the body as a machine is characteristic of the biomedical – **Cartesian** – model of the body and suggests a degree of control over the body, which is increasingly viewed as malleable or as plastic (Shilling 1993). Consumer culture encourages the view that, through the application of technology and information, the body can be endlessly modified. Therefore, the body takes on the character of an unfinished product. Moreover, consumer culture blurs distinctions between body and self (the inner/outer conflation referred to by Featherstone) such that, while body modification and transformation can provide a route to self, the reshaped body is in itself a sign of internal discipline and a marker of self-control.

Pause and Reflect: Identify images associated with current health messages. What do they tell you about underlying images of the body in consumer culture?

Distinction, physical capital and the male body

Social value

While the aesthetic impulse encouraged by consumer culture enables people to construct identities and selves through surface body modification, such 'transvaluation' (Featherstone 1982) also provides strong markers of social difference (Savage et al. 1992). Moreover, while Giddens and Beck emphasize the significance of individual and instrumental choices in the construction of self-identity through body modification – contributing to the view of the body as an unfinished project – the French sociologist Pierre Bourdieu (1984) argues that consumption patterns – of health-related products, for instance, from exercise clothes to gym memberships – reflect the choices not of individuals, but of social groups. Bourdieu maintains that the body is a bearer of **social value**, and of class in particular, in three main ways. First, the material context in which bodies are located influences shape and size. Second, bodily gestures and conduct, even in the context of health-related modes of maintenance, reveal information about the social location in which bodies develop. Even those gestures we consider automatic and deeply ingrained are markers of what Bourdieu refers to as the **habitus**, the collective culture into which people are ingrained. Third, the tastes and preferences people express for one kind of product over another (for instance, jogging or spinning over football) may appear to be individual choices, but are rooted in the material opportunities that are available to them. That is, the products, goods and services groups consume are shaped by the tastes structured by the habitus each group occupies (pre-reflexive, socially learned second natures; Atkinson 2007), and people develop preferences shaped by their habitus.

Yet choices differ between groups and distinguish one group from another. For instance, in the 1980s, jogging was the exercise regime of choice for the bourgeoisie on the grounds of its contribution to health. However, as Radley (1995) observes, this choice is meaningful only in relation to knowledge about the effects of exercise, knowledge acquired as members of the same social groups that produce such knowledge (i.e., health professionals). Dominant social groups choose exercise and health maintenance activities that differentiate them from other social groups because the choices themselves are dependent on access to time, money and opportunity. In contrast, (male) non-dominant social groups may take up activities that rely on physical competencies and bodily contact such as boxing or team sports such as football.

Sports Supplementation, Habitus and the Male Body

An ethnographic study in Canada explored masculinity, health and sports supplementation among non-elite and recreational athletes. The study suggested that sociogenic processes (such as the decline of traditional forms of work and family, challenges to hegemonic masculinity through the 'queering' of aesthetics, and the emergence of healthism) have led many white, middle-class men in Canada to express their anxieties about these changes through bodily practices such as sports supplementation (Atkinson 2007). The analysis suggested that the men in this study used supplements as a means of achieving an ideal-type male body image (lean, muscular), and as such, could be viewed as responding to a perceived dismantling of masculinity by pursuing a particular form of bodily control and self-restraint (Atkinson 2007).

Forms of capital

Not only is the body, through maintenance and care, a vehicle through which to make claims about who we are and how we would like to be perceived, but it is also a unique form of capital. Bourdieu (1984) has observed that the body is a bearer of status, of power and of distinctive symbolic forms that are critical to the acquisition of resources. The body that conforms to ideals of health, youth and beauty is recognized as possessing a particular kind of value and represents a form of physical capital, which people may use or come to rely on as a means of earning a living (Bourdieu 1984). Indeed, different forms of capital can be exchanged within particular fields.

For example, Loïc Wacquant's research among boxers in Chicago demonstrates how boys from poor, urban areas often develop a toned, fit physique through boxing or other kinds of sport as a way of earning income, respect and status from the communities of which they are part. Boxers have to invest in practical body work to achieve upper body strength, agility and endurance through 'drills' and exercises involving skipping, calisthenics and sparring (Wacquant 1995: 71). In turn, the development of **physical capital** can be seen as a tradable asset critical to the acquisition of other resources and other forms of capital such as economic, social and cultural. Since the boxer has to work on his body in order to transform it into physical capital and labours with his body, Wacquant argues that 'bodily capital' and 'bodily labour' are dependent on each other. Drawing on this argument, Frew and McGillivray (2005) suggest that the social space of the health and fitness club is a space in which the desired form of physical capital is the pursuit of a 'toned and taut' body in order to enhance one's moral worth and social capital.

Social capital refers to activities, relationships and processes that allow people access to prized material and social goods and services, while **cultural capital** refers to resources or repertoires of knowledge or taste (e.g., body image) that individuals use to build value or social status in contexts that are especially meaningful to them (or fields) (Bridges 2009). This process may be particularly acute in relation to those who make a living displaying and performing the body (and gender), such as boxers, professional athletes or models (Bridges 2009). For instance, those who pursue a career in the Hollywood system, either through cinema or the range of associated occupations that support this system, invest in a clearly defined presentation and performance of self. This investment in the body, through workouts, exercise regimes, dietary control, cosmetic surgery and other interventions and modifications, has the potential to transform the body itself into a product that has a certain exchange value. Yet the pursuit of an idealized body depends on and demands an endless, circular form of consumption. In order to reshape one's body, one must first consume a range of goods, services, products and technologies that are oriented towards reinforcing the idea that the body can be transformed and modified. As Featherstone has noted, consumerism reinforces the pursuit of an idealized self via body projects (1982).

Pause and Reflect: Using the example of bodybuilders, Bridges argues that gender capital – an interactionally defined and negotiated state – extends the concepts of cultural capital and **hegemonic masculinity** (see p. 65) by drawing attention to the social value that accrues when the gendered self is presented in a contextually relevant way. Gender capital refers to the ways in which people negotiate presentation of self in ways that are aware of, and take advantage of, the different impressions their sculpted bodies make. Do you think men and women possess different kinds of gender capital or is gender capital more fluid depending on the context in which it is negotiated?

Masculinity, identity and embodiment

Consumer culture has influenced idealized images of the male body and masculinity in advertising, media and popular culture. As many scholars now note, the male body is on display as never before through a 'new kind of representational practice' in which the male body is displayed in idealized and eroticized ways that invite the 'gaze' (or indeed, multiple gazes) (Gill et al. 2005). The dominant image of heterosexual masculinity in late modernity is the 'muscular mesomorph' (Mishkind et al. 1987), typical of advertising campaigns for personal hygiene products in men's magazines. This idealization can be attributed to at least three trends in the post-war period. First, the 'muscular mesomorph' has associations with the gay male body. Gay men have entered public space through consumer culture and have established a degree of economic power to do so, particularly in the US (Mort 1988). Where in the immediate post-war period the gay body was associated with failed masculinity (Connell 1995), the so-called 'limp-wristed sissy' stereotype of popular culture was replaced by the macho body-builder in the 1980s, through male fantasy figures (think Stallone, Schwarzenegger and Van Damme) (Mishkind et al. 1987). These fantasy figures promoted a very physical form of masculinity, as a set of prized qualities under threat, that needed to be defended by the explicit exclusion of women and the feminine (Jeffords 1994).

Second, as the participation of women in economic and political culture has expanded, and as cognitive, lifestyle and occupational differences between men and women have converged, so a muscular backlash developed. Yet while the sensibility associated with the muscularity of 1980s cinematic imagery was superseded by both the emergence of the new man and softened muscularity and the beer-bellied character of the criminal underworld (Work 2002), it was not fully displaced. Third, the declining significance of breadwinner identity as the lynchpin of male identity (as labour markets have shifted and occupational categories have been restructured) has been accompanied, as we have seen, by the growth of consumption and the pursuit of identity via the modification and care of the body. Men are typically addressed directly as consumers and users of personal grooming products, and fashion and accessory advertising (Mort 1988), a rapidly expanding domain in the last decade, directed towards men primarily through men's magazines, has fostered themes of corporeal indulgence and sensitivity.

Nixon (1996) suggests representations of male bodies changed significantly during the late 1980s due to changing commercial practices in the fashion industry and in magazine publishing. These industries, in an attempt to appeal more to men, constructed and promoted a new category of male consumer which became known as the 'new man', who would be interested in his image, reading fashion magazines and buying stylish products. Advertisements aimed at the 'new man' portrayed models who were meant to be objects of the male gaze; that is, they were presented solely to be looked at by other men (both gay and straight) rather than portrayed partaking in activities, as was historically typical in male representations in advertisements. Frank Mort (1988) argues that the male body has also been sexualized in ways that explicitly frame men as the objects of another's gaze. In the imaging of personal grooming products (aftershaves, fragrances, deodorants), the male body is exposed to the camera as the object of a male gaze in ways that foster a more open eroticism and male narcissism within the advertising lexicon. Where this exposure was initially carefully managed to draw clear distinctions between heterosexual and homosexual masculinity, advertising images in relation to men's fashion and fragrances commonly allude to both homoeroticism and androgyny in which it is often difficult to discern gender from stance, clothing or expression (see chapter 2).

Therefore, new idealized forms of the male body have emerged that emphasize a particular form of physique, encourage men to maximize their bodies through clothes and skincare products, and offer the potential to change one's body shape and size. This imagery sets up a gap between the ideal and the actual (Mishkind et al. 1987), ties identity to the material of the body and increases the demands on men to be concerned with the size, shape and appearance of the male body in the interests of achieving market value. However, while this concern with the appearance of the body may be relatively new for men (Nixon 1997), it is not for women.

Pause and Reflect: What do the kinds of advertisements carried by magazines such as *GQ*, *Esquire* and *Arena* tell us about the significance of the male body and how men define themselves?

Body Consciousness in Men

A key criticism by many scholars of the focus on the male body and its significance in consumer culture has been that the debate is too theoretical; few empirical studies exist that focus on what men in everyday life think of and feel about their bodies. A study by Brooks interviewed 140 boys and men in different parts of the UK, who were asked to reflect on topics related to bodily changes and body care, including body modification. One of the findings from the study was that, while most men engaged in practices to help them feel and look 'different' (i.e., expressive individualism via weight training or body piercing), they drew on a limited range of very similar expressions and language (or interpretive repertoires) to talk about this pursuit of difference. There was little evidence of the 'pressures' on men to focus on their bodies, as argued by some scholars, and instead, a taken-for-granted emphasis on individualism as a central norm of hegemonic masculinity that was carefully policed and disciplined.

Discipline and docility

Gender and discipline

This chapter has already introduced the idea of personal discipline in the pursuit of body-maintenance techniques and how the 'fit' body becomes a bearer of discipline as a social value. As Featherstone argues, consumer culture encourages people to discipline their bodies not only in pursuit of appearance, but also in the name of health. This relationship between body maintenance, appearance and health has particular consequences for women. More so than men, women are encouraged to take responsibility for their own health and the health of others (Graham 1979). Moreover, the forms of self-discipline embedded within body-maintenance techniques reinforce relations of power between men and women. While most of us engage in 'body work' of one sort or another, such as exercise or 'watching what we eat', women are encouraged to discipline their bodies in ways that have the potential to restrict and confine their social and political participation, contributing to their public invisibility (Dolezal 2010). Second-wave feminism has asked why the female body has been particularly subject to discipline through a continuum of practices which affect the size, shape and appearance of the body, from foot-binding in traditional China, to corsets in Victorian Britain, to cosmetic surgery (Bordo 1993). One way of beginning to answer this question has been by examining the discourses that shape and constitute femininity.

Discourse

Discourse is a term that ranges in meaning from the precise analysis of language and conversation to the role of language and practice in constituting and maintaining social order and notions of reality. Discourses establish a coherent way of describing and categorizing the social and physical world and refer to a body of ideas, beliefs and concepts that represent an accepted world-view. Hence, examining discourses provides a way of looking at the frameworks that underpin social phenomena, such as the disciplined female body.

The beauty myth and the male gaze

Simone de Beauvoir commented in *The Second Sex* ([1949] 1972) that the female body is the raw material for women's cosmetic transformation from nature to culture. Feminists have argued that the female body is viewed as an object of the male gaze (Mulvey 1975) and is looked at by men in many different and mundane everyday contexts. Hence, the female body is a body that invites transformation, and women are encouraged to transform themselves and their bodies into historically and culturally specific ideals of beauty (Smith 1990; Bartky 1988). This transformation occurs in a number of ways that focus on, for instance, the display of the body and the body as an ornamental surface. Bartky (1988) notes that contemporary Westernized ideals of femininity stress that the female body should be taut and firm; skin must be smooth, flawless and blemish-free; there should be no signs of wrinkles or lines, spots or hard skin. Moreover, hair must be removed from legs and underarms through shaving, waxing or depilation, and preparation of the skin requires regular use of cosmetics, creams, lotions, hair and nail products, hair-removing products and products designed to eradicate lines and wrinkles (or, as advertisements for Olay put it, 'the seven signs of ageing').

Though ideals of feminine beauty change and are both historically and culturally specific (Callaghan 1994), women are, says Naomi Wolf (1990), subtly coerced to embody beauty and men are encouraged to desire and possess beautiful women. The **'beauty myth'**, as the institutionalization of the **male gaze**, has consequences for women. First, the constant monitoring (examining oneself in the mirror, checking oneself in passing windows) and repairing required by the pursuit of beauty diverts women's energy and saps their confidence. Though women are still told by L'Oréal 'you're worth it!', this promotes a 'changing room culture' in which women are constantly measuring their self-worth in terms of how they compare to other women. Second, the pursuit of beauty becomes a currency for women and increases competition between them (think of all those conversations in women's toilets that focus on 'her' – the woman 'outside' – dress/make-up/hair). Moreover, visual appearances that conform to ideals and norms of beauty provide access to public life, and women seen to avoid or fail to achieve beauty standards experience overt and covert forms of discrimination. Third, the current emphasis on beauty is a form of backlash against women's economic and political gains in the post-war period. As women are seen to enter into public life, the beauty myth intensifies to the point that women in public life also need to embody beauty norms. As Synott (1993) has put it elsewhere, women place themselves or are placed under a form of **self-surveillance** by adopting 'male' values of 'ideal' female bodily form and thus reinforce prevailing discourses of beauty and slenderness. However, to do otherwise has the very real potential to restrict employment opportunities in a labour market that favours work for women on the basis of appearance (Wolf 1990).

Physical Appearance and Occupational Work

A study of flight attendants (Tyler and Abbott 1998) noted that physical appearance provided a set of criteria by which applicants were judged, and women were recruited to a number of airlines on the basis of appearance. Selection and recruitment favoured those who presented flawless professionalism without drawing attention to the work involved. Once in position recruits were formally and informally encouraged to be vigilant and disciplined about personal grooming and body techniques. Both company stipulations and regulations (such as regular weight checks for female attendants) and informal peer and self-appraisal constitute what Tyler and Abbott refer to as the **'panoptic management'** of the female body. This management is deemed necessary because of the way the female body is presented as a material expression of each particular airline and its philosophy. Hence, aesthetic performance and presenting the 'face of the company' becomes part of the job. However, flight attendants must work hard in order to achieve and maintain the required appearance, which in turn is considered a natural aspect of female embodiment.

The Male Beauty Salon

Although the body beautiful and beauty norms are associated with femininity, the male body is increasingly a sexualized object of the gaze and men with disposable income are especially able to 'do difference' through beauty work (Barber 2008). The 'metrosexual man' is the embodiment of such work and illustrates how male beauty work is deeply tied to occupation, in the sense that grooming is viewed as 'essential to the business world' (Salzman et al. 2005: 460). Indeed, Barber's (2008) ethnographic study of a male beauty salon in California suggests that for men working in professional occupations, styled and groomed hair ('stylish', 'progressive', 'superior') is essential for business, marks them as 'stylish' and in doing so, signals professional status. Moreover, these men specifically visit a hair salon in order to distinguish themselves from white working-class men they associate with barber shops, whilst at the same time distancing themselves from the feminizing character of the 'women's' hair salon. Barber argues that the use of the hair salon by these men reinforces a class-based sense of masculinity while within a traditionally feminine space. They view the barber shop as 'traditional' and 'conservative' masculinity, whilst they see their use of the hair salon as for the 'new', 'progressive' man. These perceptions allow them to negotiate a space traditionally associated with femininity without compromising their masculinity.

Visual images, advertising and the body

The persistence of the beauty myth

The beauty myth and other cultural injunctions concerning the visual appearance of the female body are deeply embedded in advertisements not only for beauty products but also for other products and ideals. Advertising offers a privileged world of appearances (Wernick 1991) providing both information and misinformation (Barthel 1989) that constructs symbolic worlds and, in turn, associates them with particular products. Advertisements shape and reflect society and the pursuit for distinction through the purchase of products (Wernick 1991). Yet distinction and the creation of self is conferred not through acquisition of the product alone but also through identification with the narrative and lifestyle in which the product is embedded. Advertisements have to translate statements about objects (material) into statements about people – about how people might use the object and about what kinds of people might use the object (Williamson 1978). Therefore, in advertising and other forms of visual imagery, meanings are generated by the way products are given a symbolic exchange value (i.e., the sign refers to both the object itself and the particular meaning which the object is given).

Furthermore, the products themselves and the images through which they are represented come to define and reinforce a sense not only of self (to others and which confirms this sense to ourselves) but also of gender.

Social change and changing themes in advertising imagery

Naomi Wolf argues that the emancipation of women and the mass production of the beauty myth, through advertising, go hand in hand. Advertising that specifically targeted women began to emerge in the late nineteenth and early twentieth centuries through the medium of women's magazines. For instance, *Harper's Bazaar* catered for and helped to broaden the appeal of clothing and fashion that had previously been the domain of the upper middle classes and the aristocracy (Davis 1994). Such magazines were initially created through capital investments but began to draw revenue from cosmetic advertising from companies such as Estée Lauder. Magazines expanded their circulation as literacy developed among lower-middle-class and working-class women and coincided with the move of women into higher education and the creation of women's colleges in the US.

If the 1920s was a period in which advertising in women's magazines signalled a degree of decadence and indulgence, the immediate post-war context was one of regrouping and encouraging women to move back into the home after time in paid work supporting the war effort. Advertising reflected this change and reinforced the post-war swing to domesticity. Magazines and the advertising contained within became resources for the hassled housewife in the 1950s, and women were addressed principally as 'shoppers-in-chief' for domestic products to be consumed by themselves and others within the household. Such products were presented to women via themes of guilt about dirt, the therapeutic value of domestic skills required for housework (Friedan 1963). Ferguson's study of magazines from the 1940s to the 1980s (Ferguson 1983) highlights the similarities in both editorial content and advertising images across magazines and suggests that these similarities were restrictive in the way they defined what it was to be a good and real woman. The key themes of editorial and advertising content during this period included getting and keeping a man, the pursuit of a happy family, self-help and becoming beautiful, and products advertised were mostly those associated with the rituals of beauty, child care, cooking and cleaning. Ferguson terms these themes as shaping and reproducing what she calls the 'cult of femininity'.

The cult of femininity

Key social changes occurred from the late 1960s that contributed both to redefining the woman addressed by advertisers and to the commodification of the female body as a medium through which many products/objects have come to be represented. Although this period was pejoratively termed the 'permissive' period in the Thatcher and Reagan years, it is clear that many changes contributed to the sexualization of the female body, and later, as Frank Mort argues, the male body. First, the authority of established religion was increasingly challenged as the arbiter of morality, and the law became the framework for establishing the parameters of acceptable sexuality in the Anglophone world (Weeks 1986). Second, legislative changes and grassroots action in relation to fertility control, such as the expansion of contraception under professional jurisdiction (Gordon 1978), the decriminalization of abortion and the development of new abortifacient technologies (Clarke and Montini 1993), made the pursuit (if not the achievement) of sexual pleasure more possible for women. Third, legislative changes concerning obscenity redefined what it was possible to talk about in public, in relation to sex. This had the effect of expanding the language and imagery of sex and contributed to greater visibility of the female body as part of advertising's lexicon.

These wider changes helped to commodify the female body: the opening up of sex as a subject which could be talked about and drawn attention to in public had the effect, too, of turning female desire into something which could be sold to both men and women. On the one hand, advertising for many products became increasingly associated with sex and, in particular, the desirability of the female body. On the other, advertisers viewed female desire as something to be developed, elicited, articulated and shaped to encourage the purchasing of products that represent a distinct lifestyle (Coward 1984).

This period was characterized by a growing emphasis on equality issues (for instance, pay and sex discrimination), particularly as married women increased their levels of economic activity (and therefore had more money in their control). Barthel (1989) suggests the movement of women into the market requires new advertising strategies which blend acknowledgement of women in paid work with the growing individualism reflected in fashion advertising ('dress for success') and the promotion of the business suit for women in employment. The business suit and themes of assertiveness and aspirational can-do attitudes infused advertising in the US from Charlie perfume (tomboy) to Virginia Slims (you've come a long way), and was used by advertisers to address women themselves as particular kinds of individuals (liberated, sexy, free). Hence, in the 1970s, advertising which targets women began increasingly to address women in terms of being particular kinds of women (elegant, sexy, alluring, free, independent, smart).

Themes associated with the 'cult of femininity' endured until well into the 1980s (Ferguson 1983), accompanied by a new emphasis on the female body, in particular 'sexiness' at work. This was reflected in fashion and its associated advertising with regard to a sharper focus on body shape in the work of designers such as Donna Karan and stretch clothes and short skirts. For instance, advertising for Victoria's Secret takes this to extremes, with cleavage displayed across a variety of media in Western urban spaces.

Negotiating images

However, while the dominant analysis of the gendered meanings created and reproduced through advertising points to the way in which women are encouraged to pursue ideals of embodied femininity, the response of women to the meanings generated in advertisements must also be explored. Although there is little research on the response of women to, and their interaction with, advertisements, research on women's magazines (the main context for advertising targeting women) suggests an alternative analysis. Joke Hermes's study of Dutch readers (Hermes 1995) highlighted how women's magazines are read quickly as something undemanding to fill empty spaces. They provide repertoires of practical knowledge and emotional learning, and allow women to explore themselves by recognizing themselves in the lives of others. Advertising is significant here too, because magazines are bought not only for their editorial content or articles, but for their look and quality: the whole package provides a form of pleasure which can be bought, consumed and dipped into in private, at intervals in otherwise busy lives. And, further, they are popular because they contain contradictory messages, which reflect the contradictions of many women's lives. Thus advertising does not simply shape definitions of gender but also provides a space in which the meanings of gendered embodiment can be negotiated and challenged.

Pause and Reflect: What does current advertising for hair products imply about beauty ideals? To what extent is hair important in women's daily struggle over cultural ideas about feminine beauty? Is it, as Rose Weitz (2003) suggests, a vehicle through which women express and resist cultural expectations about femininity, and if so, in what ways?

Consumer culture and body modification

The communicative body

Societies have developed their own culturally specific ways of reshaping, moulding and marking the human body in order to signal changes in social status (such as rites of passage whereby boys are transformed into men) or to demonstrate social value through painting or masking (Falk 1995). Body-modification techniques may be permanent and irreversible, such as neck-stretching rings (Ebin 1979), or temporary decorations, such as clothing. As Featherstone (1982) has argued, contemporary Western contexts place a premium on bodily appearance. The post-war period in the Anglophone world has been increasingly associated with preoccupations about modifying the surface appearance of the body as a key expression of self-worth (Blaikie et al. 2003). Such modification may be effected through fashion and clothes, and children and young people have been addressed as consumers in their own right with money to spend and time to spend it.

Much of this consumption is linked to self and body image (Russell and Tyler 2002). For instance, clothes made for and aimed at children are increasingly undifferentiated from clothes aimed at a more adult market and, moreover, particularly for girls, are typically endorsed by teen pop stars. For children and young people, the body is a means of affirming a collective identity in opposition to and signalling difference from adult authority. The body is used as an expressive medium and dressed distinctively to present a spectacular self that also establishes a distinct group identity that is separate from and in opposition to the identities of particular others. Both class and gender differentiate these forms of resistance to adult authority. For instance, working-class boys in post-war Britain used dress style to create a sense of resistance not only to adult authority but also to capitalist culture (Willis 1993). They flouted conventional clothing codes as comment on their relative lack of access to material power and the tension between the goal of material success invited by capitalism and the likelihood of materially unrewarding jobs. Middle-class groups such as the hippies in both Britain and the US protested against predominantly middle-class forms of bodily conduct and made a virtue of physical touch and drug using to resist the norms of the civilized body, such as bodily order and restraint (Young 1971). In contrast, though girls were absent from group cultures formed by working-class and middle-class boys and young men in public spaces (McRobbie 1991), they nonetheless developed a bedroom culture that emphasized romance and cultivated femininity as display, transforming the surface of the body through fashion and make-up. The emphasis on display and the transformation of the surface appearance of the body remains central to young women's experience of contemporary femininity, and is promoted through fashion and accessory chains such as 'Girl Heaven' (Russell and Tyler 2002).

Therefore, consumer culture encourages people to adopt instrumental strategies to combat decay and deterioration and combines it with the notion that the body is a vehicle of pleasure and self-expression (Radley 1995). As discussed above, discipline and 'calculating hedonism' appear to go hand in hand (Featherstone 1982), hence body-maintenance techniques and health-related consumption are tied to a range of social meanings that move beyond their original use value. Yet consumer culture also provides a vehicle – and mobilizes **instrumentality** – in ways that contain and alleviate people's frustration about modern life and 'keep in check the anger and discontent of a commodified, capitalist political economy in its global moment' (Langman 2008). Where the dominant (e.g., adult) culture emphasizes order, control and restraint, dissident cultures emphasize openness and celebration of the ludic and grotesque (Langman 2008). Indeed, particular forms of body modification in consumer culture, such as piercings and tattoos, may confront the degree of closedness and conformity associated with adult, civilized society (and present as part of a decivilizing process) (Langman 2008).

Pause and Reflect: Carnival culture is characterized by transgressive actions and practices (e.g., mockery, satire, use of the grotesque) that create a world full of fun, revelry and play, while also posing challenges to social and political elites. How far can contemporary practices (e.g., body modification, porn chic, sexercise) be considered transgressive and carnivalesque?

The tattooed body

Practices such as scarification, tattooing and piercing mark the body in ways that overturn ideals of bodily presentation in Western contexts.

Such body marking or inscription techniques provide a means for the individual literally to transform the external appearance of their body (Falk 1995). In consumer culture, the use of body-modification techniques that transform the surface appearance of the body differs from those in pre-modern or non-Western contexts in the sense that such techniques explicitly focus on the elaboration of one's own body. In the past, however, techniques of inscription were associated with the stigmatization of particular social groups and were less amenable to eradication (Falk 1995). For instance, tattoos were marks on skin that represented or signified people who were socially categorized as marginal groups (Brumberg 1997). In eighteenth-century France, criminals were branded to signify the crimes they had been accused of committing, such as V for *voleur*; thus the marks created a lasting trace on the surface of the body (Falk 1995).

In contrast, in modern Western contexts, tattoos represent marks of distinction that some people use to signal their difference from the dominant social groups with which they come into contact (Radley 1995). Tattoos stand as a symbol of disaffiliation and are directed at those who are seen to lead conventional lives. However, where clothing styles may represent an explicit group identity, tattoos may be more ambiguous. For instance, many people tattoo in areas of their bodies that can be concealed and displayed only in contexts of intimacy (Brumberg 1997). Whereas many women may tattoo as a form of pleasure to be shared in intimate relationships and contexts, men typically tattoo parts of their bodies that are more often on public display. Tattooing may also be used as a rite of passage, marking a personal transition from one status to another and, in this sense, provide a self-inflicted reference point that reminds us of who we are. Hence, while those who tattoo may share that experience as a group, the individual who tattoos is constantly reminded of certain kinds of personal experience through the tattoo itself (Radley 1995).

The pierced body

Similarly, the practice of body-piercing provides an example of the body as an 'unfinished project' (Shilling 1993) in consumer culture. In contrast to non-Western cultures, where piercing is associated with particular social traditions and cultural rites of passage, piercing in the West provides a means of *self*-expression. Piercing ranges from visible parts of the body, such as ears, the commonest focus, to intimate body parts such as nipples, labia and penis (Brumberg 1997). In contemporary American culture, the increasing practice

Plate 4 Modern Primitive
Nicor, Wikimedia Commons

of piercing is associated not only with a *National Geographic*-inspired fascination with non-Western societies such as the Maori of New Zealand, but also with the 'homosexualization' of American life (Altman 1978), and represents a key social practice in popular culture. While piercing offers an example of the body's role in the exhibitionism central to consumer culture (Brumberg 1997), it is also associated with the emergence of Modern Primitivism (Eubanks 1996). Modern Primitivism seeks affinity with non-Western cultures as a way of signalling discontent with the modern social order and confronting categorical distinctions between normal and deviant. In particular, it confronts the 'simulacrum society' in which images are privileged over text and representation over reality in ways that undercut notions of personal identity and authenticity. In doing so through the appropriation of non-Western practices such as piercing, Modern Primitivism reclaims what it views as 'the sensual self' (Eubanks 1996). Hence the marking represented in practices such as piercing, tattooing and scarification is perceived by Modern Primitivism as a 'radical gesture' against dominant norms.

Carnival culture?

Scholars increasingly note that contemporary body transformations (such as piercing and tattoos) are now less easily interpreted as 'compulsory signs of collective belonging' than as individualized marks of differentiation (Ferreira 2009). The diversity of modifications suggests how central the body is as a symbolic resource, as a way of establishing somatic affinity. However, this affinity is less easily codified as a form of collective belonging to a highly visible, well-defined group, than as an individuated affinity with others who regard modifications as a way of 'celebrating the emotional and bio-graphical value of a particular moment in their lives' (Ferreira 2009). Therefore, contemporary body modifications such as tattoos and piercings are undertaken as a means of individuation, rather than as a mark of collective belonging, and signal 'commitment to self', rather than a means of expressing resistance against adult, class and gender norms. Seen this way, the body (especially skin and its surface) increasingly offers a canvas for inscribing identity through consumer culture (tattooing is big business after all; Patterson and Schroeder 2010). However, tattooed and pierced bodies constitute relatively new 'forms of embodiment' (Mellor and Shilling 1997) that can also be viewed as transgressive examples of the carnivalesque.

There may be limits in a society where the human body is already marked, for instance, as female or black (that is, as 'other'), to the level of defiance represented in body-modification practices. Moreover, while those who participate in body-modification practices such as tattooing or piercing may claim to be participating in the construction of an 'authentic' self, they do so in ways that consume cultures that to the West are already marked as 'other' (Clifford 1988). Indeed, 'carnivalization' via practices such as body modification is itself deeply implicated in consumer culture and already highly commodified (Langman 2008). Hence, in consumer culture, the body is a communicative body (O'Neill 1986) that people may use as a canvas on which to create or inscribe marks of distinction that not only help to bind themselves to a particular group, but also have the effect of marking the distance between themselves and others.

The tyranny of slenderness

Disciplining hunger

Bordo documents changes in ideals associated with women's size and shape in *Unbearable Weight* (1993) and places such ideals in the context of changes in women's social, economic and political position. For instance, the nineteenth-century hourglass figure was promoted by corsets (Brumberg 1997), which restricted breathing, digestion, circulation and movement. The hourglass figure morphed into the matronly curves of the 1950s but was rejected and replaced by the more androgynous figure of the late twentieth century – the long-legged, small-breasted, slender silhouette. As women have moved into the public sphere in the context of paid work and other forms of public participation and visibility, the slender body – a body that takes up less physical space – has been internalized as the current Western ideal.

Though not all women restrict food intake in the pursuit of the ideal of slenderness, it would appear that a continuum of dietary control underpins women's relation to food. It is common to hear women say 'I must go on a diet', and many studies (Charles and Kerr 1988) demonstrate that women typically over-estimate their weight or have a negative image of their own body. Recent scholarship reinforces the connection between body image, eating behaviours and gender and the high levels of dissatisfaction that women report about their bodies compared with men (Algars et al. 2010). As studies of food preparation and use in families show, women are under pressure to maintain their appearance through food control – a point understood all too well by the food industry, with its proliferation of low-calorie foods, artificial sweeteners and appetite suppressers (Lupton 1996).

Bordo (1992) argues that the restriction of food intake disciplines women's hunger in ways that have the potential not only to control size and shape but also to culminate in eating disorders, such as bulimia or anorexia. However, rather than define eating disorders in terms of individual – psychiatric – pathology, feminist writers have sought to locate the control of food intake in the context of gendered power relations. Feminists such as Susie Orbach (Orbach

1988) drew on Freudian concepts to examine eating disorders in terms of relations between (female) children and maternal figures. A decade or so on, feminists identify the control of food intake as part of the pursuit of slenderness, a form of tyranny that 'distorts' the female body and creates a sense of alienation for women from their bodies.

This observation has been sustained through contemporary studies that focus on women's experiences of food and eating. For instance, Macsween (1993) notes how anorexia in particular is accompanied by a sense of revulsion towards one's own body and consists of cultural contradictions about contemporary femininity. Concomitantly, Urla and Swedlund (2000) note that, if the female body actually took on the anthropometrically narrow-hipped and taut proportions of Barbie, the epitome of Westernized femininity, fertility levels would grind to a halt. The expurgation of the body through control of food intake both captures the contradictions associated with obedience to social injunctions to pursue slenderness (and the docility this produces) and operates as a form of protest. Female protest is often channelled through the body. For instance, central characters in literature have voiced protest via psychosomatic conditions such as wasting diseases or fevers (*Anna Karenina* or *Tess of the d'Urbervilles*).

Women of colour also experience the tyranny of slenderness. Empirical research in the US shows that binge eating disorder (BED), the most prevalent eating disorder, is observed across racial and ethnic groups. A large study using aggregate data from treatment trials for BED showed that efforts to control food intake were associated with concerns and stress about body shape and weight among Caucasian, African American and Hispanic women (Franko et al. 2012). Qualitative studies flesh out this story. For instance, Poran (2006) argues that while popular theories suggest Black women are protected from negative effects of body representations because of a 'Black Culture' that promotes high body esteem, Black and Latina women experience pressures to be thin as a consequence of the preferences of men of diverse ethnicities; competition with other Black women in relation to beauty; and a strong feeling that media images of Black women are too thin (see also Cheney 2011).

Docile or empowered?

Bordo (1993) argues that the anorexic body can be seen as a protesting body. The pursuit of slenderness, by making the body smaller, appears to conform to idealizations of contemporary feminine appearance. The anorexic body takes up less physical space, loses the curves associated with the hourglass version of the female form, controls hunger and suppresses desire. However, the anorexic body also denies those cultural stereotypes associated with contemporary femininity, such as weakness, precisely because the pursuit of slenderness requires obedience and self-discipline. A similar case is made for the daily struggles that women have with their hair. In her study of how women manage their hair – simultaneously a cultural artefact, personal/embodied and highly malleable – Weitz (2003) argues that women are both acutely aware of the cultural expectations regarding their hair and adopt strategies to increase their social and cultural power. She notes the power associated with both 'doing femininity well' and in resisting mainstream ideas about attractive hair. Thus, for Weitz, women are far from 'docile bodies'. Therefore, though diet, hair and exercise regimes need to be seen as practices that train the body in 'docility', they are contradictory in that they are also experienced as empowering practices that enable women to feel they have control over their own bodies and lives.

Pause and Reflect: A majority of studies concerning diet, fatness and bodily reduction focus on women and femininity. However, men too are subject to these preoccupations and exposed to the tyranny of slenderness and the contemporary 'malevolence' towards fat and fatness. Although the 'fat man' has been largely invisible in much contemporary feminist scholarship, Bell and McNaughton (2007) argue that men too are affected by weight dissatisfaction and eating disorders, such as bodybuilders who engage in the pursuit of excessive body size. In addition, they argue, many men experience the bodily alienation and self-surveillance that is generally associated with femininity, especially men who are overweight, in whom fat signals 'weakness' and sexual impotence. Yet, although there has been public outrage directed towards media figures who have ridiculed overweight women on national television, the same persecution of fat men has been overlooked. Bell and McNaughton argue that fatness has implications for men as it undermines normative forms of masculinity (see chapter 5 too, on obesity).

The body and exercise

The female body is subject to discipline through other contemporary transformation practices, such as aerobic exercise, which are generally directed towards women as ways of resculpting specific body parts. The impact of such practices on body and self appear to be mixed. For instance, one recent qualitative study that focused on both men and women found that men and women used aerobics as a means to attain a better bodily appearance, and both expressed positive and negative experiences of their bodies in the aerobic context (Loland 2000). There were differences, though, in how aerobics helped the participants in this study achieve a stronger, healthier, more powerful body. Echoing what some feminist writers have claimed in fictional work (such as Marge Piercy in *The High Cost of Loving*), women were more likely to feel empowered and that they could challenge traditional femininity ideals in terms of bodily appearance and use. However, men were more likely to express feelings of insecurity and a sense of being under critical scrutiny during training. Nonetheless, evidence continues to support the claim that exercise regimes such as aerobics reinforce established standards of feminine beauty and disempower women in a covert way. Drawing on Elias's process sociology approach, Maguire and Mansfield (1998) refer to aerobics as part of an 'exercise-body beautiful complex' which forms part of a configuration of social constraints that combine with embodied experiences to reinforce the rationalized management of the female body.

The management of the female body is a dominant theme in the analysis of female body-building. Though female body-building is perhaps a more exaggerated example of the self-discipline to which Bordo refers, it nonetheless demonstrates the fragility of the boundary between body and self. Mansfield and McGinn (1993) observe that women who body-build are engaged in developing musculature according to highly specified criteria and showing their bodies in ways which draw attention to muscle shape, size and definition. However, female body-builders are acutely aware of the need to carefully maintain the presentation of femininity. Indeed, one of the features of female body-building is the extent to which the contenders 'feminize' themselves in competition, by using make-up, jewellery and other accessories and, at times, cosmetic surgery. As Mansfield and McGinn note, because the male and female body are pushed to extreme physical limits, and women can develop similar kinds of musculature to men, the use of cosmetics and other accessories help to 'make safe' body-building, and to maintain clear boundaries between masculinity and femininity.

Cutting the body to size
Homogenizing the body

Exercise regimes are not of course the only way to maintain and modify the body, and various forms of technology now contribute to the modification and transformation of the body in consumer culture in ways that help to construct a particular identity or view of oneself. For instance, though access to cosmetic surgery is clearly dependent on people's material circumstances and socio-economic position, cosmetic surgery now provides a wide variety and range of body-modification techniques. These include eyelid correction, rhinoplasty, lip enlargement, collagen implantation, facelifts, chemical peeling and dermabrasion, breast correction, reduction and enlargement, fat removal and liposuction. In such 'body sculpting' clinics, flesh is either taken away or added to (Davis 1995) in the pursuit not only of body maintenance and self-enhancement but also of exchange value.

Cosmetic surgery and other forms of body maintenance and work have particular implications for women, because of the ways in which they have the potential to reproduce dominant discourses about idealized femininity. For instance, Balsamo (1996) observes that surgical intervention for cosmetic (and sex-altering) purposes has the potential to homogenize the female body. Drawing on anthropometric tables, cosmetic surgeons establish the parameters of normality in which surgical intervention occurs and define what a normal nose ought to look like, how wide apart eyes ought to be or how full lips should be, and so on. The painter Jenny Saville (BBC/OU 1991) has commented on this process and its social and personal implications in some of her work. She has talked to surgeons and their clients and used a process that allows her to focus on and suggest the degree of distortion implicit in cosmetic surgery. For instance, one of her techniques requires her to lie naked on large sheets of perspex through which her partner and collaborator takes photographs of her body as it is pushed and squashed against it. The process through which Saville makes her art is thus tantalizingly analogous to the process and implications of cosmetic surgery as the images produced distort the shape of the body.

Body technologies and racial capital

Balsamo (1996) makes the point that anthropometry in practice actively shapes and constructs beauty norms in ways that not only homogenize female size and shape, but also feed a racialized imagination. bell hooks (1992) notes how body-modification techniques such as cosmetic surgery encourage its practitioners to pursue white ideals of beauty and thinness. This seems particularly apparent in the case of Cher (Cherilyn Sarkisian LaPierre) (see also p. 112), whose facial and body transformation over three decades has, arguably, erased her cultural and ethnic origins. Moreover, the alleged amount of cosmetic work undertaken on Cher's face and body has been discussed and evaluated in moral terms. Franckenstein (1997) conducted an analysis of how the German print media discussed Cher and observed that dominant themes in reference to the star are that of 'artificiality' and the absence of 'authenticity'. It would seem then that a critical issue for women who use cosmetic surgery in pursuit of body modification and self-enhancement is its potential for inviting moral comment about its impact on the 'natural' female body.

This issue is especially notable in discussions about cosmetic surgery and other body-modification practices among people of colour. Skin lightening or bleaching has increased across the globe as people in Africa, Asia and Latin America pursue not only lighter skin but also the social and economic status and lifestyle imbued with racial meaning that it confers (Hunter 2011). 'Yearning for whiteness' has been historically associated with nations formerly colonized by European nation-states (Glenn 2008); however, the desirability of whiteness is increasingly valorized by a mass media that reinforces a message that 'white is right' (Thomas 2009). This valorization creates a form of racial capital that can be bought, in which light skin is valued more than dark skin and in which light skin is attainable through various technologies of the body (Hunter 2011). Cosmetic surgery is also increasing. For instance, between 2000 and 2008 in the US, the number of cosmetic surgeries performed on Whites increased 31 per cent, while that number increased 145 per cent for African Americans, 240 per cent for Latinos, and 290 per cent for Asian Americans (Hunter 2011).

Pause and Reflect: Mike Featherstone (2006) notes that even though images of youth, fitness and beauty within magazines, advertising, television and the urban landscape abound, people do not necessarily believe or follow the naive cause-and-effect self-improvement logic with its 'if you look good you feel good' rationale. What other explanations are there for body transformations through practices such as piercing or cosmetic surgery?

Aesthetic healing or conformity to norms?

Yet women who participate in surgical body modification may reject the idea that cosmetic surgery reproduces dominant discourses of femininity and, instead, break the rules and use surgery to stage a critique of normalization, pursue a kind of 'aesthetic healing', or use surgery to transform how the body is lived, rather than how it looks (Featherstone 2010). For instance, several studies suggest that cosmetic surgery may enhance women's experience of bodily presence and thereby facilitate perception and successful intentional action; in doing so, such surgery may be seen as benefiting women (Dolezal 2010). By making the choice to have surgery, such women are taking control, empowering themselves, as indicated in a widely cited study conducted by Kathy Davis (1995) which examined how women themselves rationalized and made sense of their decisions to undertake cosmetic surgery. Access to cosmetic surgery in the Netherlands differs from that in other industrialized societies such as the UK or the US in that it is not open only to the economically advantaged. Therefore the sample of women interviewed by Davis was drawn from diverse socio-economic circumstances. Davis's analysis of her transcripts presents a view of cosmetic surgery consistent with ideas about its role in establishing personal control over women's lives rather than as evidence of conformity to beauty norms. A dominant view among the women in her study was that cosmetic surgery offered a way of establishing a sense of feeling at home in one's body and of making one's body fit one's sense of self. Hence, cosmetic surgery made sense to the women in Davis's sample in terms of reinvention and self-empowerment, rather than in terms of body modification in pursuit of cultural belonging (or 'fitting in'). However, such an analysis may not fully account for the complex contexts of facilitation and constraint in which cosmetic surgery takes place, and the cultural norms that underpin the ability to invest resources in one's body (Gimlin 2007), especially the post-industrial context in which such transformation typically takes place.

Cosmetic Surgery and Masculinity

There is evidence that cosmetic surgery procedures in North America are increasing for men, including invasive procedures (e.g., rhinoplasty, eyelid surgery, liposuction, hair transplantation and breast reduction) and non-invasive procedures (e.g., chemical peels, hair removal, Botox and collagen injections, and microdermabrasion) (Atkinson 2008). Such expansion may suggest a collective shift in how men are negotiating the conventional parameters of masculinity (outlined in chapter 2). As the power bases of modernity have fractured (work, family, politics), male anxieties have increased, especially in response to what many men view as a cultural war against them (Atkinson 2008). Men have responded to broader social changes and challenges to masculine hegemony through body ritual, which also serves to improve their self-perceived social powers within the context of a perceived crisis of masculinity. For the men in this study, cosmetic surgery was a tool that allowed them to reconstruct a sense of masculine identity and challenge the doubt and anxiety they feel in relation to their masculine status. Men used the reconstruction of their bodies in order to 'reframe' their masculinity and feel empowered. The male-feminine body described in this work is one that is firm, fit, flexible, fat-free and open to exploring non-traditional (feminized) forms of body work in order to construct a new male identity and respond to changing roles, statuses and identity of 'new men'.

In a similarly critical fashion, ORLAN, a French visual artist, uses her own body to provoke and challenge cultural ideals concerning visual appearance and raise questions about the relationship between body modification and self (Davis 1997). She engages in what she refers to as 'on-going self-portraits' involving cosmetic work that is filmed and screened as it occurs. The surgeons become her 'tools' in the reconstruction of her face to reflect fragments of faces deemed 'beautiful' in works of visual art (such as Botticelli's *Venus*). This kind of enactment or performance forces us to consider not only the relationship between natural bodily appearance and a body that is unfinished and malleable but also the boundary between body modification as a means of personal control and as a disciplinary technique that fosters conformity to norms.

Finally, in the context of rising obesity and associated ill-health, weight loss (or bariatric) surgery has emerged as a distinct form of 'cutting to size' that many see as a legitimate and necessary intervention to improve health. This intervention is also widely viewed as a moment of 'rebirth' (a 'new me') that demonstrates the individual's ability to exercise discipline and control over consumption, and in doing so, the body. However, as Throsby (2008) notes in her study of weight loss surgery recipients, this rebirth is fraught with risk, because any weight gain following surgery is likely to be attributed to the individual, rather than to failure of surgery, in ways that reinforce a moral connection (or a tyranny) between slimness and self-worth.

Summary

This chapter has reviewed material concerning the emergence of consumer culture and the value it places on visual appearance – especially notions of youth, vitality and beauty – as a source of self-worth. One of the implications of the emphasis placed on external appearance in consumer culture is that the choices we make over the purchase of goods and services – dietary products, clothes, body-modification techniques – are interpreted as statements about who we are. Moreover, what we consume is judged for symbolic meanings, whether or not we actively make consumption choices or seek to reject the very notion of choice in consumption. A thread running through some of the literature here is that the body is a socially plastic resource that supports identity exploration (Pitts 2005). Yet the choices open to people to modify their bodies, to work on their body projects, are determined largely by habitus and reflect not only the kinds of claims they seek to make as individuals but also their social location. In Bourdieu's term, the body becomes a bearer of social value and is the materialization of class taste. Moreover, achieving the body beautiful, so desired and stimulated in consumer culture, invites disciplinary techniques that may, on the one hand, inscribe or mark the body as a radical gesture and, on the other, reinforce gender relations. Hence, one of the – disquieting – implications of living in a consumer culture is that it is impossible to live beyond it, because we are always defined within its terms.

Further Reading

For material on health and the body, see:
Dworkin, S. L. 2009. *Body Panic: Gender, Health and the Selling of Fitness.* New York: New York University Press.
Moore, S. E. H. 2010. Is the healthy body gendered? Toward a feminist critique of the new paradigm of health. *Body & Society*, 16 (2), 95–118.
These are good for thinking about the significance of identity, physical capital and body modifications:
Adams, J. 2009. Bodies of change: A comparative analysis of media representations of body modification practices. *Sociological Perspectives*, 52 (1), 103–29.
Brubaker, S. J. and Johnson, J. A. 2008. 'Pack a more powerful punch' and

'lay the pipe': Erectile enhancement discourse as a body project for masculinity. *Journal of Gender Studies*, 17 (2), 131–46.

Spencer, D. C. 2009. Habit(us), body techniques and body callusing: An ethnography of mixed martial arts. *Body & Society*, 15 (4), 119–43.

For an elaboration of the body and media representations, see:

Neal, S. 2008. Feared and revered: Media representations of racialized and gendered bodies – A case study. In C. Malacrida and J. Low (eds) *Sociology of the Body: A Reader*. Oxford: Oxford University Press.

Pompper, D. 2010. Masculinities, the metrosexual, and media images: Across dimensions of age and ethnicity. *Sex Roles*, 63 (9–10), 682–96.

Poran, M. A. 2006. The politics of protection: Body image, social pressures, and the misrepresentation of young black women. *Sex Roles*, 55 (11–12), 739–55.

And for material on the postmodern body and self, see:

Orend, A. and Gagne, P. 2009. Corporate logo tattoos and the commodification of the body. *Journal of Contemporary Ethnography*, 38 (4), 493–517.

Patterson, J. and Schroeder, J. 2010. Borderlines: Skin, tattoos and consumer culture theory. *Marketing Theory*, 10 (3), 253–67.

See these for material on beauty and modification:

Adams, J. 2010. Motivational narratives and assessments of the body after cosmetic surgery. *Qualitative Health Research*, 20 (6), 755–67.

Black, P. 2006. Discipline and pleasure: The uneasy relationship between feminism and the beauty industry. In J. Hollows and R. Moseley (eds) *Feminism in Popular Culture*. Oxford: Berg.

Cheney, A. 2011. 'Most girls want to be skinny': Body (dis)satisfaction among ethnically diverse women. *Qualitative Health Research*, 21 (10), 1347–59.

Cooke, G. 2008. Effacing the face: Botox and the anarchivic achive. *Body & Society*, 14 (2), 23–38.

Dolezal, L. 2010. The (in)visible body: Feminism, phenomenology, and the case of cosmetic surgery. *Hypatia*, 25 (2), 357–75.

Holliday, C. and Cairnie, A. 2007. Man made plastic: Investigating men's consumption of aesthetic surgery. *Journal of Consumer Culture*, 7 (1), 57–78.

Kang, M. 2010. *The Managed Hand: Race, Gender and the Body in Beauty Service Work*. Berkeley, CA: University of California Press.

Shildrick, M. 2008. Corporeal cuts: Surgery and the psycho-social. *Body & Society*, 14 (1), 31–46.

Discussion Questions

How is identity embodied for you and what body practices make you feel powerful?

How is racial capital a form of physical capital?

5
Regulating the Body

Introduction

Social order has been a prominent theme in the writings of a range of social theorists and sociologists from Hobbes to Emile Durkheim, Max Weber to Talcott Parsons. For instance, what mechanisms do societies develop to ensure that people conform to dominant norms? What sanctions are applied to deter people from breaking the rules? What forms of power are necessary to establish those sanctions? An increasingly pressing question for sociologists interested in the significance of the human body in everyday life is, thus, how central it is to the creation and maintenance of social order. An initial and influential attempt to address the body sociologically was Bryan Turner's classic *The Body and Society* (Turner 1984, 1996), which viewed the body as a problem of order. Turner's aim was to demonstrate the mechanisms and processes societies developed to contain and manage the human body in the interests of social order. The framework he put forward emphasized key processes, which worked upon and within the body across time and space. This framework elaborated four 'Rs' – reproduction, representation, regulation and restraint. These kinds of questions were also the explicit focus of one of the most influential writers of the twentieth century on the body, the French philosopher-historian Michel Foucault.

Michel Foucault
Foucault studied at the Sorbonne in the 1940s and worked in many different institutions (until his death in 1984) developing a rather unconventional approach to the study of a range of substan-

tive issues (Eribon 1992). Foucault's writings dealt with diverse topics, including madness, medicine, sexuality and penality. What linked these topics was their connection to issues of social order and power, but what distinguished Foucault's approach from other studies of these topics was his method. Foucault was not interested in accepting what other disciplines held as fact – such as medicine or law. Rather, he was interested in understanding how things come to be known as fact. Hence, he focused on the conditions and circumstances that enable some groups and not others to make claims that come to be regarded as truth. In particular, his approach emphasized the importance of understanding how language, practice and perception shape the world in ways that enable some groups and not others to exercise power. One of the central claims made by sociologists and social historians has been that social struggles and practices actively shape knowledge and understandings of the human body. Foucault takes this claim further by arguing that the human body can be understood only through the discourses that produce it and, in particular, that a new form of power governs modern societies. This form of power targets the human body with a gentler touch than pre-modern regimes, but with a wider reach.

The regulated body

The birth of the clinic

Foucault's influence is keenly felt within the sociology of health and illness, the sociology of the body and feminist theory. There are clear reasons for this. While Foucault was not a sociologist, his work addresses areas of interest to these groups. Some of it directly addresses the relation between medical knowledge, power relations, historical changes in collective perception and the government of the body (1973, 1979). It also focuses on the **regulation** of female sexuality (1990) and issues of power, knowledge and the body (1980). His methodological approach is of interest particularly in the way it challenges liberal humanist approaches that view the development of rational knowledge as progressive, continuous and emancipatory (Silverman 1989). In contrast, Foucault stresses discontinuities in the development of knowledge and in the exercise of power. To this effect, he emphasizes the importance of discourses, which are:

> practices that systematically form the objects of which they speak. . . .
> it is through discourses, that is, the mix of beliefs, ideas and concepts
> which make up and organize our relation to reality, that power and
> knowledge come together. (Foucault 1972: 48)

Foucault suggests that particular socio-historical frameworks that
comprise a mix of ideas, beliefs and practices shape knowledge of
the world. Various developments in the eighteenth and nineteenth
centuries (in relation to medical practice, crime and punishment and
education) corresponded with changes in ideas about the human
body and, in particular, in the relationship of the body to the state
(Foucault 1980). During this period, population growth and urban
and capitalist expansion produced new problems for emerging
nation-states, which became increasingly concerned about the fitness
of people to engage in productive labour, to reproduce the next generation and to participate in military conflict with other nation-states
(Turner 1984, 1987). Power and control in the interests of social
order were no longer in the hands of a sovereign, but became much
lighter, subtler and more effective (Garland 1990). The new forms of
power that emerged during this period were located in specific spaces
and institutions, namely the school, the hospital and the prison.
Foucault (1979) observes the growth of examinations, timetables,
registers and classification systems as means of establishing not only
information about populations but also ways of monitoring their
movement across time and space.

Public health, for instance, expanded during this period as a set
of practices based on the systematic surveillance of populations on
the part of the state (Fee and Porter 1992). The development of the
British welfare state created a need for information about the health
and well-being of people in terms of their social relationships and
activities as well as in terms of the human body (Armstrong 1983,
1995; de Swaan 1990). The expansion of population surveillance by
the state, to which public health was central (Lupton 1995), created
a new body: the body of society, or the social body (Scheper-Hughes
and Lock 1987), which required regulation and discipline.

The clinical gaze

These processes, through which governments target the body as
a means of creating 'good citizens' (Woodward 2009), are tied to
the birth of the clinic and the emergence of a new model of power
by which modern societies are governed based on the clinical gaze.

Foucault developed this model of power by synthesizing his observations in not only *The Birth of the Clinic* but also *Discipline and Punish*, which examines the ways in which prisoners are observed in emergent prison regimes. The **clinical gaze** is key to rendering the body as an object amenable to expert scrutiny. This gaze was based on new kinds of practices such as anatomy and pathology, and relies on visual observation, touch, and opening up the body. The clinical gaze is an active mode of seeing the body that defines the reality of the body and has helped to establish a biomedical monopoly over the construction of bodily reality (Illich 1986). It is this active mode of seeing that is central to modern understandings of the human body as a machine that can be repaired and tinkered with.

Three principles – continuous surveillance, specialized knowledge and corrective measures – form the basis of the clinical gaze and represent this new form of power that does not use force, but nonetheless has control over people because of their visibility to those in authority.

Pre-modern medicine

Conventional histories of medicine emphasize its evolution as a form of scientific rationality, based on empirical observation and clinical examination. They explain the development of medicine in terms of discoveries (such as germ theory in the nineteenth century) and technological improvements (the stethoscope, antibiotics and X-ray) and its successes in the eradication of infectious diseases. The power of medicine, by implication, rests in its knowledge base – expert, established on scientific objectivity and, thus, incontestable. In contrast, Foucault argues that the knowledge allied to modern medicine has been produced through changes in the form of power associated with modern societies.

Pre-modern forms of healing (which included interventions such as blistering and blood letting) were practised by an unregulated assortment of people, many of whom were women, and were accompanied by a range of theories. Disease was understood in quite different terms from that associated with a modern medical framework and viewed as a set of generalized disturbances, a response to contagion or to the environment (Jordanova 1989). In order to make a diagnosis, practitioners of healing visited the patient in their home and listened to their story, and either placed it in a wider social and environmental context or made judgements according to the personal characteristics of the sick person (Jewson 1976). Moreover, hospitals were qualitatively different from the modern teaching hospital and served religious culture as a generalized last resort for the poor, sick and destitute (Turner 1987). Hospitals began to grow in number around the eighteenth century, financed by merchants and philanthropists, and experienced rapid growth in the nineteenth century in the context of both urban and population growth. The growth of hospitals underpinned the capacity for clinical observation and continuous surveillance.

Continuous surveillance

The modern hospital, associated with industrial capitalism, was a very particular kind of social space and contributed to the development of medical practice and its consolidation as a modern profession. Changes in the status of the hospital clinic in eighteenth- and nineteenth-century Paris provided Foucault (1973) and other writers (e.g., Jewson 1976) with data from which they made a number of observations. The growth in hospitals presented doctors with an increasing number of patients to observe and examine, all gathered in one central space. This gathering also allowed patients to be examined by more than one doctor and provided a place in which the bodies of the dead, rather than the bodies of living patients, could be opened up, inspected, mapped and classified in greater number. The practice of observing and examining living and dead bodies in a centralized space – touching, listening, looking – helped to shape a new examining apparatus that included auscultation, percussion and palpation (Armstrong 1983). Hence, clinical observation replaced the history given by the patient to the doctor and became a cornerstone of modern medical practice (Jewson 1976). Moreover, the accessibility of the body through physical examination, the development of a new form of anatomical recording and the rigours of pathology established a new language through which the body could be interpreted (Armstrong 1983). What this implies is that practitioners approached the bodies of patients, ready to listen, touch and observe, *already knowing* what they should hear, feel and see.

Specialized knowledge

The examination and observation of patients in hospital space by many practitioners became more systematic and provided an 'examining apparatus'. Observations and their results were recorded, stored and analysed. The analysis of records produced classifications of diseases and conditions, which were used to establish similarities and differences between and across cases. Clinical examination was increasingly accompanied by a reliance on laboratory science and technology (Sturdy 1992), which contributed to the subordination of other forms of knowledge – notably that of the patient's own knowledge about their own body (Jewson 1976). In turn this new kind of systematic comparative observation contributed to a new knowledge and understanding of disease as individualized pathology rather than generalized disturbance. This preoccupation with the examination of bodies is unique to modern societies:

> the details of human bodies are perpetually subject to scrutiny, and the knowledge of bodies, in aggregate, contributes to the development of social policies, which in turn are aimed at the alteration of policies. For example, babies are repeatedly weighed, standard weights are deemed appropriate, and those who deviate from them are considered to be in need of dietary controls. (Nettleton 1995: 113)

Corrective measures

Many hospitals, and those who practised medicine within them, were more frequently attached to universities, which provided them with legitimacy and the resources for a formal education. Hence, entry into medical practice became formalized and dependent on socio-economic circumstance. Those men with the available means could gain access while others could not. The Medical Regulation Act of 1858 further assembled support for restricted entry to medicine, and its particular impact was to effect closure in terms of gender (Witz 1992)

Pause and Reflect: What are some of the body practices that help you feel like a 'good citizen' but that are also 'required' in some way by the state, your doctor or your mother? How does the state (or your mother) make sure (regulate) that these practices get done? Are there differences in the means they use to achieve your participation?

Foucault's model of power

Disciplinary power

In pre-modern regimes, power was centralized and held by the sovereign, who had the authority to demand allegiance from his subjects and could physically punish and kill those who were disobedient. Moreover, sovereign rule was displayed to society through public hangings and exhibitions of torture so that people were reminded where power lay and to whom they must be obedient.

However, changes in the structure of society created through urban and population growth and industrial expansion transformed the nature of power. Sovereign power has been displaced by what Foucault refers to as **disciplinary power**. This term denotes the way the human body is regulated to fit the requirements of modern capitalist societies (Lowe 1995). First, as state bureaucracies and agencies have grown and the capitalist class has expanded, power has become more dispersed throughout society. Power in modern regimes no longer resides in the body of the sovereign but is invested in particular persons and practices. For instance, punishment was transformed from physical incarceration and torture to incorporate more subtle controls that regulate prisoners' lives through continuous surveillance. Second, urban and population growth generated considerable anxiety for the state in relation to the physical proximity of people, and capitalist expansion created societal needs for health and productivity (Turner 1984, 1996).

Biopower and biopolitics

Therefore the state became more concerned about the management of life (**biopower**) and the governing of populations in three main areas. The proximity of men and women brought with it a concern to regulate sexuality and control disease. New forms of work required distinct forms of supervision and ways of maintaining the health of labourers, concerns that were shared by moral entrepreneurs and philanthropists such as Joseph Rowntree in England. The threat of military invasion raised concerns about maintaining a well-disciplined military. These concerns about discipline in relation to education, welfare and health generated new specialized knowledge and disciplines, for example, psychology, criminology and sociology, that helped to establish corrective measures such as lifestyle modifications or the prison drill. These new problems of management defined population as an object of surveillance, analysis, intervention and correction across space and time (Nettleton 1992). Moreover, biopower depends on technologies through which the state and its agencies manage 'the politics of life to shape the social to accord with the tasks and exigencies faced by the state' (Hewitt 1991: 225). According to Foucault, the body (individual and collective) is the raw material for this undertaking, and he refers to the knowledges, practices and norms that have developed to regulate the quality of life of the population as **biopolitics**.

Governmentality

How does disciplinary power govern populations? First, distinct physical spaces – the school, the hospital, the prison – provide new points of collection in which people are monitored and in which those in authority can observe them with minimum effort (Nettleton 1992; Armstrong 1983). The spatial layout makes it possible for one person to watch over a number of other persons in ways that reinforce relations of authority. Relations within such spaces are based on the observation of many by the watchful eyes of a few, or on the 'gaze', which judges as it observes and decides what fits – what is normal – and what does not. Think of the school classroom, university lecture theatre or Nightingale hospital ward.

Second, disciplinary power is exercised through the clinical examination or the military inspection, which generates detailed information about those under surveillance. This information about individuals is recorded and held centrally in files or registers, or in a database that requires an administrative system in order to develop ways of tracking and channelling populations across time and space (e.g., timetables and examinations channel populations through the curriculum). Third, therefore, people become conceptually visible as an individual case among cases, and information produced about individuals is aggregated to establish averages and norms that are used by disciplines as a basis for comparison. In this manner, knowledge is produced in ways that support the development of a discipline (medicine, education) and help shape corrective interventions (remedial work, surgery). As such, disciplinary power is part of what Foucault terms *governmentality*, in which expert knowledges monitor, observe, measure and normalize individuals and populations via diffuse mechanisms (e.g., discourses) that promote health through modes of personal conduct such as self-surveillance, biopower and technologies of the self (Rose 1996, in Clarke et al. 2003).

However, power for Foucault is a productive power. That is, it works by persuading people to undertake activities and practices because they believe them to be in their best interests (Greco 1993). As many studies have demonstrated, this is particularly evident in health behaviour, such as that associated with disease prevention, pregnancy and childbirth. According to Foucault, practices and

knowledges of surveillance through observation and monitoring regulate the phenomena they constitute. However, individuals are not
coerced by the state to behave according to the norms that it establishes. Rather, practices of surveillance, for instance, through public
health or welfare policies (Hewitt 1983), encourage individuals to
observe and monitor their own behaviour. This **self-surveillance**
represents a lighter mode of liberal governance (Rose 1990), which
has been of great interest to feminists and sociologists of health and
illness.

From Medicalization to Biomedicalization

Medicine itself is increasingly under scrutiny as new forms of
regulation have been devised to scrutinize practitioners (especially
doctors) and ensure they are accountable and transparent in their
procedures and decision-making processes. The 'audit culture' in
welfare societies in particular has created constraints for practitioners in terms of working hours, standardization of training in
ways that potentially limit their practical experience, the development of guidelines and protocols that doctors must now follow in
their practice and the emphasis on consumer needs and desires
(Nettleton et al. 2008). This scrutiny is linked to what Clarke
et al. term **biomedicalization**, which refers to the increasingly
complex, multi-sited, multi-directional processes of medicalization that rely on new technoscientific knowledge and practices and
that are characteristic of late modernity (Clarke et al. 2003). In the
US, for instance, the health care sector has grown enormously in
size and influence, in ways that have made it possible for parts of
the body, such as genetic and tissue samples, to become increasingly commodified (Clarke et al. 2003).

In biomedicalization, biomedicine is itself recognized as being
reorganized from the inside out (as Nettleton's focus on audit
suggests) through clinical innovations, the expansion of the
clinical gaze from disease to health, and the development of an
institutionally complex biomedical sector. In biomedicalization,
'technologies of the self' are increasingly important in governing
health and pervade more aspects of daily life.

Disease prevention, surveillance and visualization techniques

Disease prevention

Disease prevention has been vital to the development of modern medicine in the Anglophone world. Not only has the state become increasingly concerned with managing and maintaining the health of populations but also it has supported the role of medicine in policing a social and moral order through public health (Wear 1992). Disease prevention occurs within a framework of governance which, following Foucault, exerts subtle degrees of moral control over individuals (Turner 1997). Within this framework, populations are more and more subject to informal and formal forms of surveillance (for instance, various kinds of population screening, immunization programmes, workplace health check-ups). Moreover, individuals are encouraged and indeed are expected to subject themselves to scrutiny and to incorporate into their everyday repertoires a 'duty to be well' (Herzlich and Pierret 1987; Lupton 1995; Greco 1993). Hence, participation in preventive initiatives is produced through a specific form of power that encourages individuals to take responsibility for their own health and well-being, ensuring social regulation through individuals' own self-discipline (Turner 1997).

Disease-prevention initiatives such as cervical screening exemplify what Turner (1987) has termed the 'Foucault paradox'. That is, in industrial capitalist societies, where welfare systems make provision for equity in health and where health is seen as a desirable though limited resource, the state establishes a correspondingly greater degree of regulation over its citizens. Such regulation includes population surveillance through disciplinary power, which encourages individuals to monitor their own conduct and measure it in relation to dominant health discourses. For instance, adhering to dietary regimes represents 'practices of self'. Concomitantly, preventive regimes that necessitate population monitoring engender a series of mechanisms through which new populations and new aspects of people's lives come under expert scrutiny (such as diet, lifestyle and sexuality).

Surveillance medicine

This new form of health governance is characterized by 'surveillance medicine' (Armstrong 1995) through which populations are managed via expert forms of knowledge in relation to diet or exercise, which shape conduct (Lupton 1997). These expert forms of

knowledge become dispersed throughout the everyday, embodied
practices of both expert and lay people (Turner 1997), where the
former 'set up the markers of compliance' (Higgs 1998). Moreover,
individuals are encouraged to view such knowledge as crucial to their
own health interests, often by way of risk assessments that calculate
degrees of risk of acquiring a condition or becoming ill and so per-
suade people to engage in self-monitoring (e.g., breast checks) or by
submitting to standardized risk assessment monitoring (e.g., cervical
screening) (Clarke et al. 2003). Hence, the disciplinary techniques
of the 'late modern clinic' encourage people to identify themselves
with a particular moral position in the domain of health and regulate
populations through enabling techniques (for instance, schools that
promote health through physical education that incorporates teachers as tools of surveillance in ways that reproduce gender relations
through the male gaze; Webb et al. 2010) rather than restraining and
coercive means (Higgs 1998). These techniques also rely heavily on
ideas about the normal or normative body, which, as Shildrick notes,
is 'always and everywhere open to challenge' (2008).

Pause and Reflect: If normative discourses are open to challenge
as Shildrick suggests, how is the obesity discourse challenged and
by whom?

The Obese Body

Disciplinary technologies and surveillance medicine are evident
in the case of obesity and the obesity epidemic in Europe and the
US. As Rail et al. (2010) observe, no one can have escaped the
'avalanche' of information about obesity and its link to ill-health
and disease (diabetes being one of several diseases to which obesity
is linked, prompting the US Surgeon General to refer to obesity
as 'domestic terrorism'). Rail et al. argue that the epidemiological
evidence about obesity is part of an obesity discourse (a clinical
gaze), in which obese people are deemed lazy and at risk, and
therefore in need of expert surveillance. Although scholars are
challenging the extent to which obesity constitutes an epidemic, or
even a disease, nonetheless, the media persistently fuels the obesity
'epidemic' with panic stories that reproduce the idea that obesity
represents a failure to engage in technologies of the self that are
considered 'healthy'.

Consequently, disciplinary technologies have emerged to

'control' obesity (e.g., self-assessment through fat leagues and fat report cards), and a range of institutions now contribute to surveillance, including governments, schools and the media (e.g., *The Biggest Loser*). In this discourse, 'not being fat' is a predominant notion of what the normal body should be, and being fat invites moral approbation. Furthermore, as Crossley (2004) notes, the putative rise in the prevalence of (unintended, unanticipated) obesity challenges the imperative to pursue bodily perfection (see chapter 4) in ways that have triggered a strong reaction from government and expert agencies that is oriented towards strategies to ensure normative regulation. Thus, social and political responses to obesity reinforce the body-consciousness by which contemporary society is characterized.

Disease prevention and gender

Disease prevention has been vital to medical practice since at least the 1960s and is central to health policy in the UK and other European countries (Allsop and Freeman 1993). Prevention practice has increasingly emphasized self-responsibility for health (Nettleton 1997) at the expense of addressing the material causes of disease (Crawford 1980), and good citizens are expected to comply with prescriptions for health (Rose 1990; Howson 1999). Yet many prevention strategies are gender specific and focus on the female body, from antenatal screening for syphilis in the inter-war period (Davidson 1993) to contemporary screening for foetal abnormalities (Lane 1995). Moreover, preventive discourses typically address women as mothers and guardians (Graham 1979; Nettleton 1992) and as carers in the community charged both with self-responsibility (Lupton 1993) and with the responsibility for maintaining the health of others (Stacey 1977). Disease prevention also relies on strategies and discourses of containment (see *cordon sanitaire*, chapter 3) that work to 'protect' society from sources of symbolic pollution, such as the HPV vaccine. Experts argue that the vaccine prevents recipients from some strains of the human papillomavirus, which can lead to cervical cancer. However, conservative organizations and entities argue that the vaccine symbolizes the potential contamination of young women by sanctioning sexual activity, or 'promiscuity' (Carpenter and Casper 2009).

Disease prevention and protective discourse

This gender focus is characteristic of the protective approach to women embedded within welfare states (Holmwood 1993; B. Marshall 1994), though many feminists and women's health activists view disease-prevention initiatives as potentially empowering for women (Doyal 1983; Hastie et al. 1995). However, despite the emphasis on individual responsibility and consumer choice within contemporary prevention strategies, most initiatives assume that people – women especially – will comply with their directives. Howson (1999) found that, though there was an increasing emphasis on information provision and informed choice in cervical screening delivery, nonetheless, smear tests were presented to the women in her study as something in which they were expected to participate. Furthermore, a sense of social obligation and indeed moral duty accompanied the experience described by many of the women not only in Howson's study (see also Bush 2000), but also more generally in women's experiences of health and health care (Oakley 1998). This sense of obligation is further illustrated by Merck's accompanying publicity campaign supporting the launch of Gardasil, the HPV vaccine, which encouraged parents to consider vaccinating their daughters and urged young women to consider vaccination through messages such as 'Roll up your sleeves. It's your turn to help guard against cervical cancer' and 'The power to prevent cervical cancer is in your hands. And on your daughter's arm' (Carpenter and Casper 2009).

Visualizing the body/alienated embodiment

The body can be objectified via techniques of visualization. The development of techniques of inspection that inform the clinical gaze (Armstrong 1983; Laqueur 1990) have penetrated the surfaces of the body and rendered its interior amenable to public observation (Cartwright 1995). Techniques of examination and visualization have been crucial to the establishment of a biomedical monopoly over the construction of bodily reality (Illich 1986) and have consolidated biomedical practitioners as knowledgeable experts of the body (Turner 1987). Yet while the clinical gaze fixes the body of the patient as an object of clinical practice and intervention (Armstrong 1983), the post-Enlightenment shift towards visual strategies for imaging the unseen (Stafford 1991) have had particular consequences for women. Indeed, the development of medical visualization techniques and the new ways of affixing meaning to the interior spaces of the body that these support have been made possible largely because of the unparalleled access to the bodies of women achieved by biomedicine (Oakley 1998). Moreover, some feminists have claimed that the imagery and discourses of biomedicine shape women's understandings of bodily experience (e.g., Birke 1999) and reinforce a sense of fragmented, objectified and alienated embodiment.

This observation is supported by research that examines women's experience of cervical screening and examination for cervical abnormalities (Howson 2001), a process of professional mediation through which women come to 'know' their own body in a particular, somewhat problematic way (Blomberg et al. 2008). For some women, examination included cervical visualization via a television monitor used both to magnify the cervix and for teaching purposes. Many women thought that the opportunity to see their own cervix imaged on screen might help them to develop an enhanced awareness of their bodies and provide a means of understanding the implications of cervical abnormalities. However, those who were able to see their own cervix did not find the experience constructive. First, the image of the cervix available to the women was distorted in terms of size and shape. It is magnified, stained and shaded in ways not necessarily associated with the bodily interior. Second, the imaged cervix was available not only for women themselves but also for a range of others (nurses, medical students, clinicians). The exteriorization afforded by visualization renders the cervix into an object separate from one's own body, and images of it being touched or manipulated may highlight the vulnerability of the cervix as a functional and symbolic gateway to the womb (Thomas 1992). Similar observations have been made about breast screening (mammography); mammographic technology may visualize the breast in ways that create a fragmented sense of the body, and separate the at-risk breast from embodied experience (Griffiths et al. 2010).

Visualization techniques such as those associated with colposcopic investigation of cervical abnormalities create images that require expert interpretation. Moreover, the degree of abstraction, and the 'close-up, vivid, hyper-realization of the corporeal' (Stafford 1991) embedded within such imagery, underpins the power of the medical expert to define the significance of the cervix. It 'fixes' the cervix as a primarily medicalized object and potentially undermines the capacity for women to develop an appreciation of the cervix beyond the boundaries of medical discourse.

Biometrics: a new mode of visualization

A range of new technologies such as biometric passports and DNA databases are transforming how we think about visualization and its role in surveillance of the body (Ball 2005). As Aas observes (2006), these technologies work to codify the body and construct new forms of social identity that rely on digital data and not only contribute to the regulation of people in public spaces (e.g., airports), but also work to establish trustworthiness between people who are other-wise strangers. One consequence of the increasing importance of biometric data in identity verification is the downgrading of speech and language in human communication. Another is the extent to which our bodies – or rather, the unique physiological characteristics that are turned into biometric data – have become what Aas terms 'passwords' that allow or deny us entry to regulated spaces (across borders, through airports, into commercial facilities), especially in, though not exclusively as a result of, the post 9/11 world.

As Aas points out, codifying the body as a way to delineate risk and danger is not new, and is a thread that runs through the eugenic movement of the early twentieth century, the human genome project – which has contributed to the potential for using DNA analysis to identify risk of certain diseases – or urine testing to screen for drugs not only in sport, but also in the workplace (Aas 2006). However, these technologies of surveillance, which create a new, standardized and seemingly unambiguous language of identity, are increasingly used not only to confer privilege (entry to regulated spaces) but also to exclude those deemed 'untrustworthy' and possibly 'dangerous', because the data they generate, and so make the body 'readable' (Ceyhan 2008), are viewed as infallible. In this vein, Kruger et al. (2008) compare biometric technology in airports and in the US welfare system and examine how this technology reduces individual bodies down to body parts and reassembles them as 'data' cases. They suggest this process is a regime of techno-biopower that crimi-nalizes, dehumanizes and excludes certain bodies in ways that are not race, gender, class or (dis)ability neutral. Indeed, Kruger et al. suggest that biometric technology makes possible the multiplication of discrimination and categorization on the basis of race, gender, class and disability, by deeming certain bodies 'untrustworthy', and categorizing 'untrustworthy' bodies as 'terrorist' or 'security threat'.

Visualization technologies that generate biometric data do so via a one-way power relation that creates 'culture at a distance', by increasing the gap between nature and culture. The consequence of these technologies is that life is transformed to abstract information patterns in which the body is the supplier of information that cannot be contested, and the self is apparently irrelevant. As discussed in chapter 3, according to Mary Douglas, bodily control is a way of containing disorder – and so it is with biometrics. However, Aas and other theorists (e.g., Ajana 2010; Alterman 2003) ask us to consider what kind of order is being established through body codification and what kind of truth is being revealed by purging the self from the body.

Pause and Reflect: Consider the ways your body is reduced to parts and re-assembled as biometric data when you move through airport security (Kruger et al. 2008).

Embodied experience and technoscience

As discussed in chapter 1, embodiment refers to the lived dimensions of human experience, and the dynamic interplay of the individual body, the social body and the body politic (Scheper-Hughes and Lock 1987). This concept is acutely significant in relation to the medicalization of the female body and its impact on the embodied experience of health and well-being. As Martin (2010) notes, once a condition is medicalized, 'its boundaries are not static' (p. 528). As feminist scholars have long argued, the female body itself has been subject to medicalization, as a long list of conditions that arguably emerge from women's social and political status have been construed as pathologies.

The women's health movement

From the late 1960s, feminist activism and scholarship challenged the ways in which health was defined in the language of biomedicine and rejected expert constructions of the female body as deviant. In contrast, feminists focused on the embodied experience of health and health care (e.g., Lewin and Olesen 1985). Feminists noted the general tendency in medical practice for women's experiences and knowledge to be disregarded by practitioners (Lawler 1991; Ruzek 1978), and research began to refocus on women's experiences of those aspects of embodiment defined as pathological. For instance, women invariably report that common procedures associated with

Plate 5 'Your body is a battleground': Barbara Kruger
Courtesy of the Mary Boone Gallery, New York

reproductive and sexual health are often accompanied by a sense of violation and discomfort (e.g., Graham and Oakley 1981; Kitzinger 1992). These kinds of indignity are typically provoked by the practices and techniques marshalled by biomedicine to visualize the body.

The emergence of the women's health movement in the Anglophone world, the development of body consciousness and the publication of radical texts such as *Our Bodies Ourselves* (Phillips and Rakusen 1978) or *Spare Rib* place particular emphasis on self-knowledge. Many feminists argued that acquiring knowledge of one's own body was vital to challenging medical culture and its problematic definitions of female embodiment. Self-help involved 'learning the language of the professional' (Ehrenreich and English 1979) in order to challenge medical authority and enhance personal autonomy. Moreover, self-help and, later, health education and health promotion were important to feminists as a way of challenging the medical model of health. They contributed to the development of alternative sources of information for women about various aspects of health and tried to be sensitive to the diversity of experiences and choice with which women are faced (Hastie et al. 1995).

Embodied experience/embodied health

The emphasis of this approach was to reclaim what was perceived as the authenticity of embodied experience through body consciousness groups (Ruzek 1978), which encouraged practices such as cervical self-examination; the advocacy of 'traditional' female approaches to health and healing; and 'well-woman' clinics (Gardner 1982). For instance, the women's health movement quite vigorously politicized the cervix, and self-visualization was identified as an empowerment strategy that would enable women to 'own' their cervix. Such ownership and knowledge could be used to dispute medical expertise (Frankfort 1972), and indeed, has informed the emergence of feminist perspectives on embodied health that contend that women are not (nor need be) passive recipients of medical expertise, but active participants in 'medical power relations' who draw on their own embodied knowledge (as emphasized in the women's health movement) in order to engage in a process of negotiation (Lorentzen 2008). However, as chapter 2 outlined, women's health continues to be managed primarily within a biomedical framework and as Clarke et al. (2003) note, biomedicalization co-opts ideological movements – such as the women's health movement – and their knowledge base. For instance, in the 1990s, AIDS activists lobbied for access to experimental drugs and changes in the approval process for new drugs which have become commonplace in contemporary clinical programmes administered by the US Food and Drug Administration (Clarke et al. 2003). Therefore, despite shifts within this framework to a more preventive approach to health care, women continue to be incorporated into wider and subtler webs of surveillance, buttressed by apparently benign techniques of visualization and technoscience.

Technoscience and the normalized body

Body practices and projects are 'situated in a technologized culture', such that it is difficult to think (or theorize) about the body *without* considering technology (Pitts 2005). We are, as Ihde remarks, 'bodies in technologies' (2002). Technoscience is an example of this linkage between the body and seemingly disparate forms of technology, such as visualizing or information technologies. Although electronic health and medical records offer the potential for a central point of access to patient information that could support coordinated health care, they also allow more aspects of patient life to be scrutinized by more people and underpin the application of molecular biology and genomics to medicine, as biotechnology and pharmaceutical companies use computer software to trawl through genome interactions to find potential points of intervention (Clarke et al. 2003). In addition, technoscience customizes difference through, for instance, cosmetic surgery, as we saw in chapter 4, conceptive technologies offering 'rhetorics of choice' and individualized medicine through gene therapy and pharmacogenetics (Clarke et al. 2003).

For instance, sexuality has become increasingly subject to 'enhancement technologies' via vaginal tightening, labia reduction and other procedures (Tiefer 2010). While such surgeries are premised on addressing sexual function, their impact on appearance has engendered new identities and expectations based on negative self-perception, disgust and fears about social rejection (Tiefer 2010). As Tiefer notes, 'pudendal disgust' and vulvar ambivalence are long-time phenomena, underpinned by cultural mislabelling ('down there' or 'vajayjay') and brought to light in the *Vagina Monologues*. However, specialist emphasis on transforming this bodily area through surgery offers a further example of how biomedicalization creates norms in ways that harness prevailing gender and sexual anxieties and so invite people to engage more deeply in the practice of self-surveillance.

While body enhancements are driven at least in part by consumer culture, enhancements make us reflect on what the normal body is and how bodily normality is shaped by the social, economic and political processes that have contributed to the emergence of bio-power. As described above, biopower is a mechanism that relies on controlling and normalizing bodies (e.g., through statistical information and categorizations such as body mass index) (Hogle 2005); thus, the idea of normality is also a moral idea of what *ought* to be (Hacking 1990).

Pause and Reflect: Genetic history and DNA is increasingly the focus of surveillance, from *in vitro* and embryo testing (e.g., pre-natal genetic testing) to the privatization of genes through patents, to storing genetic data in biobanks (Le Breton 2004). Utopian or dystopian?

Obstetric surveillance and the late modern 'clinic'

Just a gaze. An inspecting gaze, a gaze which each individual under its weight will end by interiorizing to the point that he [sic] is his own overseer, each individual thus exercising this surveillance over, and against, himself [sic]. (Foucault 1980: 155)

The transformation of childbirth

Pre-modern experiences of pregnancy and childbirth were very different from the process with which people in Western societies are familiar at the beginning of the twenty-first century. In a pre-modern era, pregnancy was not separated from everyday life as a special kind of experience, and women expected it to be accompanied by discomforts (Donnisson 1977). There was very little formal advice given to women – a very early attempt to formalize knowledge consisted of an inventory of symptoms experienced by women themselves – and knowledge about pregnancy and childbirth was acquired through relations with other women and shared orally across generations.

Historically, childbirth attendance was mainly the preserve of women. Women who specialized in such attendance – midwives – assisted women in childbirth alongside their kin and friends. Though midwife attendance was not subject to any kind of scrutiny, a struggle to formalize the practices and knowledge associated with childbirth attendance dawned in the eighteenth century and centred on intervention. The rise of organized medicine in the nineteenth century consolidated the process of redefining pregnancy as pathology and childbirth as a clinical event. Moreover, the medical men who practised birthing were increasingly located within the space of the hospital, which enabled them to systematize knowledge and argue for intervention techniques to aid the process of birthing. In particular, the development of forceps provided a means for such practitioners to deliver babies that would otherwise not have survived birth and to discredit midwives. The development of birthing technologies provided a way of restricting the informal practice of midwifery, and technical intervention emerged as the hallmark of obstetrics. Though midwives continued to provide care for women in the nineteenth century, wealthy women tended to consult the 'physician-accoucheur' in the context of confinement (Oakley 1980).

New technologies of childbirth

Processes of specialization helped to shape a specialty within the profession of medicine dedicated to the management of reproduction and childbirth. There are good historical and sociological studies of the way in which women's role in and knowledge about Western birthing has been marginalized and masculinized (Ehrenreich and English 1973). Indeed, obstetrics was established at the expense of midwives' knowledge and practice (Donnisson 1977). The introduction of forceps (Wajcman 1991) and the association of midwifery with witchcraft and superstition further contributed to the deskilling of women's traditional healing roles (Gamarnikow 1978). Moreover, practitioners aspiring to obstetric practice operated processes of closure to ensure that midwives were precluded from entering obstetric training (Witz 1992). Thus, not only has women's knowledge about birthing been sidelined by professional medicine, but also pregnancy and childbirth are treated as pathologies that require examination and intervention (Oakley 1984). New technologies further define the pregnant body as a pathological body in need of medical supervision, in particular, ultrasound. Before the development of ultrasound, the mother's experience, some hormonal tests and the foetal stethoscope confirmed pregnancy (Oakley 1984).

Ultrasound

The development of ultrasound revolutionized obstetrics and secured its status as a specialism within the medical division of labour (Mcleod 1986). In particular, ultrasound provided a 'window on the womb' that enabled obstetrics to view the foetus as an entity distinct from the mother. Oakley's study of the development of ultrasound documents the initial development of sonar and its application in a naval context to a routine form of antenatal **surveillance**. Ultrasound was used sparingly in the 1960s but routinely in the 1970s to monitor growth and detect foetal abnormalities. Its routine use in the first trimester of pregnancy (sometimes twice) makes the foetal body visible to professionals and pregnant women, defining it rather than the pregnant woman herself as the subject of obstetrics. The systematic use of ultrasound has two particular consequences.

First, its identification of so-called 'soft markers', or anatomical and chromosomal variations in the unborn child, bolsters the potential for further interventions such as amniocentesis and potentially leads to clinical and ethical dilemmas and raises maternal anxiety (Getz and Kirkengen 2003; Green et al. 2004). Second, ultrasound technology displaces the source of women's knowledge about pregnancy from embodied or corporeal experience – what it actually feels like to be pregnant, for instance, nauseated, breast tenderness – to the expert (Rowland 1992; Stabile 1994). While women who become pregnant may experience a range of bodily changes that signal the growth of new life, it is the visual image of the foetus that is used to confirm the reality of pregnancy. This may be both reassuring for women and contribute to early bonding with the growing baby, but it may also undermine the significance of experiential knowledge in ways that diminish women's confidence in their own bodies (Marshall 1996). Moreover, technologies such as ultrasound help to define the foetus as potentially at risk of abnormality and complication (Lane 1995) and help to centralize birthing care in the space of the hospital. Not only is pregnancy defined as a medical event, but also medicine defines which embodied experiences of reproduction contribute towards a 'diagnosis' of pregnancy (Rowland 1992).

Extending the obstetric gaze

There was also a radical shift in the location of childbirth in the twentieth century. During the inter-war years, the majority of births occurred in domestic space. According to official statistics for the UK (Macfarlane and Mugford 2002), over 99 per cent of births now occur in hospital. There have been many studies of hospital-based childbirth that compare modern pregnancy and childbirth to a process of industrial production (Martin 1989), define modern childbirth as the medicalization of a life event (Oakley 1984) and criticize its capacity for intervention. The biomedical framework in which pregnancy is experienced entails compartmentalization, segmentation and fragmentation (Oakley 1984; Stacey 1988; Martin 1989). Recent figures reveal an upward trend in intervention and in the practice of elective Caesarean section in particular (rising from 5.5 per cent to 7.3 per cent between 1991 and 2000 in Scotland alone). However, the routine use of techniques such as forced recumbence and stirrups, monitoring, forceps, artificial induction, shaved pubic areas and enemas have been replaced by a lighter form of obstetric care.

Accompanying changes and criticisms of hospital-based obstetrics has been an increase in forms of antenatal care in the community that is supported not only by women but by professionals who recognize pregnancy and childbirth as a life event rather than as pathology. This expansion into the community relies on incorporating pregnant women as 'joint adventurers' in the obstetric project (Arney 1982). The establishment of antenatal screening, classes and care by general practitioners and midwives in the community has also been in part a response to criticisms of intervention. Arney (1982) conducted a study of the development of obstetrics in the US and observed that obstetric care had expanded out into the community. This expansion was a partial response to women themselves and to more organized lobbying from the Natural Childbirth movement and other groups. These groups argued for less professional intervention and more inclusion in decision making for women. However, this development of antenatal care in the community is part of a more general trend that expands the reach of the **obstetric gaze** and widens the potential for surveillance in a way that shores up obstetric power.

Disease potential, risk and genetic testing

In contemporary childbirth, professionals still play a key role in confirming not only pregnancy, but also the onset and stages of labour in ways that can be objectifying, for instance, through foetal monitoring (Akrich and Pasveer 2004), which has increased the visibility not only of the pregnant female body, but also of the foetus. Arney (1982) notes the development of foetal monitoring in 1819, a practice that involved listening to the foetal heart through an instrument designed for auscultation. Foetal heart auscultation was designed to monitor the developing heart for potential pathology and relied on the establishment of categories of normal and abnormal in order to develop classification systems and preventive interventions. The redefinition of the foetus as the object of obstetric scrutiny and as a subject at risk has also raised the ethical profile of the foetus (Lane 1995), and created new legal uncertainties in cases where medical practitioners recommend intervention (such as forceps delivery or Caesarean section) to protect the health of the foetus, but this is refused by the pregnant woman. As the foetus becomes more autonomous, the law faces the difficulty of balancing the rights of the foetus with those of the woman carrying it. As Lupton (1994) notes, perinatal endangerment is an imminent moral discourse in which the rights of the foetus are potentially privileged over those of the pregnant woman. Debates about protecting the foetus from unhealthy maternal conduct such as smoking demonstrate how social and cultural boundaries between the female body and medicine are potentially being redrawn.

The expansion of the obstetric gaze is part of a more general trend within modern medical practice (Armstrong 1995). First, the focus of the clinical gaze has moved from the physical body of actual patients in the hospital or the clinic to the identification of disease in the community. Second, the identification of disease is related to its potential rather than its localization. Where in the past the patient sought out the doctor, now the doctor, or more generally, medicine, looks at the community and identifies potential patients. Third, the identification of disease potential in the community is tied to the assessment of risk in specified populations (Howson 1998), especially in the maternal body (Lane 1995). Risk factors are derived from large-scale computerized databases that provide information about target populations in need of surveillance. Surveillance may take the form of screening (such as for cervical cancer) or advice and information (tied to lifestyle, such as smoking, diet, exercise). Finally, this shift towards community-based surveillance (rather than observation of the body in the clinic) and self-surveillance is enshrined in health policy across Western Europe and beyond (Allsop and Freeman 1993), and is exemplified in pre-genetic diagnostic technologies, which reinforces maternal responsibility for the foetus (Reed 2009), but is, nonetheless, 'shaped by forms of self-government imposed by the obligations of choice, the desire for self-fulfillment, and the wish of parents for the best lives for their children' (Rose 2007: 69).

The obstetric gaze thus has established a 'new mode of social control' over childbirth that is softer and lighter, because it extends into a wider community of reproductive women, with that community's consent. Because antenatal care is framed in the language of prevention, it not only expands the number of births that are subject to the obstetric gaze, but also legitimizes the expansion of the obstetric gaze into wider aspects of women's lives. This exemplifies what Foucault defines as a process of 'normalization' in which people are subject to surveillance and monitoring with a view to classifying the observations such practices produce into degrees of normality/ abnormality. However, normalization processes work by inviting women to participate in their own observation as active collaborators, by taking personal responsibility for conduct and actions.

If you haven't yet read Margaret Atwood's *The Handmaid's Tale*, an imagined dystopia about reproduction, now is a good time.

Maternal conduct

The routine use of visualizing technologies such as ultrasound (and earlier, the *in utero* foetal photography pioneered by Leonard Nilsson) has had the effect of establishing a social and legal distinction between the foetus and the woman carrying it. This separation has not only been politicized by pro-life groups but has also contributed to an approach to antenatal care that defines all foetuses as potentially at risk of abnormality and/or poor development. This definition has fostered an emerging discourse of responsibility in which pregnant women are required to adhere to proliferating health discourses concerning responsible pregnancy conduct.

As Lupton (1994) observes, these forms of health advice now extend well beyond pregnancy and increasingly pertain to preconception care and conduct, such as advice on diet and vitamin intake. Hence, the expansion of the obstetric gaze from hospital to community space may soften the edges of antenatal care, but it also opens more aspects of women's lives to expert scrutiny. The midwife/ obstetric relationship becomes a space in which women are encouraged to confess their failings as obstetric: patients, opening up spaces for experts to provide information and advice. Similarly, antenatal observations undertaken in the community produce information that requires expert interpretation. In particular, screening for raised alpha-foetal proteins (AFP) in maternal blood detects the potential for certain kinds of abnormalities. Where these proteins exceed certain limits, women are offered further investigation to detect the likelihood of foetal abnormalities. However, in many hospitals, many obstetricians do not offer tests such as amniocentesis unless women are willing to undergo termination should abnormalities be confirmed. In such cases, the prior relationship established with the foetus not only through embodied experience, but also through visual confirmation via ultrasound, may increase women's ambivalence about pregnancy (Hubbard 1984). Moreover, maternal conduct is increasingly a matter of public comment and scrutiny not only by professionals but also by other parties. For instance, in the US, government warnings are put on bottles of alcohol, and visibly pregnant women may be refused alcohol in bars. Therefore, in the new lighter mode of obstetric surveillance, women are encouraged to comply with health discourses and defined as deviant if they fail to do so or choose not to comply. In this way, all of us are invited to scrutinize and judge maternal conduct.

Indeed, modern pregnancy is a public experience. The 'bump'

invites people to reach out and touch it. Pregnant women are much more visible in the workplace and other public spaces, and popular culture has encouraged women in the public eye to display the barely clothed and naked pregnant body. Indeed, many naked, discernibly pregnant stars have graced the covers of magazines, such as Demi Moore (*Vanity Fair*), Britney Spears (*Harper's Bazaar*) and Nia Long (*Ebony*). Demi Moore's shot on *Vanity Fair* was recently mimicked by an image on the cover of *New York* magazine of a grey-haired, 63-year-old woman, apparently pregnant and certainly naked, accompanying a story about women over 50 having children. Moreover, with the development of foetal photography and ultrasound, the obstetric gaze has expanded not only into the community but also into the womb. The pregnant woman is more subject to the scrutiny of professionals through blood tests, antenatal visits (from GPs, midwives, health visitors) and visualizing techniques and also to the scrutiny of friends, colleagues and the media. As Janice Kaplan put it in 1989:

> A woman who is pregnant immediately knows that her body is no longer her own. She has a tenant with a nine-month lease; and should he spend every night kicking or hiccuping . . . there is nothing she can do. Sharing one's body with a small being is so thoroughly wondrous though, that one can generally overlook the disadvantages. The real problem is sharing one's pregnant body with the rest of the world. (Kaplan 1989)

Pause and Reflect: Identify examples in which pregnant women have behaved in socially and culturally 'inappropriate' ways. What do these examples reveal about the 'normal body' and surveillance?

Commodification and reproduction

As we saw in chapter 3, commercial traffic in body parts has become a problem within the global economy in which wealthy groups exploit the bodies of socio-economically disadvantaged people (Scheper-Hughes 2000). Even professionally organized and regulated procurement processes through which blood and organs are transferred from donors to professionals (e.g., blood banks, organ donation organizations) are characterized by an uneven flow of 'resources' from poor to rich (Healy 2006). This unevenness and commodification is perhaps especially discernible in relation to reproduction (Rapp

1999), and contemporary reproductive technologies such as steri-lization, RU486, the use of hormones to stimulate superovulation, egg harvesting and embryo implantation. Some scholars argue that these technologies create a hierarchy of experience, in which white women's reproduction is valued and privileged and the reproduction capacities of women of colour are exploited (Roberts 2009), and in which affluent white women have access to reproductive technologies to create genetically linked children (e.g., through *in vitro* fertilization and genetic selection; Inhorn 2007), while women of low income and colour often struggle for access to basic reproductive care (Roberts 2009).

Although many of the issues associated with reproductive tech-nologies give cause for concern, scholars have argued that some tech-nologies, such as egg freezing, or oocyte cryopreservation, empower women by potentially offering a method for combating age-related infertility. While some see this reproductive technology as an illustra-tion of reproductive autonomy, in that it offers a way for women to potentially extend their fertility (see Klein 2008 for a review of this position), it also potentially commodifies the unfertilized egg, and exploits women who are vulnerable (women over the age of 35 who have not yet tested their fertility and who want to consider having children) (Harwood 2009). Such exploitation is possible, argues Lauren Jade Martin, not least because discourses of empowerment (such as taking control of anticipated infertility, planning reproduc-tive futures) may be fuelled by anxiety and fear about what it means to *not* have children, the persistent stigma associated with childless-ness and the emerging 'genetic imperative' that increasingly defines motherhood (Martin 2010).

Regulation, reproduction and the male body

The male body is not untouched by the regulatory practices associ-ated with reproduction. Marcia Inhorn (2007) focuses on men's reproductive bodies in the Muslim world via interviews with 250 men from Middle Eastern IVF clinics in Egypt and Lebanon as sites of bodily practice. Men talked about their anxieties and experiences with IVF, which has resulted in new forms of 'embodied agony' for men in general, and Muslim men in particular, due to their religiously derived ambivalence towards masturbation and semen. In the modern IVF clinic, men's bodies do not escape unscathed. Inhorn suggests there are tensions inherent in men's experiences of IVF because the requirement for sexual performance (masturbating a semen sample) conflicts with the complex meanings of sin, guilt and illicit pleasure amongst men in the Muslim world. In this context, semen is viewed as polluting, as impure and requiring ablution before prayer; masturbation is viewed as an illicit sexuality, which some men deem to be the cause of their own male infertility. Furthermore, Muslim men may feel guilty about masturbation and may believe their own infertility is a result of their practice of masturbation during their youth.

As such, Muslim men may experience difficulty when having to provide a semen sample to the IVF clinic, especially when clinics do not provide adequate privacy or promote 'guilty pleasures' by providing pornography to aid sexual stimulation. The introduction of intracytoplasmic sperm injection (whereby sperm is removed from men's bodies through testicular biopsies and aspirations) contributes to further psychic and emotional agony. In conclusion, Inhorn argues for greater attention to be given to what men have to say about their reproductive bodies, their sexuality and their biomedical encounters.

Pause and Reflect: Under what circumstances could your body become property that can be transferred to a different owner?

Summary

This chapter has described Foucault's approach to power and his observations about new forms of bodily regulation within modern regimes. The shift from sovereign to disciplinary power is associated with the growth of the state and its bureaucracies, new concerns about welfare, health and education and the fitness of the population for productive work. These concerns were pursued by the development of the professions and new disciplines oriented to the surveillance and monitoring of populations in order to find ways of correcting deviations from behaviours and practices they themselves establish as normal. Surveillance (or the 'gaze') underpins the regulation of populations and creates knowledge that is used to specify and establish new populations as the object of particular gazes. Foucault's challenge seems to be: scratch the surface of habitual conduct and you will find a concerted effort to instil it into populations. Yet disciplinary power is not a coercive form of power, because people believe that practices associated with health improvement and physical enhancement are, largely, in their own best interests. Questions remain, however, about the relation between regulation, responsibility and desire.

Further Reading

See the following for material on regulation and childbirth:

Brubaker, S. J. and Dillaway, H. E. 2009. Medicalization, natural childbirth, and birthing experiences. *Sociology Compass*, 3 (1), 31–48.

Davis, D. L. and Walker, K. 2010. Re-discovering the material body in midwifery through an exploration of theories of embodiment. *Midwifery*, 26 (4), 457–62.

Namey, E. E. and Lyerly, A. D. 2010. The meaning of 'control' for childbearing women in the US. *Social Science & Medicine*, 71 (4), 769–76.

Walsh, D. J. 2010. Childbirth embodiment: Problematic aspects of current understandings. *Sociology of Health & Illness*, 32 (3), 486–501.

For material on reproduction, commodification and embodiment, see:

Almeling, R. 2009. Gender and the value of bodily goods: Commodification in egg and sperm donation. *Law and Contemporary Problems*, 72, 37–58.

Budiani, D. 2007. Facilitating organ transplants in Egypt: An analysis of doctors' discourse. *Body & Society*, 13 (3), 125–49.

Carter, S. K. 2010. Beyond body: Body and self in women's childbearing narratives. *Sociology of Health & Illness*, 32 (7), 993–1009.

Curtis, A. 2010. Giving 'til it hurts: Egg donation and the costs of altruism. *Feminist Formations*, 22 (2), 80–100.

Goodwin, M. 2006. *Black Markets: The Supply and Demand of Body Parts*. Cambridge: Cambridge University Press.

Hoeyer, K., Nexoe, S., Hartlev, M. and Koch, L. 2009. Embryonic entitlements: Stem cell patenting and the co-production of commodities and personhood. *Body & Society*, 15 (1), 1–24.

Roberts, D. E. 2008. The future of reproductive choice for poor women and women of color. In C. Malacrida and J. Low (eds) *Sociology of the Body: A Reader*. Oxford: Oxford University Press.

Seale, C., Cavers, D. and Dixon-Woods, M. 2006. Commodification of body parts: By medicine or by media? *Body & Society*, 12 (1), 25–42.

Discussion Questions

Have you noticed how the human body is central to the creation and maintenance of social order? Provide examples from your own experience.

How does racial/ethnic variation transform ideas and ideals about the body and embodiment (e.g., body techniques and somatic expressions)?

6
Vulnerable Bodies

Introduction

The final chapter of this book examines the vulnerability of the body in relation to childhood, ageing and death. It takes the life course as its central concept, in order to address the relationships between the chronological, physiological and social components of ageing (Arber and Ginn 1995). Whereas chronological age refers to the number of years achieved by a person, physiological age is defined in terms of biological stages and processes, and social age represents social events and practices that occur at various points across the life course (such as entry into paid work) and the expectations associated with them. The chapter first examines childhood, second, ageing and, third, death. These topics are addressed through considerations of the impact of images and imaging on embodiment.

The Historical Emergence of Childhood

For historian Philippe Ariès, childhood is a thoroughly modern phenomenon, emerging towards the late seventeenth century. Ariès makes key observations in his comprehensive, though controversial, survey of images of childhood gleaned from visual art, architecture, literature and costume. First, he argued in *Centuries of Childhood* (1972) that there is little evidence of differentiation between adulthood and childhood in pre-modern periods. In medieval times, there were few special clothes, games or toys, for instance, and little special provision for children, who were, on the whole, expected to work, play, eat and sleep alongside adults. Moreover, children were punished in much the same way as adults, since they were viewed as small adults who were capable of sin (for instance, Ariès found evidence that children as young as seven years old could be hanged).

Second, the development of Ariès' analysis by subsequent authors suggests this absence of differentiation could be attributed to parental indifference. There is certainly evidence that children in pre-modern eras were beaten, exploited, murdered and abandoned, which might suggest they were in fact treated quite casually. Further, pre-modern mortality rates were high, which might account for a low emotional attachment between adults and children. However, this particular observation has been subject to considerable scrutiny and criticized in particular by Pollock (1983). Drawing on an analysis of diary evidence, Pollock suggests that parents exhibited concern about children and anguish on occasion of their death. Moreover, Ariès' source material is French, and cannot be generalized to the rest of Europe and other Western countries. His analysis of this material tells us about representations rather than about actual relationships between adults and children. In contrast, other studies have demonstrated significantly higher levels of emotional attachment between adults and children and, in particular, between mothers and infants (Pollock 1983).

Notwithstanding such criticisms, Ariès identifies changes in the representation of children and childhood across time and, specifically, an increasing emphasis on innocence and a new concern for the physical protection and welfare of children. Changes in representation were influenced first by Christianity's insistence on the soul as unique, open to salvation and in need of protection from the corrupt world of adults. Enlightenment ideals and a decline in the belief of original sin informed the writing of theorists such as John Locke and Jean-Jacques Rousseau, who emphasized the innocence of children. This was reflected in visual images of the child as pretty and delicate (such as *Pretty Baa Lambs* by Ford Madox Brown, 1851–9) and in literary images of innocence (such as Blake's *Songs of Innocence and Experience*). Further historical analysis of images of children and the body of the child suggests that representation of the child has been increasingly based on establishing its physical difference from the body of adults (Higgonet 1998), a difference that embodied sexual innocence as well as innocence of the world. These new emphases mark a shift in concepts of childhood from the late seventeenth century that

expanded in the late eighteenth century and were consolidated by
the mid-twentieth century.

Contemporary images of childhood and the body of the child

The first part of this chapter explores how childhood is defined in
the West and the images with which it is associated before moving
on to consider some of the ways in which the body is central to how
children experience childhood. Childhood in contemporary Western
cultures is typically viewed as a time of innocence and joy and is seen
as being distinct from adulthood. Children are viewed as dissimilar
to adults in biological, psychological and moral terms. Consequently,
the contexts and institutions in which children 'grow up' are oriented
towards enabling them to achieve adulthood (James et al. 1998),
or towards 'becoming' – that is, becoming adults or future selves
(Brownlie 2006) – based on an assumption that the bodies of children
are supremely 'unfinished' (see Williams and Bendelow 1998). Such
achievement is dependent on becoming civilized, or as Mayall (1998)
puts it, civilizing and regulating children's unruly selves. As chapter 3
outlines, the civilizing process is as much a process that occurs across
biographical time as it does across historical time. Therefore, much
of childhood is consumed with being encouraged to control one's
own body and learn appropriate forms of bodily conduct over time
and in particular places or contexts.

Protective discourse and the child's body

Important changes in Western perceptions of children and discourses
concerning the body of the child occurred in the early years of the
twentieth century, which have, in turn, had an impact on children's
embodied experiences. First, by the late eighteenth century, there
had emerged a bourgeois concern about children's labour, and both
images and writings of the period increasingly represent children as
vulnerable and physically unsuited to particular kinds of work associated with danger and even death. For instance, in Britain, chimney
sweeps' use of children as climbing boys (and girls), immortalized in
Charles Kingsley's *Water Babies*, was considered untenable because
of the danger of falling on pins or fires, of developing cancer or even
of death. By the end of the twentieth century, the child's body had
become increasingly viewed – and constructed in political and legal

discourse – as a body in need of protection (Brownlie 2006), because of the potential risk for harm or violation. Accordingly, childhood also became increasingly equated with the management of risk (Brownlie 2001), a preoccupation with the prevention of disease and harm, and with constant vigilance – surveillance of the physical body of the child, or parts of the child's body – in order to forestall potential threats to children's well-being (Scott et al. 1998).

As chapter 5 outlined, an assortment of surveillance techniques were developed in the twentieth century in relation to the regulation of health and welfare, many of which focused on the body of the child. By the early years of the twentieth century, the measurement and analysis of the bodies of children (in the school, in the home, in the hospital) helped shape the categorization of the 'normal' child and chart the parameters of normal mental and physical development (Armstrong 1995). For instance, in parts of Europe, the US and Britain, psychiatry, psychology and medicine established ways of charting 'normal' progress through discernible stages in development. These professional discourses set specific milestones and provided information and advice to parents to ensure children achieved them (Armstrong 1995).

Moreover, both home and school became crucial sites for the observation and monitoring of children to ensure they met the markers of normality established by experts (Donzelot 1979). For example, in Britain, the 1918 Maternity and Child Welfare Act focused on the monitoring of children in schools to ensure they were receiving the right kinds of diet at home. Similarly, a growing emphasis on dental hygiene was typical of the kinds of British welfare reforms of the early twentieth century, where children were collectively taught how to brush their teeth and given toothbrushes of their own (Nettleton 1992). Moreover, the body of the child was increasingly constructed as a problem within paediatrics as it shifted its concern from diseases of childhood to concern about the health and development of children as a whole (Armstrong 1995). These measures of surveillance created new categories of children (nervous children, difficult children, delicate children; Armstrong 1983: 14) and new discourses about the body of the child as vulnerable and in need of protection by parents and professionals (Brownlie 2001). Furthermore, these discourses raise questions about the body of the child as a particular kind of object and its relation to self.

The body of the child, self and intercorporeality

In Scotland in 2002, new legislation was proposed to revise the scope of the physical chastisement of children. This proposal, while not ultimately enacted (though a similar proposal became law in England and Wales in 2005), allowed parents to physically punish their children (termed 'justifiable assault') for purposes of discipline, but banned the use of implements, shaking children and blows to certain parts of the child's body (principally the head). Drawing on qualitative interviews with 85 parents and a survey of 692 parents in Scotland as part of research about parental beliefs and attitudes concerning the physical chastisement of children commissioned by the Scottish Executive, Brownlie (2006) suggests that when parents talk about physical punishment, they often engage in a process of what McGillivray (1997) calls 'zoning' the child's body. Through this process, parents draw lines and boundaries on the child's body about what is permissible and justifiable to chastise (that is, to hit or hurt without, as these parents see it, causing harm). In doing so, parents reinforce a notion of the child's body as a pre-rational 'object' (or what Christensen 2000 terms the somatic body, a body objectified beyond subjective experience). This theme of the child's body as a pre-rational 'object' is similarly reflected in scholarship concerning infants, which suggests that within sociology, infants are conflated with their bodies (or framed in sociological research as 'biobundles') and have been, therefore, largely invisible within the sociology of the body and of childhood.

However, as Brownlie and Sheach Leith (2011) point out in their discussion of parents' talk about immunizing their children, when talking about their infants, parents also acknowledge the messy 'unboundedness' of the infant body (see also p. 110), and the various ways in which their relation to their infants is *intercorporeal*. Parents talk, for instance, about the pain they feel and share when their tiny babies are immunized, when the skin of the infant body is breached via vaccination. This reference to sharing pain suggests that the skin of the infant body is less a fixed boundary between nature and culture than a site of 'relationality', to the extent that the infant 'through contact with his/her caregivers gains a sense of self as bounded by skin – a self produced through intercorporeality' that in turn shapes – in an embodied and emotional way – parents' own sense of self (p. 202). Thus, the infant body is interconnected and interdependent with the bodies of parents and others in ways that require us to interrogate the ongoing metaphorical power of the complex interrelationship between nature and culture (Brownlie and Sheach Leith 2011).

Temporality, the child's body and innocence

Although childhood is perceived in the contemporary West as a literal category, defined by physiological, psychological and anatomical norms, it is, as Hockey and James (1993) suggest, also symbolic. There are at least four themes that symbolize and shape contemporary concepts of the child and childhood. First, childhood is perceived as a distinct period in time in which children themselves are temporally set apart from adults and their world. Moreover, the social distance between childhood and adulthood is reinforced through special games, toys and socially sanctioned freedoms. The body of the child is both literally and metaphorically viewed as smaller, younger and less mature than that of the adult, and emphasis is placed on encouraging growth in physical and developmental terms. This temporal setting apart of childhood contributes to establishing the child as other, as *not* adult (indeed, as a particular kind of pre-rational object – see above), and is reinforced by the emphasis on age and size. The social importance of accumulating years is marked by birthdays, candles, badges which all underscore that accumulation (James 1992). Yet emphasis on progress through time is not in itself necessarily a modern feature of the movement from childhood into adulthood, as analysis of Renaissance visual art suggests (Ariès 1972). However, it is generally accepted that images such as Titian's *Three Ages of Man* (1511–12), which depicts a child, an adult and an ageing man, serve as a *reminder* of mortality (*memento mori*) rather than evidence of discrete stages through which children pass across the life course. Therefore, what seems to be distinctly modern is the emphasis on temporally defined ages and stages and the requirement to pass through them en route to adulthood.

A second image underpinning contemporary Western concepts of childhood is that of the child as innocent. By the mid-twentieth century a dominant image of childhood in children's literature emphasized childhood as a carefree time symbolized by shiny, happy faces (Scott et al. 1998). Similarly, contemporary photographic images of children produced for public and popular consumption accord special social significance to the child as the embodiment of innocence and a 'timeless utopia' (Higgonet 1998: 77). Higgonet observes that images such as those produced by the Australian photographer Anne Geddes are assembled in ways that not only emphasize the fleshiness of the child's body but also reinforce the association of childhood with innocence through the material objects that accompany its representation (such as flowers, angel wings).

Moreover, the surface of the body of the child is associated with newness and flawlessness. For instance, Christensen (2000) remarks that there is an 'embedded cultural understanding' of the body of the child as divided into a 'visible, exposed and specific outer nature' that adults attend to through grooming, observing, touching, and so on, and 'a hidden, wild and vulnerable inner nature' that is nurtured 'via food and knowledge' (pp. 47–8). This theme of flawlessness and innocence in contemporary childhood has been termed Apollonian (Jenks 1996), as Apollo was characterized by sunshine and light.

In this version of childhood, children are seen to embody essential goodness, especially the bodies of infants (Murcott 1993), untainted by the world they enter, possessing clarity of vision that is not often shared by adults. In contrast to pre-modern concepts of the child in which children were viewed first as innately sinful and then as *tabulae rasae* (Jenks 1996), in the Apollonian model children are celebrated and encouraged. While innocence remains a crucial motif in the concept of childhood, its loss is increasingly the focus of public and academic anxiety. This loss is addressed via debates about the ways in which, for instance, visual culture explicitly addresses the body of the child as a surface of consumption (Russell and Tyler 2002), and therefore of bodily transformation and modification in accordance with adult norms, just as pop culture quite explicitly contributes to the hypersexualization of children's bodies, especially adolescent girls. However, as Casper and Moore (2009) note, 'innocent bodies may also be missing bodies, in part because the production of innocence requires silence' (p. 23). That is, despite the pervasiveness of imagery promoting the idea of innocence via particular representations of the child's body, children themselves are often denied the status of speaking subjects capable of narrating their own lives, as others – parents, the law, the state – speak for them.

The dependent child and social change

A final theme shaping contemporary notions of childhood emphasizes childhood as a period of dependency, fostered by Western modes of parenting, in which children are not expected to hold responsibilities, and priority is given to their protection and welfare. Such dependency is seen to be physical, economic, social, psychological and intellectual and reinforces the social distance between adults and children through, for instance, child-specific games, toys, television and the general absence of opportunities to enter the adult world. Yet the emphasis on fostering dependency is contradictory as it potentially reduces the degree of autonomy available to children and, crucially, opportunities, especially for girls, to develop physical confidence and competencies (Young 1990; see pp. 71–3).

Though these images of contemporary childhood vary in their intensity, they are buttressed by changes in the size and shape of families in the Western world. Despite variation according to religion and ethnicity, family size in modern Western societies is typically smaller than that of one hundred years ago. Moreover, children are generally closer in age to each other than in previous eras, which has contributed to a more concentrated focus on children as a social group and to a perception of the body of the child as qualitatively distinct from the adult body. Equally, the loss of a productive role in the economy has contributed to children's growing subordination and dependence, though in the last decade, fostered by visual media and pocket money, children are developing a new role as consumers. Differences rather than similarities between children and adults are reinforced, and the *futures* of children are emphasized, in both expert and commonsense understandings of childhood, rather than their present. Children are 'social only in their potential future but not in their present being' (James et al. 1998: 6) and, consequently, consideration has rarely been given to the impact of contemporary images of childhood on children's experiences.

Pause and Reflect: In your experience, what makes children dependent on adults and how might dependency reduce children's autonomy?

Children's experiences of childhood

Contemporary images of childhood are potent, but what bearing do they have on how children themselves experience 'growing up'? So potent are these images that academic interest in children has been largely restricted to childhood itself as a period of time distinct from adulthood, as a period of becoming rather than being. Social scientists of many disciplinary persuasions have focused their attention on the institution of childhood, what it is, how it is shaped, the boundaries between normal and abnormal, without paying much attention to children themselves. In other words, until the last two decades, children have persistently been conceptualized as 'other', as non-adult, as pre-social. In contrast, Alison James conducted a piece of research that centred on the experience of children in order to explore the impact of images and concepts of childhood (1992). She employed an ethnographic approach in order to develop understandings of children's concepts of self and the significance of relationships with both children and adults in these concepts. Her interviews with children in schools and observations of playground conduct reveal the significance of the body in children's sense of self.

Growing up: age and size

First, growth is an important aspect of children's talk about themselves, and children are well aware of its significance. Bodily stereotypes pepper children's talk about themselves in relation to others. Physical size and chronological age are both conceptual filters through which children measure themselves not only in relation to adults but also against other children. Children become aware of their own bodies at an early age and, in the context of primary school, very young children are aware that 'size matters'. Physical smallness sets children apart from other children and is experienced as a form of negative differentiation. For instance, established nursery-school children talked about their own size as a way of comparing themselves to both new entrants and primary-school children. Being 'big' marks social progress, but the meaning of size is established by the institutional context in which it is experienced. Children also use size as a means of claiming degrees of autonomy, for instance, 'when I am big I will get more pocket money/be able to walk to school/ have my own bedroom.' Size is also a source of anxiety for children, particularly where physical difference is concerned. Indeed, children develop a sharp awareness of what is deemed normal such that any form of difference (disability, sickness, anxiety) sets them apart from other children. The appearance of the physical body in relation to comparisons is especially significant for children with disabilities and, as discussed in chapter 3 (p. 23), for children whose lives depend on medical technologies and who, therefore, engage in considerable work to manage discrepancies between virtual and social identities that are in transition (Kirk 2010).

Restraint and risk

Second, though the predominant images of childhood emphasize a time of relative freedom, in practice, children are subject to a high degree of restraint and discipline. In part, this is an effect of risk society (Beck 1992) and the rising anxiety which many parents experience in relation to their children, in which the world beyond the home is identified as 'risky' and from which their children must be protected and shielded (Scott et al. 1998). Consequently, the social spaces in which children move are highly circumscribed and limited to supposed spaces of safety such as parks, playgrounds, schools, high chairs, car seats, playpens. Children's mobility is restricted because of their perceived vulnerability to harm from traffic or strangers, and public spaces are increasingly monitored by closed-circuit television (in part to contain the threat that children, usually older ones, themselves are seen to pose). Hence, though childhood is understood as a time of freedom, children's own experiences point to increasingly high levels of protection and bodily regulation across space and time. This shift may be counter-productive in the sense that children are not provided with opportunities to develop the physical and mental skills necessary for the acquisition of independence (Scott et al. 1998). In addition, ordering, disciplining and restricting of bodily practices may also contribute to the construction of bodily differences, particularly in terms of gender. As Karen Martin (1989) has argued, the hidden curriculum in schools contributes to gendering by requiring children to act or behave in certain ways (e.g., girls are encouraged to develop quiet voices and control their sound), and fostering an environment in which boys and girls monitor each other's bodily practices and physicality.

Time and timetables

Third, childhood is temporally ordered and the world of the child is bounded by adult time. For instance, home life may be shaped by regimes and routines instigated by adults. At school, children are channelled through the day in ways that subordinate bodily needs to those of the timetable. Children have to ask permission to go to the toilet and can only exercise and eat/drink at times specified by adults. Mayall (1998) observes both how children have to learn how to manage their bodies in the context of school, for instance, going to the toilet at specified times, and how children's bodily conduct is supervised by the adult gaze. Eating, going to the toilet and play are all activities that require degrees of adult supervision (or that of older children). Consequently, children have to learn to manage their bodies in highly restricted contexts.

Though contemporary images of childhood emphasize freedom, innocence and dependency, they are often contradicted by children's experience of 'growing up'. Evidence suggests that children go through considerable anxiety about their bodies in relation to those of others and in terms of attaining the established norms of maturity. The experience of childhood is shaped by protection and restriction in ways that limit the degrees of freedom available to children, and many participate in paid and unpaid work in ways that are at odds with ideas about childhood as a time of play and leisure.

Borderliners

Peter Høeg's novel *Borderliners* (1995) provides a fictional account of the experience of being at an experimental Danish school during the 1960s where time is used as an instrument of control and regulation. Timetabling is endured by the children as restrictive and as a form of surveillance, and the novel chronicles their attempts to resist time as a form of control. The context of school provides an ordered passage through childhood marked by moves from one level to another higher than before. Childhood is therefore defined as a hierarchy in which the normal passage of movement is onward and upward and eventually out. It is shaped and regulated by temporal frameworks and processes that configure the experiences of children themselves.

Ageing and the life course

Understanding ageing

This chapter suggests that images of the body play a substantial role in perceptions and experiences of ageing across the life course and are mediated by social and cultural context (Nettleton and Watson 1998). Images of ageing provide models against which we can measure ourselves as we age, and changes in physical appearance are part of the process of physical ageing (Fairhurst 1998). As chapter 3 suggested, the civilizing process is a process occurring not only across historical time but also across biographical time, and much of the social learning that takes place in childhood is oriented towards instilling social and bodily competencies within particular biographies. Entry into adulthood or independence – becoming adult selves, as outlined in chapter 1 – is premised on and associated with bodily control, emotional restraint and the presentation of a 'mature' self. Ageing and, in particular, old age is similarly associated with changes and alterations in the shape, appearance and function of the body that may cause pain or discomfort and contribute to the social devaluation of ageing and old people (Tulle-Winton 2000).

Furthermore, the processes and experiences associated with ageing occur in a context marked by cultural emphasis on images and values of youth and beauty (Featherstone 1982).

Ageing has been examined primarily within the discipline and practice of social gerontology, which is based largely on biological understandings of the human body and is typically focused on the policy and management issues produced by ageing (Bury 1995). Ageing, like many other aspects of embodiment, is defined in biomedical terms primarily as a biological process, and clinical medicine (through geriatrics) has been the dominant framework through which the ageing body is understood and collectively managed. Changes in nutrition, levels of health and fertility control have contributed to longevity and an increase in the numbers of people living beyond retirement age. This demographic change is interpreted by policymakers and professionals (and perhaps the lay public too) largely as a social problem. After all, bodies that age may get sick and become frail or physically compromised. Added to this, the structure and provision of both welfare and pensions is deemed insufficient to meet the needs of a growing elderly population.

Old age as a foreign land

Old age (as understood in medical, biological, psychological and welfare terms) in particular has become a problem for Western societies that demands new techniques of government, especially as people of a particular chronological age become surplus to the requirements of capitalism and industry. Political economy approaches to ageing have focused on the structural components of ageing and the ways in which the loss of a productive role in the economy, increased welfare dependence and loss of status compound ageing and contribute to old age as a problem. Indeed, there is some evidence that the identification of old age as a problem occurred simultaneously with changes in the age of retirement and in welfare provision (Phillipson 1982). Consequently, old age has increasingly come to be defined in terms of productivity, the absence of which leads to social and economic marginalization. There is a large social gerontology and demographic literature on ageing and the social, political and economic challenges it presents. However, sociologists have begun to examine more closely the lived experience of ageing and the various ways in which the body and images of the body contribute to both understandings and experiences of ageing. Therefore, the following section looks first at images and second at experiences of ageing.

Think first of all about popular images of ageing and old people in the contemporary West. What springs to mind may include some of the following: bodily disease and decay, physical incompetence and bodily betrayals (such as dribbling or shaking), lack of activity, isolation and/or institutionalization, dependency, fear of physical deterioration and/or pain, false teeth. As Hepworth observes, the 'look of age' is 'considered unwelcome and undesirable' (2000: 40), and the physical signs and experiences of ageing invoke value judgements and stereotypes that reflect fear and anxiety (Woodward 1991). For many of us, old age in particular represents a 'foreign land' (Blaikie 1999). Though these images of ageing may be peculiar to modern industrial societies, their potency relies on a sense of a 'lost golden age' in which ageing was not associated with loss of place and function.

Representations and images of ageing reveal something of the widespread cultural and social fear and apprehension about ageing and contribute to 'visual ageism' (Blaikie 1999). While there may not be an exact 'fit' between images and experiences of ageing, nonetheless, such images provide material for gauging assumptions and ways of seeing age. Consumer culture and visual presentation is central to the experience of the contemporary period, thus, visual and textual images become a crucial part of how phenomena are defined and understood. As Hearn (1995) puts it, images are not solely *of* a particular individual, event or phenomenon. Rather, social categories (e.g., 'old people') and phenomena are actively *imaged* and imagined through processes that entail producing, presenting and looking at images. Visual images, and in particular photographs, create a 'cultural iconography' of ageing (Blaikie and Hepworth 1997) that highlights the dependencies associated with ageing and suggests ways of 'ageing gracefully'. The imagery of ageing typically reproduces negative stereotypes about the ageing body or presents idealizations to which people ought to aspire (Hepworth 1995a). Though there are 'few graphic representations of old bodies' (Tulle-Winton 2000), such that exist are marked by particular characteristics that emphasize the problems of ageing, such as bodily decline and changing physical appearance (wrinkles, loss of hair, stooping). Moreover, such images typically evoke reactions from people such as disgust or revulsion.

Changing images of ageing

Blaikie (1999) provides an inventory of changing images of ageing in Western societies over the twentieth century. While images of

ageing differ according to the contexts in which they are produced
and presented, there are, nonetheless, continuities in the ways old
age has been portrayed in the media, in film and in television. First,
in general terms old age is typically characterized as a phase accompanied by decrepitude, oblivion and senility, and images of old age
reflect the distance from and fears about age held by the non-aged.
Predominant in the representation of ageing and older people are
notions of infantilization, whereby ageing people are reduced to
childlike status (see Hockey and James 1993 for accounts of how
infantilization contributes to relationships between old people and
their carers).

Second, there are significant gender differences in representations of ageing. Whereas women are subject to negative judgement
on the basis of physical appearance and are desexualized, physical
manifestations of age in men are more likely to be interpreted as
distinguished or as signs of wisdom (Blaikie 1999). For instance,
one study (Lambert et al. 1984) of images of men in the media (television) found that the majority of those over the age of sixty were
accounted for by reference to men in positions of power (world
leaders, politicians, businessmen). Moreover, while it seems evident
that women in the media are required to pay attention to their physical appearance, the physical appearance of their male counterparts is
unquestioned.

There are also differences in class and period in images of men and
women. While Victorian grandmothers were represented in paintings
as genteel and frail (Hepworth 1995b), twenty-first-century images of
grandmothers are typically working class, portraying a no-nonsense
and fixed stoicism consistent with idealizations of working-class older
women (Blaikie 1999). In cinema, though it is generally accepted
that three-dimensional parts for actresses over the age of forty are
rare, men of sixty can still reasonably expect to be playing scenes
of intimacy (typically with women less than half their age). Though
there have been a number of parts for older women in the last decade
or so, they generally portray women who are stubborn, powerless
or self-sacrificing (Markson and Taylor 1993). Nonetheless, images
of ageing and of older people have been transformed in magazines
aimed at this particular market and reflect demographic expansion,
concerns about maintaining health and well-being across the life
course and the relative affluence of the ageing 'baby boom' generation (see Featherstone and Hepworth 1984).

Experiences of ageing

Awareness of age-related change

Though ageing was the focus of professional and academic scrutiny for much of the twentieth century, the tendency was to examine the problems associated with the *losses* of physical capacity and social status. Notable exceptions to this approach include ethnographies and oral histories of the experiences of today's elderly population (Blaikie 1999). An approach that takes embodiment into account has been notably absent from research until relatively recently. Such research concerns the experiences of midlife, ageing and health and of the social organization of caring for older people. Within the collective experience of ageing, people draw on the visual signs of ageing as a topic of comparison (Bytheway and Johnson 1998). However, as Diehl and Wahl (2010) observe, the experience or awareness of ageing is multidimensional, and involves not only an awareness of bodily decline and loss of capacity but also perceptions of the gains associated with ageing, especially those associated with environmental, social and biomedical change (Jones and Higgs 2010). Diehl and Wahl outline the parameters of awareness of age-related change (AARC) in terms of people's expectations about what ageing will bring (cultural norms tied to chronological age and age-related events); the internalization of stereotypes about ageing, which can influence behaviour; and the experiences that people have of ageing, as well as the contexts in which ageing occurs. As Jones and Higgs (2010) argue, the contexts of ageing in modern societies have been transformed; they are increasingly constituted by a reflexive focus on fitness (chapter 4) that disrupts normative assumptions about ageing and reinforces the importance of mobilizing 'technologies of the self' in order to age 'well'. One consequence of such technologies (e.g., hormone replacement therapy) is the emergence of a new 'normal' based on a moral imperative of working toward the goal of fitness, which constitutes social value on those engaged in pursuing that goal.

Pause and Reflect: 'Keeping a youthful look becomes *more* important with age' (Oberg and Tornstam 2001). Do you agree?

Gender and ageing

As in many other areas of life, there are gender differences in the experience of ageing. Moreover, there is evidence that some aspects of midlife are more likely to be medicalized – that is, viewed and responded to within a predominantly medical framework. For instance, the period of women's lives in which menstruation ceases, menopause, is generally treated and viewed within biomedical terms and largely associated with oestrogen deficiency or ovarian dysfunction (Freund and McGuire 1999). In Western culture, menopause is associated with a range of symptoms (such as hot flushes, fatigue and depression). It is viewed as 'a biological certainty' (Cunningham-Burley and Backett-Milburn 1998: 7), and intervention typically focuses largely on treating oestrogen deficiency. Yet there is considerable variation in how women in different cultures respond to the cessation of menstruation (Lock 1991), suggesting the experience of menopause is associated with social and cultural expectations for women. The attachment of meanings about menopause to hormones is associated with the various ways the female body has been defined within the biomedical model as a body 'in trouble' (Hughes and Witz 1997). Given the ways in which women in Western societies have been reduced to the body and defined in particular by the capacity for reproduction, it is perhaps unsurprising that the cessation of menstruation marks a transitional point in women's lives. However, the image of menopause has tended to emphasize the end of one period of women's lives (their potential to reproduce) rather than the beginning of another phase.

Moreover, images of menopause typically reinforce ideas about older age as a period of declining use, value and function, and consolidate notions about older women as 'crones' (thus reinforcing a double standard in which, as women age, their source of power – beauty – is diminished, while men's is enhanced; Twigg 2004). Indeed, Greer (1991) argued that menopause symbolically and literally marks women's decreasing sexual powers, which correspond with their diminishing social status. She raises critical questions about the use and effects of hormone replacement therapy and suggests that medicine and pharmaceutical companies manipulate Western societies' expectations of women to retain youthful looks. Though menopause tends to be viewed as a condition requiring medical intervention and treatment, there is considerable ambiguity about how women respond to menopause and how they negotiate this aspect of embodied experience. For some women, the cessation of menstruation brings a degree of freedom. The participants in Martin's (1989) study of the imagery and experience of menstruation and menopause observe that menopause brought relief from the discomfort and inconvenience of menstruation and freedom from the fear of pregnancy. Martin comments that, for many of her respondents, menopause was simply 'part of life' rather than a medically defined condition or event. In similar though more notably phenomenological vein, Rothfield (1997) comments that, though menopause is essentially defined as a biological event in Western societies, the embodied experience of menopause is shaped by social and cultural practices and circumstances that suggest wide variation in the meaning of menopause and, more generally, of middle life.

Though people age in physical and chronological terms, many report that they are not aware of their bodies as ageing or old or that they do not 'feel' old. For instance, the participants in Cunningham-Burley and Backett-Milburn's (1998) study of ageing and midlife found it difficult to talk about their bodies in terms other than of health and well-being. The women referred to experiences of tiredness and a loss of physical stamina rather than to ageing in and of itself. Therefore one of the questions asked by the authors of this study is whether the experiences alluded to by the women are a direct consequence of physiological changes or an effect of the various ways in which women are expected and encouraged to 'slow down' in midlife, particularly in the post-menopausal phase.

This study hints at the central issue in relation to embodiment and the ageing body; that is, the ways in which local cultures and public discourse – in this case, negative notions of ageing – may construct the subjective experiences of the ageing body. As discussed in chapter 2, body work (make-up, fashion, hair, exercise) is critical to the production of docile female bodies; as many scholars now argue, body work – through age-resisting practices that promote functionality and the appearance of youthfulness – is also critical to the experience of ageing for both women and men. Indeed, as Slevin (2010) notes in her study of ageing experiences, resistance to old age 'makes sense' because 'it is a way of fighting invisibility, of resisting exclusion, of trying to maintain positive cultural capital' (p. 1017).

Beauty and Older Women

Many studies have identified the importance of touch and beauty maintenance in constructing subjective experiences of gender (e.g., Furman 1997; Gimlin 2002). An ethnographic study of beauty therapy training explored how particular body-maintenance techniques and body talk constructed the lived experience of ageing. Beauty therapists are trained to provide facial and body skin care, including electrolysis and massage, and in doing so, use bare, rather than gloved hands. This direct skin-to-skin contact creates a therapeutic charge and, as Paulson (2006) notes, affirms the value of the ageing body and, for the women in the study, created an experience of ageing that was based on feelings of well-being. These feelings, argues Paulson, contrast with the women in Furman's study, who experienced a sense of loss of beauty associated with ageing, and further endorse Gimlin's claim that different bodily practices associated with particular contexts – and the cultural knowledge associated with these contexts – create distinct bodily experiences. In Paulson's study, beauty therapy practices such as massage created a synergy between internal and external beauty that created feelings of well-being for ageing women and embodied a nourishing and affirming culture of beauty. Furthermore, Paulson's observations about the experience of touch as healing lend weight to Burkitt's (1999) claim that in the modern, fragmentary world, the body is an important focal point for relational networks that enable individuals to integrate aspects of themselves into whole persons.

Embodied Ageing – Gender, Sexuality and Ethnicity

Social position such as gender, race/ethnicity, sexuality, class, all play a role in shaping the experiences of ageing. Kathleen Slevin (2010) interviewed 57 women and men between the ages of 60 and 89 about their experience of ageing within a culture that places a great deal of value on youth and youthful appearance. She notes the gay men in her sample experienced 'accelerated ageing' (Bennett and Thompson 1991) because physical appearance is highly valued amongst gay men, and gay culture reinforces youthful and hegemonic masculinity more than heterosexual male culture. Consequently, the gay men she interviewed worried about telling their partners their real age in case they felt they were 'too old'. Indeed, these older gay men experienced stigma and disadvantage when trying to find partners. Slevin notes that the gay men in this study were similar to heterosexual women in relation to their anxieties about their appearance, and engaged in considerable body work to maintain a youthful appearance, and were more likely than heterosexual men to consider cosmetic surgery.

In contrast, the Black women and men who participated in this study showed little interest in cosmetic surgery. Their attitude to ageing was that they ought to accept who they are and do their best with their natural appearance. One of the Black female participants explained this difference as being because Black women 'had more problems to deal with, and this [ageing] is almost immaterial'.

The mask of ageing

As with other phases in ageing, the middle years are typically patholo-gized with expert focus on its 'problems'. Yet the 'bodily betrayals' that may accompany and signify midlife 'derive their primary signifi-cance from the fact that for a majority of men and women, there *is* a lot of life left to live' (Hepworth 1987: 137). As bodies age, they may be 'brought to mind' in ways that are uncomfortable for people's sense of self. In turn, reflexivity may become more pronounced when bodily limits are experienced (Hallam et al. 1999). Featherstone and Hepworth (1991) observe that many people make sense of the expe-rience of ageing and its attendant changes in appearance and capacity by holding on to a sense of self that is separate from and concealed by these changes. They refer to this phenomenon as the '**mask of ageing**', which conveys the sense of alienation experienced by older people when others perceive them as 'old'. The metaphor of the mask refers to the duality between what is displayed by the external sur-faces and competencies of the body and the sense of self experienced by the individual. This mask may also become part of a strategy to 'masquerade' (Biggs 1993) and conceal the signs of old age by using cosmetics and clothes or participating in exercise regimes (Hepworth 1995b). It's interesting to note, however, that empirical studies have identified a converse mask of ageing, in which individuals feel older than they look. Wainwright and Turner's (2006) study of ballet dancers suggests that as dancers age, while they may continue to look youthful (energetic and flexible), they may feel their bodies 'tighten-ing up' and become painfully – in a literal way – aware of their ageing bodies. Bones crack and joints ache in ways that continually remind them of embodied change, even though, from the audience's per-spective, their bodies apparently continue to function at a high level of performance.

Gender, age and body work

'Self-work' or body work may also be gendered in the context of ageing, in the sense that women are more likely to be encouraged to conceal the physical signs of age than men and are indeed rebuked if they fail to conceal such signs in socially and culturally appropriate ways (Fairhurst 1998). Yet while the transition from midlife to later life need no longer be marked by a change in wardrobe (Lurie 1992), there is nonetheless, as Fairhurst (1998) notes, a fine line between 'growing old gracefully' and becoming 'mutton dressed as lamb'. Such work contributes to an emerging gap between midlife and old age in which the former is increasingly prolonged and in which there is growing convergence in the embodied experiences of men (Gullette 1997). While there is considerable ambivalence about the meanings and even doubt about the existence of male menopause, the greater anxieties men are expressing about their bodies as they move into the middle years (Hall 1991) are connected with a range of socio-economic and cultural changes that have destabilized male identities (Hearn 1995).

Though the approaches of these various studies differ, they make reference to a tension between the lived experience of ageing and its external manifestation. People may 'feel' 'young at heart' and yet visibly present the signs of physiological ageing consistent with chronological advancement in years. Such an analysis is in harmony with the view that definitions and categorizations of age and ageing are dependent on the social contexts and relations in which they occur. Physical signs of ageing are interpreted in culturally specific ways that in turn contribute to individuals' awareness and experiences of ageing. This may help to explain the imperative towards the concealment of ageing because the ageing body has become a site of social and cultural devaluation in the contemporary West.

Positive ageing: youth, fitness and morality

Health policy and public health practices have increasingly emphasized new ways of producing and maintaining healthy and fit bodies through 'lifestyle' changes (Burrows et al. 1995). These policies and practices are the product of many different kinds of changes in the socio-economic and political landscape, but there is a general consensus among commentators that they are informed by images of youthfulness and vitality. Though public health and health-promotion practices are increasingly concerned with developing new techniques for combating the decay and disease attendant with ageing, they are also based on and contribute to moral distinctions between 'styles of ageing and old age' (Hepworth 1995a: 176). Moral here refers to judgements made by self and others that contribute to the social categorization of people in terms of social acceptability (Goffman 1968). In this sense, as Hepworth (1995a) argues, ageing and old age can be seen not only (if at all) as objective biological states, but as 'socially constructed moral categories' that reflect prevailing dominant values.

These values, as chapter 4 suggests, are associated with youth and vitality, and consumer culture has contributed to the advent of such values within the context of health (Featherstone 1982). Consumer culture offers the view that the individual can be modified in ways that demand body work but also contribute to the maintenance of well-being across the life course. Therefore stereotypes about 'normal ageing' are constantly being challenged not only by health policies and practices that emphasize the necessity of maintaining physical fitness and well-being, but also by the activities of the 'baby boom' generation, who are equipped in economic and educational terms and expectations to participate in new ideas about and experiences of ageing (Hepworth and Featherstone 1998). Part of this process involves confronting the negative stereotypes associated with ageing in order to promote health and well-being. Yet this process is also bound up with ageing as a moral enterprise, with, as Williams (1990: 66) observed in his study of older people in the north-east of Scotland, a sense of duty to resist the onset of 'late old age'. Such resistance increasingly requires or entails physical activity – the physically fit body. Here, health is identified as a moral standard to which people are expected and encouraged to aspire, and evidence of dependencies is interpreted not only by professionals but also by the lay public as failure to achieve this standard (Crawford 1984). The pursuit of health is considered a positive virtue, and one that represents the demedicalization of later life (Hepworth 1995c); it is also increasingly embedded in images of positive – and thus normal – ageing.

Hence, 'positive ageing' in the contemporary period is typically presented through the framework of health and well-being. People in their middle years and beyond are encouraged to participate in activities that are thought to have some impact on biological and physiological processes of ageing in order to maintain levels of health and prevent the onset of disease and/or disability. As a corollary of 'positive ageing' people are encouraged to foster positive attitudes towards life and living. Yet it is worth considering that the efforts directed towards positive ageing betray an underlying and deeply rooted cultural understanding of ageing. They betray 'hostility to physical decline' and define old age in particular as pathology and as social deviance (Hepworth 1995c). The increasing emphasis on positive ageing contributes to the social distance from 'normal physical ageing' and perpetuates midlife as stretching endlessly beyond (Biggs 1993).

Bodily decline

The ageing process can be accompanied by bodily decline and decay. These processes elicit, as Lawton notes, disgust and revulsion in contemporary society because they undermine the notion of self-containment and boundedness that is associated with the autonomous, adult self (Lawton 1998), especially if accompanied by leaks and smells (Douglas 1970). Urinary and faecal incontinence are examples of such leaks, or bodily betrayals (see chapter 1), that are often accompanied by odours which, as chapter 1 discussed, elicit disgust and undermine an individual's 'mastery' over health and bodily control (Brittain and Shaw 2007). In doing so, such betrayals undermine the very basis of self and self-identity, as understood in modern societies (Lawton 1998) and has the potential to stigmatize the lives of others, via the body work and 'dirty work' involved in caring for those who suffer from incontinence (Brittain and Shaw 2007). In addition, such decline often occurs in deep old age, or the Fourth Age, which is, as Twigg (2004) notes, predominantly female due to increasing longevity. However, as Twigg also points out, there is as yet little sociological appreciation of the lived experience of this phase of life; most studies focus on physical frailty and decline, rather than intersections between decline and subjectivity, and in doing so, objectify the body.

Death, dying and bereavement

Death, dying and bereavement are challenging to deal with in modern industrial societies, and somewhat contradictory experiences. As a student then, later, qualified nurse, I witnessed death at various points in my career. My first experience was of a woman in her eighties who apparently died in her sleep. I discovered her and immediately drew curtains around her bed. It was visiting time and we would need to attend to her body with minimum attention and fuss. In other words, our practice as nurses at that time (circa 1983) was to 'carry on as normal'. This entailed preparing the dead woman's body for the mortuary: washing her, wrapping her body in a fresh sheet and placing an identification label around one of her big toes without drawing attention to her 'passing on', a ritual described in Sudnow's book of the same name (Sudnow 1967). Although there is considerable sociological debate around the extent to which death, dying and bereavement are taboo subjects in Anglophone society (Exley 2004), there is at the least a tension between public and private experiences and images of death and dying.

Changing understandings of death

Whereas in pre-modern contexts, where mortality rates were much higher than in contemporary Western contexts, death was viewed as an unpredictable and random event, in the late modern (rationalized) era, death is seen as the ultimate failure (Bauman 1992). It has been argued that death exposes the absurdity of modern societies' collective pursuit of instrumentality and rationally calculated longevity. In particular, the advent of professional medicine has framed death and dying (Williams 1997) in ways that foster the idea that life is enduring. Advances in medical technologies and therapies have increasingly meant that people can be 'kept alive', attached to machines, tubes and wires, even though they may be unable to feel, speak or think. Even the categorization of death is subject to rational processes and practices that attribute to each death a particular and special cause in order to render it calculable (Prior and Bloor 1993). Concomitantly, there is a tendency in Western societies to invest in lifestyles that will reduce the chances of dying from a particular disease, such as cancer or heart disease (Williams and Bendelow 1998).

In this way, death is rarely viewed as a natural and inevitable event and its presence is actively repressed by the *conscience collectif*, an inevitable consequence perhaps of the extent to which self-identity is concentrated on the body (Mellor and Shilling 1993). Death in the modern industrial period has been gradually concealed and sequestrated from public consideration and acknowledgement (Ariès 1983), shifting from domestic to hospital space. Most people will die in a hospital or institutional environment 'attended to by professional strangers' (Exley 2004: 112). Even in community settings, however, it appears that death, dying and the dead body are less community centred or collectively managed, but have become increasingly domains of life that are handled by professionals (Clark 2002).

Death and dissection

In institutional spaces, the body is an object of scrutiny and analysis, used to document the cause of death involving post mortem or autopsy (Armstrong 1987). It becomes, as Haddow (2005) puts it, a resource. Dissection of the dead body was once considered a form of punishment for criminal conduct, albeit accompanied by moral and religious prohibitions (Richardson 1998). However, by the sixteenth century, dissection of the human body was viewed as a means of developing anatomical knowledge, though one still imbued with awe and circumspection. In Renaissance Italy, for instance, the anatomist Vesalius performed anatomical dissection in a theatrical style that highlighted the spectacular nature of the event (Sawday 1995). Though dissection remained subject to moral and religious constraints until the nineteenth century, specialization within medical practice and the expansion of both anatomy and surgery was dependent on access to bodies for the purposes of dissection. However, medical schools in Britain, for instance, had difficulties in acquiring such access and surgeons began to pay 'resurrectionists' to supply a source. The use of bodies as a commodity in such a way was morally intolerable, hence legislation such as the 1832 Anatomy Act in Britain sanctioned the requisition of the bodies of those on the margins of society for the purposes of anatomical dissection (Richardson 1998).

Dissection in contemporary Western contexts remains an important practice for forensic, educational or knowledge-producing purposes. For instance, the education and training of medical students in the US and Britain have hitherto required that they participate in the dissection of human corpses in order to acquire knowledge about anatomy. However, fears and concerns about the vulnerability of bodies under dissection are aired in popular culture through films such as *Coma*, in which prestigious surgeons compel patients into a coma in order to 'harvest' their organs. While many people regard organ donation as an act of altruism (or, as Mauss 1990 would have it, a 'gift'), others see donation and transplantation in terms of the commodification of body parts.

The body in parts

The expansion of organ transplantation in the developed and developing world has placed a premium on organ procurement, and the absence of sufficient donors has led to a global traffic in human organs through which the developing world supplies the developed world (Scheper-Hughes 2000). Moreover, though many people view organ donation (as with the donation of blood) as a voluntary expression of unselfishness (Titmuss 1970), others consider it as a form of social obligation that could be subject to compulsion. Socio-cultural beliefs shape how people feel about specific body parts, and evidence suggests that some parts are considered more sacred than others and that the use of body parts from the dead to prolong the lives of the living challenges deeply held socio-cultural beliefs concerning the boundaries between bodies (Helman 1991).

In Australia, the US, Britain and parts of Europe, practices concerning the retention of tissue and organs acquired during 'routine' post mortem and autopsy have, in a way that is similar to anxieties concerning organ donation (Scheper-Hughes 2000), contributed to emergent concerns about the relation of body parts to the whole and to the person. In the late 1990s, knowledge emerged in Australia, New Zealand, Ireland and the UK that hospitals and coroners were retaining organs and tissues from the bodies of babies and infants. Beyond the public sense of scandal and concern about the issue of consent (parents had not been asked if the organs and tissues of their children could be retained for teaching and research purposes) (Sheach Leith 2007), the issue of organ retention raised the visibility of how Western societies organize death, dying and the disposal of bodies. What happens to bodies after death? Are bodies 'disposed of' in similar ways regardless of where, when or how they die? How do those who come into contact with the bodies of the dead deal with this situation?

Death and dying in popular and promotional culture

Despite the concealment of the realities of death and dying, images of death and dying bodies clutter the visual iconography of Western art. For instance, representations of death and dying in the fifteenth and sixteenth centuries (associated with engravers such as Dürer) highlighted the ubiquity and inevitability of death. Paintings in the Renaissance period emphasized the moral and religious aspects of death, whereas 'post-mortem portraits' in the nineteenth century provided photographic images of deceased loved ones for family albums and domestic display (Hallam et al. 1999). Arguably the late modern age has witnessed a new openness about and acknowledgement of dying and death, and, concomitantly, there is a new emerging imagery of dying and dead bodies, especially in popular culture.

For instance, the broadcast and print news provide obituaries and coverage of death where a rail or road accident has occurred or where death has occurred by murder (Walter et al. 1995). Similarly, popular culture increasingly focuses on the body in death, as represented in a range of crime narratives that feature forensic pathology from *Silent Witness* in the UK to *Bones* in the US. Analysis of narratives that feature a female pathologist (such as Cornwell's heroine Dr Kay Scarpetta) suggest a gendered dimension to the representation

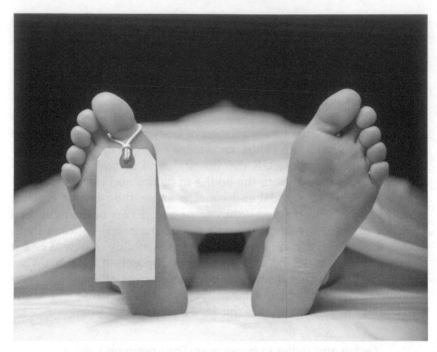

Plate 6   The body in death: tagged cadaver
© Eric Simard/iStockphoto

of the body in death in which, it is argued, female forensic patholo-
gists offer a device to bring the reader/viewer closer to the messiness
of death and 'give voice' to the dead (Horsley and Horsley 2006).
In so doing, such narratives raise questions about the boundaries
and borders between life/death, male/female, bodily interior/exterior
(Kay 2002).

Finally, images of death have been used as part of promotional
culture (Wernick 1991). The Italian clothing company Benetton
used an image of an American man dying of AIDS as part of their
advertising campaign in the early 1990s. The photograph, taken
originally in black and white by Therese Frare and subsequently col-
ourized by Tibor Kalman and Oliviero Toscani of Benetton, depicted
David Kirby, a 32-year-old man from Ohio, dying of AIDS, sur-
rounded by his family. The viewer looks directly onto his deathbed
and becomes a consumer of a representation of dying that is designed
to disturb. In such a way the supposedly private experience of dying
becomes part of a public lexicon of death.

Exhibiting corpses

In similar fashion, contemporary artists and exhibitions manipulate images in ways that force us to consider the relation between death, the dead body and the disposal of the dead. For instance, in 1997 at the London Contemporary Art fair, the sculptor Anthony Noel Kelly displayed a number of human cadaverous casts that he painted silver. Questions were raised about the legitimacy of his access to these body parts and he was charged with stealing human corpses (Wilson 2002). Other artists have used simulations of human and animal body parts and fragments (such as Damien Hirst or Marc Quinn) but none more controversially than Professor Günther Van Hagens in his *Body Worlds* (*Körperwelten*), which has toured globally and has been described by the *New York Times* as 'among the most popular attractions at American science and natural history museums' (Barboza 2006). The subject of documentaries and media discussion, Van Hagens neither identifies himself as an artist nor views his display of bodies and body fragments as art. Indeed, he is an anatomist by trade and produces 'exhibits' that have been subject to a preservation process of 'plastination'. The people whose bodies he has plastinated have all bequeathed their bodies to medical science and provided informed consent for Van Hagens to undertake this procedure (though questions have been raised about his plastination of foetuses).

As discussed above, the exhibition of corpses is not new. The development of medicine as a profession was based on access to and practice on the bodies of the dead (Sawday 1995), and public dissection was a common practice from the sixteenth to the nineteenth centuries in the 'anatomy theatres' of Europe and in the display by governments of executed bodies and body parts as an element of penalty (Bates 2010). Yet the display of the anatomical body as exemplified by *Body Worlds* in the contemporary period reminds us of how distanced we are from both death and the dying body (Lawler 1991). Though Western medical schools 'exhibit' body parts to which the general public have some access, Van Hagens' exhibitions of bodies and body parts sharpen the felt distance between live and dead bodies. These bodies are plasticized and presented in parts in ways that remind us of the special or moral significance of human remains and the extent to which 'the human body, in whole or in parts, is never just an object like any other' (MacDonald 2006). Indeed, these images of dead bodies and the presentation of body parts reflect the sense of **abjection** and disgust associated with decay and death and in doing so affirm people's sense of a bounded, embodied self (Shilling 1993).

Body, self and death

The importance of a bounded, embodied self has been explored in the context of dying, which is a lonely business in the late modern age (Elias 1985) that may involve periods of time spent in institutional, sanitized and impersonal spaces such as hospitals or hospices. In part the location – or sequestration, as Mellor and Shilling (1993) would have it – of dying within such environments is a consequence of Western intolerance of the disintegrating, decaying body (Featherstone and Hepworth 1991). However, it is not necessarily dying in general that assures the sequestration of the dying body but a particular kind of dying (Lawton 1998). Situations in which the body physically and visibly disintegrates (such as through loss of urinary control, for instance) demand a space that allows for such 'unboundedness' and the bodily emissions and odours that may accompany it (Lawton 1998). In contrast to non-Western societies, where the self is not necessarily bounded by the individualized physical body (Jackson 1983), in the contemporary West the privatization of bodily functions effected by the civilizing process has produced a body with clearly defined boundaries (Elias 1994). Hence, in dying processes where the body lacks 'boundedness', because of its uncontrollable emissions and odours, the self is also endangered and the dying patient potentially becomes a non-person (Lawton 1998).

Therefore, apparently new openness about death and dying sits awkwardly with the way death and dying are corralled as individualized and privatized experiences (Mellor and Shilling 1997). Concomitantly, while examples such as *Body Worlds* make death visible, they also conceal the 'material reality of embodied death' (Hallam et al. 1999: 24) and of dying. Many of the modern processes through, and circumstances in, which death occurs raise important questions about the relation between body and self. When a person dies, how do we know? What evidence is used to pronounce the death of a person and who has the authority to do so? It is difficult in the contemporary period to think about the body outside a biomedical framework. The living body is predominantly viewed in biological terms and it takes a great deal of reflection to think otherwise. Similarly, to identify a body as dead in the contemporary West, we call upon the skills and knowledge of biomedicine, of practitioners who are the 'gatekeepers' between life and death (Pellegrino 1986). We may 'know' a person has died (we may be with them when they cease breathing) or we may be told by others in whom we place our trust (nurses, doctors, kin, friends). Yet definitions of death have changed over time and it is only in relatively recent times that medicine has been involved in the diagnosis of death.

Denial of death and uncertainty

Although modern societies are viewed as death-denying, there is considerable sociological debate about this claim (e.g., Seale 1998). An alternative view suggests that 'denial of death' is itself a powerful discourse functioning at both the individual and collective level; that is, while fear and denial of death are discussed as though they are modern problems, in fact, such fear and denial is not necessarily historically new (Zimmerman 2007). Moreover, the denial of death discourse may underpin the development of particular ways of defining and dealing with death and dying, and, especially, the role of medical authority in 'brokering' death (Timmermans 2005). As many studies have shown, medical experts have long played a role in staging or orchestrating the dying process in clinical settings (e.g., Glaser and Strauss 1965; Seymour et al. 2004). In modern societies, however, medicine has established itself as the prevailing authority on whether and when death has occurred.

The rise of scientific medicine replaced earlier mechanical ways of identifying death with instruments that recorded bodily functions and their cessation (Hallam et al. 1999). The development of new technology in particular (such as the respirator and the electrocardiograph) contributed to new degrees of precision concerning the point at which death occurs (Giacomini 1997). Knowledge concerning the point at which death occurs (pupils become fixed and dilated and a range of reflexes are absent) is based on a binary division between life and death, and assumes that the point at which life ceases can be objectively identified. Yet this binary between life and death, between the body and the self, is imperfect (Harré 1991) and, though what we recognize as the self in modern societies may cease to exist, the body may live on.

Hence, death and, indeed, the process of dying (McKechnie and MacLeod 2007) continue to be accompanied by uncertainty. For instance, it is often difficult for the kin and friends of persons who undergo brain stem death to accept that the person is dead (Sque and Payne 1996). Families asked to consider donating the organs of kin who have died typically experience confusion when confronted with a body that looks as though it is living and, though the body has ceased to exist independently, they look for signs of a self. As noted in chapter 4, the late modern age is characterized by a highly attuned awareness of self (Giddens 1991) that increasingly invests in the body as the external manifestation of self (Shilling 1993). The corollary of this argument is that body and self are intimately intertwined and, in a phenomenological sense, inseparable.

Death, Embodiment and Organ Transplantation

Haddow's (2005) qualitative study of 19 Scottish organ donor families illustrates the inseparability of body and self. In the UK, organ procurement for transplantation is based on a voluntary system in which people may opt to donate organs following brain stem death (BST), providing their families do not object. However, some cultural groups have lower donation rates than others (Shaw 2010) and about 49 per cent of families object and refuse to allow the organs of their loved ones to be harvested. The accounts of donor families suggest that this objection arises because of the views of death, and in particular, the newly dead body, that people hold. For instance, some families did not want the bodies of the deceased to be cut or to have surgery to retrieve organs; they saw this as a form of mutilation and disrespect, as a practice that might compromise the body's integrity. Thus, Haddow argues, for some people, 'the newly dead body remains a powerful representation of the self'. Furthermore, for many of the families who did agree to donation, the body part in question in some way provided a means for their loved one to 'live on', and symbolized the continuation of social bonds with the deceased.

Social death

Recent research suggests that there may not be equivalence between body and self in all contexts and circumstances (Hallam et al. 1999). Analysis of 'bodily crises' associated with death raises questions about the meanings of biological and **social death**. While the predominant image of death in Western societies entails recognition and negotiation of the cessation of both biological and social life, there are many instances in which the body may be biologically dead but socially alive, or socially dead and biologically alive (Hallam et al. 1999: 3). 'Social death' refers to the disintegration of social interaction between dying patients and their loved ones (Glaser and Strauss

1965; Sudnow 1967), and to the disentangling of the person from their body. As Mulkay and Ernst observe:

> A hospital patient can become implicitly a permanent non-person whilst still alive, as other people foresee the patient's biological death and change their conduct with the patient's biological termination in mind. (1991: 174)

Similarly, the experience of living with Alzheimer's disease may entail a 'social death' that precedes bodily death (Hallam et al. 1999). The person with Alzheimer's may exhibit a bodily presence but this is not enough to secure full social acceptance or membership. It may also be indicative of the experience of Alzheimer's disease in which the loss of verbal communicative skills redefines the sufferer as socially dead. Hence, for those working within ethnomethodological and anthropological traditions, death is a social category that is made to emerge through social practices and procedural definitions (Sudnow 1967; Prior 1989). These perspectives challenge the elision of the body and the self and suggest both that social death may precede material death and that social presence may 'outlive' the death of the material body (Hallam et al. 1999). People may die in a biological sense but the person continues to be thought of, talked about and be 'present' in the lives of the living in ways that suggest the self lives on 'beyond the body'.

Summary

Despite its apparent malleability, the human body is nonetheless vulnerable, not only in terms of what we do to the body, but also in ways that images and perceptions affect experiences of self and others. Many sociologists who study images across the life course do so from a substantiated conviction that the experiences of becoming associated with childhood and with bodily ageing are shaped by and apprehended via the visual, textual and perceptual categories through which they are represented and experienced. Analysis of such images suggests that ageing is not solely a biological process but one constituted through and experienced in particular social and cultural contexts. Furthermore, the experience of ageing and dying is *intercorporeal*, in which bodies are viewed as sites of 'relationality' that, even in death, may 'live on', as the case of organ donation suggests.

Further Reading

For material on children and their bodies, see:

Bridgeman, J. 2002. The child's body. In M. Evans and E. Lee (eds) *Real Bodies: A Sociological Introduction*. Basingstoke: Palgrave.

Isaacson, N. 2002. Preterm babies in the 'mother-machine': Metaphoric reasoning and bureaucratic rituals that finish the 'unfinished infant'. In K. A. Cerulo (ed.) *Culture in Mind: Toward a Sociology of Culture and Cognition*. New York and London: Routledge, pp. 89–100.

Williams, S. J. and Bendelow, G. A. 2003. Childhood bodies: Constructionism and beyond. In S. J. Williams, L. Birke and G. A. Bendelow (eds) *Debating Biology: Sociological Reflections on Health, Medicine and Society*. New York: Routledge.

For studies on ageing and frailty, see:

Calnan, M., Badcott, D. and Woolhead, G. 2006. Dignity under threat? A study of the experiences of older people in the United Kingdom. *International Journal of Health Services*, 36 (2), 355–75.

Charmaz, K. and Rosenfeld, D. 2006. Reflections of the body, images of self: Visibility and invisibility in chronic illness and disability. In D. D. Waskul and P. Vannini (eds) *Body/Embodiment: Symbolic Interaction and the Sociology of the Body*. Aldershot: Ashgate.

Corden, A. and Hirst, M. 2011. Partner care at the end-of-life: Identity, language and characteristics. *Ageing & Society*, 31 (2), 217–42.

Gilleard, C. and Higgs, P. 2008. Aging, Alzheimer's, and the uncivilized body. In C. Malacrida and J. Low (eds) *Sociology of the Body: A Reader*. Oxford: Oxford University Press.

Slevin, K. F. 2010. 'If I had lots of money . . . I'd have a body makeover': Managing the aging body. *Social Forces*, 88 (3), 1003–20.

Discussion Questions

Casper and Moore (2009) note that 'innocent bodies may also be missing bodies'. What do they mean and, if this insight is accurate, what are the implications for children and the child's body in contemporary culture?

In what ways do racial/ethnic variation transform ideas and ideals about the ageing body and embodiment?

Glossary

Abjection: Julia Kristeva develops Mary Douglas's analysis of pollution to argue that bodily boundaries should be seen as potentially disruptive and subversive. There are three categories of the abject – food, bodily changes and the female body – that provoke disgust because of challenges to bodily boundaries created by the movement of these categories.

Action: Action is developed through a phenomenological framework that highlights the emergence of self as embodied, constituted through the practical actions of the body upon the world in which it is situated.

Actual social identity: The range of social, cultural and physical attributes a person actually possesses.

Agency: Agency is a concept derived from the symbolic interactionist framework and relates to the body's role in responding to and creating social worlds by giving meaning to the intended and unintended actions and gestures of others.

Beauty myth: The beauty myth changes over time and varies cross-culturally but denotes the various ways in which women are encouraged to measure up to ideals of beauty and men are encouraged to possess beauty (Wolf 1990).

Berdache: An institutionalized tribal system that allowed persons who were anatomically of one sex to dress, act and talk like those of the other sex and undertake work and activities associated with the gender roles usually taken by the other sex.

Biomedical model: The biomedical model of the body views it as a relatively stable, predictable, objective entity. It is seen as a complex biochemical machine that can be fixed by medical intervention (Freund and McGuire 1999). A **biomedical model of disability**

reduces disability to individualized, physical impairment (Paterson and Hughes 2000) and perpetuates an understanding of people with impairment as a 'problem' for society (Morris 1993).

Biomedicalization: Increasingly complex, multi-sited, multi-directional processes of medicalization that rely on new techno-scientific knowledge and practices and that are characteristic of late modernity.

Biopolitics: The knowledges, practices and norms that have developed to regulate the quality of life of the population.

Biopower: Refers to the management of life and the government of populations through technologies of surveillance, specialized knowledges and corrective measures.

Bodily betrayals: These are physical responses such as blushing, trembling or stuttering that people are not always able to control. Loss of bodily control has the potential to undermine social situations or encounters by damaging self (through the experience of embarrassment and shame) and social identity (Seymour 1998).

Bodily conduct: Bodily conduct refers to the range of ways people move, gesture and use their bodies. The work of Norbert Elias suggests that bodily conduct has been historically shaped by the civilizing process in which attention is increasingly paid to levels of detail in relation to gestures and expressiveness. Bodily conduct (or **techniques of the body**) also refers to the various ways in which body movements and gestures are shaped by social class and milieu (Bourdieu 1984) and moulded by techniques of self-discipline and control in contemporary Western societies (Foucault 1980).

Body idiom: Denotes the physical gestures, positions and conduct that are recognizable as conventional aspects of everyday life of a given culture (e.g., in Western culture, handshakes, smiles, gait). The concept of body idiom may bear a family resemblance to anthropological notions of 'techniques of the body' (Mauss [1934] 1973), which in turn denote the practical, embodied know-how associated with particular cultural and social contexts.

Body image: A broad concept that refers to the sense that people have of their physical appearance, which depends, in part, on how effectively individuals present themselves to others and whether encounters confirm or nullify self-conception.

Body maintenance: Techniques associated with a distinct and new consciousness that focus on transforming the outer appearance of the body and enable a person to transform their own body into a commodity (Featherstone 1982) or a form of capital that can be exchanged for other forms of capital.

Body-modification techniques: See **Body work**

Body work: In societies that place a premium on visual appearance as a way of measuring social value and judging self-worth, body work or maintenance becomes an important way for people to exert some control over external appearance through **body-modification techniques** that influence the shape, size and appearance of bodies. These may range from control of food intake and diet and exercise, to cosmetic surgery and scarification processes such as piercing and tattooing.

Cartesian: See **Mind–body (Cartesian) dualism**

Clinical gaze: The continuous surveillance, specialized knowledge and corrective measures that render the body as an object amenable to expert scrutiny with a view to classifying the observations such practices produce into degrees of normality/abnormality.

Closed body: Iris Marion Young uses this term to refer to the restricted use of space associated with female comportment.

Commodification: Cultivation of the body or body parts for social or symbolic exchange.

Communicative body: The body is used as an expressive medium and dressed distinctively to present a spectacular self that also establishes a distinct group identity that is separate from and in opposition to the identities of particular others.

Consumer culture: A dominant characteristic of late capitalist society is the consumption of goods and services not necessarily for their 'use' value but because of the kinds of statements they make about the consumer. Consumer culture emphasizes self-indulgence, self-interest and the satisfaction of desire through the acquisition of not only goods and services but also lifestyles.

Cultural capital: Resources or repertoires of knowledge or taste that individuals use to build value or social status in contexts that are especially meaningful to them.

Deep acting: Deep acting involves working on the feeling in order to alter it or exchange it for another feeling.

Dimorphism: A model of the human body in which it is categorized into two distinct, mutually exclusive sexes (Garfinkel 1967). This model has influenced the 'natural attitude' to the body in Western societies, which emphasizes that there are two distinct sexes (male and female) and that sex is assigned to the body on the basis of scientifically derived criteria that remain constant.

Dirt/pollution: Anything that is defined as 'dirt' in any one society is simply **matter-out-of-place**. In relation to the body, notions of dirt refer to anything that challenges the order of things and moves across boundaries between the natural world (the body) and the social world. **Taboos** reveal what is considered pure or polluted in any one society.

Disability: The social and political repercussions and difficulties that may be encountered through impairment. Biophysical norms are part of the assumptions people make about each other but are neither historically nor culturally universal.

Disciplinary power: Refers to a lighter, softer form of power associated with modern regimes through which the human body is shaped to fit the requirements of modern capitalist societies (Lowe 1995). Individuals are encouraged to monitor their own performances and conduct and be vigilant in ensuring their conformity to norms and the production of **docile bodies**. However, where there is power there is resistance, and disciplinary power can also be developed by individuals in ways that confront dominant discourses.

Discipline: Refers to processes and techniques that have the potential to restrict, control and define the human body (e.g., dietary control 'disciplines' women's hunger). **Self-discipline** alludes to techniques and practices that individuals adopt in order to achieve a degree of power over their own bodies. However, such practices may contribute to and reproduce dominant bodily norms.

Discourse: Discourses establish a coherent way of describing and categorizing the social and physical world. They refer to a body of ideas, beliefs and concepts that represent an accepted world-view and constitute notions of reality and social order.

Docile bodies: See **Disciplinary power**

Dramaturgical model: Erving Goffman develops a dramaturgical model to emphasize how individuals, social groups and institutions manage information (by engaging in performances) in order to present particular impressions to those with whom they interact.

Embarrassment: Embarrassment occurs where there is a discrepancy between what is expected and what occurs in a given social encounter, and may be signalled via bodily betrayals such as blushing or trembling.

Embodiment: Embodiment is used in a range of ways but generally signals attention to lived experience as the main starting point for sociological analysis of the body in society. Elizabeth Grosz (1994) suggests it is preferential to use embodiment as a way of challenging the legacy of Cartesian dualism that privileges mind over body.

Feeling rules: Rules that govern the sorts of emotions we are expected to display and how we might display them.

Gender: See **Sex/gender distinction**

Habitus: This notion refers to acquired and apparently durable patterns of taste, movement and bodily conduct that are produced through social practices (agency) and in turn reproduce social structures.

Hegemonic masculinity: This refers to the prevailing set of norms that actively shape self-presentation and bodily conduct necessary to such presentation (Connell 1987).

Hermaphroditism: Hermaphroditism refers to a group of conditions in which there is a discrepancy between external and internal genitals and the term is derived from the Greek god Hermes, and the goddess Aphrodite. In medical parlance, hermaphroditism refers to disorders of sexual development (intersex).

Imaginary space: Iris Marion Young uses this idea to refer to the sense in which women feel 'closed in' by the way their bodies are confined in social space.

Impairment: Loss of physiological or anatomical capacity. Impairments that are visible may lead to processes of categorization that may be stigmatizing in their consequences (Zola 1993).

Instrumental(ity): Using the most efficient or cost-effective means to achieve a specific end, but not in itself reflecting on the value of that end.

Intercorporeality: Within Merleau-Ponty's philosophy of embodiment, not only are mind and body interrelated and indivisible, but also body-self is developed and experienced in relations with the physical environment and other body-selves.

Lifestyle: A distinctive way of living that involves acquiring desired goods that suggest shared symbolic meanings and codes of stylized conduct.

Looking-glass self: The looking-glass self represents the way in which self-development is associated with mirroring and in particular the ways in which the external appearance of our bodies is mediated through what we imagine others think of us. The metaphor of the mirror is potent because it refers to a dynamic, ongoing process through which 'connections are made between the personal subjective self of the viewer and the external world of other people' (Hepworth 2000: 46).

Male gaze: First identified by Laura Mulvey (1975), the 'male gaze' refers to the ways in which the female body is objectified, sexualized and idealized through processes and practices of representation (such as painting, photography and cinema).

Mask of ageing: Featherstone and Hepworth (1991) have developed this concept to refer to the duality between what is displayed by the external surfaces and competencies of the body and the sense of self experienced by the individual.

Matter-out-of-place: See **Dirt/pollution**

Medicalization: The expansion of medicine's scope of interest and practice in a way that defines social experiences as problems that require medical solutions.

Mind–body (Cartesian) dualism: René Descartes postulated that minds and bodies are qualitatively distinct from each other. If the body were to be altered or damaged in some way, this would make little impact on one's sense of self or on personhood. For Descartes, the person cannot be reduced to the body, which in this view of the world becomes an object that can be manipulated, handled and treated in isolation from the self.

Modernization: Long-term processes that underpinned the shift from traditional to modern society (e.g., urbanization, industrialization, rationalization).

Natural symbol: Natural symbols are those that are common to people and which are used to express ideas about the social world and the social order. The human body in this view is a classification system which symbolizes the social body, and the degrees of care that social groups exercise over the physical body reflect concerns about what is important in the social body (Douglas 1970).

Normative: Subtle rules and expectations associated with particular social situations or social states.

Obstetric gaze: Processes through which the profession of medicine identifies the maternal and foetal bodies as objects of examination and monitoring.

Ontology: Refers to forms and relations of being.

Panoptic management: Refers to a means of managerial control in relation to service-sector employment through which the organizational body is governed via practices of peer and self-surveillance (Tyler and Abbott 1998).

Passing: Achieving a competent performance according to the norms and expectations associated with the opposite gender.

Performativity: 'A *stylized repetition of acts*' . . . understood as the mundane way in which bodily gestures, movements and styles of various kinds constitute the illusion of an abiding gendered self (Butler 1990: 140).

Phenomenology: Phenomenology focuses on the ways in which people 'sense and make sense of reality', the social processes people depend on to categorize sense data as phenomena and the extent to which these phenomena are shared.

Phenotype: Physical markers that are used to categorize bodies into specific groups (e.g., male/female).

Physical capital: The body may be used or developed in ways that can be exchanged for other forms of capital (social or economic). The transformation of the body into physical capital entails 'bodily labour'.

Physical reductionism: The biomedical model of the body with which physical reductionism is associated locates disease within individual bodies to the exclusion of the wider environments and contexts in which disease develops.

Pollution: See **Dirt/pollution**

Profane: The profane is categorically distinct from the sacred. While in traditional societies religious ceremony establishes and maintains the boundaries between the sacred and the profane, in secular societies pollution beliefs and taboos uphold this distinction.

Reflexivity: Processes of modernization have contributed to a new awareness of uncertainty and new anxieties about risk (Beck 1992). These anxieties establish a sense of personal responsibility for self and of being able to control self-identity. This is accompanied by a tendency for people to become ever more concerned with visual appearances and to view the body as a vehicle for self-expression (Lasch 1979).

Regulation: Social control in modern regimes is effected via regulatory processes that are executed through institutions (e.g., education, medicine) and ensure conformity to norms or through individual internalization.

Sacred: Refers to ideas, events, objects or persons that are considered special and beyond the ordinary. Things that are considered sacred are usually treated differently and kept physically separate from the profane through ritual enactments and ceremonies. These also remind people of the special nature of the sacred object.

Self-discipline: See **Discipline**

Self-idea: Cooley (1902) refers to the notion of the self-idea as a way of emphasizing how people develop a sense of who and what they are through social interaction with others who reflect back to us an image of who we are.

Self-surveillance: Practices or policies that encourage individuals to observe and monitor their own behaviour as a lighter mode of liberal governance.

Sex/gender distinction: Where sex refers to perceived biological and anatomical differences between men and women, gender refers to established psychological, social and representational differences between men and women (Oakley [1972] 1985). Such differences are neither inevitable nor unalterable, but differ according to social and cultural context as well as temporal location.

Shame: The civilizing process has increasingly emphasized the control and management of bodily functions, impulses and rhythms. As societies have moved from the grotesque to the civilized body, people have internalized shame as the most appropriate response to bodily functions. The elevation of the shame threshold means that people have become increasingly restrained not only in their partici-pation in proscribed forms of bodily conduct (such as urinating in public spaces) but also about discussing them.

Social capital: Refers to activities, relationships and processes that allow people access to prized material and social goods and services.

Social death: Refers to the disintegration of social interaction and relationships between people who are dying and their significant others (Glaser and Strauss 1965).

Social model of disability: Refers to the ways physical and social environments are *dis-abling*. Disabilities transpire when society fails to accommodate physical impairment or denotes such impairment as in need of 'special' arrangements.

Social order: Refers to the various ways in which societies establish social cohesion in accordance with dominant norms. Turner (1984, 1996) argues that modern societies do so via practices and processes that regulate and discipline the human body.

Social self: Lee and Newby (1989) define the social self as 'those aspects of the personal life of each individual which have been created through social participation, which shape the way in which we come to experience the world and which contribute to a consciousness of being a member of society'.

Social status: Processes through which individuals and groups are ranked and organized according to bodily value (e.g., shape, size, gestures, tastes).

Social value: The body as the materialization of class taste (Bourdieu 1984).

Somatic perception: Though Mead acknowledged that 'we are trained by our society to keep our bodies out of our minds' (Mead 1949), he also argued that mind and body are ontologically interre-lated, difficult to separate (Mead 1934), and constitutive of a somatic perception of the world through which we become objects to our-selves (Mead 1938).

Somatic work: An original concept that denotes sensing as a social and symbolic practice, and that speaks to the issue of how it feels to be and have a body – that is, to hear, feel, see, taste and move through everyday life (Hockey 2009).

Spoiled identity: Spoiled identity occurs when a discrepancy becomes apparent between virtual and actual social identity. Instances where individuals need to achieve a competent performance in order to 'pass' as credible (such as cross-gendering) require ongoing attention to details and gestures that others take for granted. Failure to achieve competent performance may result in spoiled identity and the threat of exposure.

Stigma: Stigma refers to discrepancies that may arise between virtual and actual social identity and threaten the integrity of social encounters. Such discrepancies carry moral connotations in that differences in, for instance, visual appearance may be interpreted as symbols of cultural and moral inferiority (Williams 1987).

Surface acting: Entails changing our external appearance or adopting a strategy of pretence in order to give the impression of a particular feeling.

Surveillance: Panopticism depends on technologies of surveillance that observe and monitor the movement of populations through time and space. Technologies of surveillance range from the 'gaze' of the practitioner upon the body of the patient to the visual supervision of particular groups (in the classroom, in the workplace) to the gaze of the CCTV on people moving through public spaces.

Symbolic interactionism: A theoretical tradition associated with the work of a number of sociologists linked to the Chicago School of Sociology that emphasizes symbol manipulation and meaning production; interaction process; development of self; and social processes (G. Marshall 1994).

Taboo: See **Dirt/pollution**

Techniques of interpersonal exchange: Forms of performance through which feelings are expressed (e.g., smiles, tears).

Techniques of the body: See **Bodily conduct**

Virtual social identity: The range of normative expectations associated with who and what a person ought to be in a given social context or encounter.

References

Aas, K. F. 2006. 'The body does not lie': Identity, risk and trust in techno-culture. *Crime Media Culture*, 2, 143–58.

Adams, M. L. 2005. 'Death to the prancing prince': Effeminacy, sport discourses and the salvation of men's dancing. *Body & Society*, 11, 63–86.

Adkins, L. 1995. *Gendered Work: Sexuality, Family and the Labour Market*. Buckingham: Open University Press.

Adorno, T. W. and Horkheimer, M. 2002. *Dialectic of Enlightenment*, trans. Edmund Jephcott. Stanford, CA: Stanford University Press.

Ajana, B. 2010. Recombinant identities: Biometrics and narrative bioethics. *Bioethical Inquiry*, 7, 237–58.

Akrich, M. and Pasveer, B. 2004. Embodiment and disembodiment in childbirth narratives. *Body & Society*, 10, 63–84.

Alcoff, L. M. 2000. Philosophy matters: a review of recent work in feminist philosophy. *Signs*, 25, 841–62.

Alcorn, K. 1988. Illness, metaphor and AIDS. In P. Aggleton and H. Homans (eds) *Social Aspects of AIDS*. London: Falmer Press.

Algars, M., Santtila, P. and Sandnabba, N. K. 2010. Conflicted gender identity, body dissatisfaction, and disordered eating in adult men and women. *Sex Roles*, 63 (1–2), 118–25.

Alimahomed, S. 2010. Thinking outside the rainbow: Women of color redefining queer politics and identity. *Social Identities*, 16 (2), 151–68.

Allsop, J. and Freeman, R. 1993. Prevention in health policy in the United Kingdom and the NHS. In M. Mills (ed.) *Prevention, Health and British Politics*. Aldershot: Avebury.

Alterman, A. 2003. 'A piece of yourself': Ethical issues in biometric identification. *Ethic and Information Technology*, 5, 139–50.

Altman, D. 1982. *The Homosexualization of America/The Americanization of the Homosexual*. New York: St. Martin's Press.

Annandale, E. 1998. *The Sociology of Health and Medicine*. Cambridge: Polity.

Arber, S. and Ginn, J. 1995. *Connecting Gender and Ageing: a Sociological Approach*. Buckingham: Open University Press.

Ariès, P. 1972. *Centuries of Childhood*. Harmondsworth: Penguin.

Ariès, P. 1983. *The Hour of our Death*, trans. Helen Weaver. Harmondsworth: Penguin.

Armstrong, D. 1983. *The Political Anatomy of the Body*. Cambridge: Cambridge University Press.

Armstrong, D. 1987. Silence and truth in death and dying. *Social Science and Medicine*, 24, 651–7.

Armstrong, D. 1995. The rise of surveillance medicine. *Sociology of Health and Illness*, 17, 393–404.

Arney, W. R. 1982. *Power and the Profession of Obstetrics*. Chicago, IL: University of Chicago Press.

Atencio, M. 2008. 'Freaky is just how I get down': Investigating the fluidity of minority ethnic feminine subjectivities in dance. *Leisure Studies*, 27, 311–27.

Atkins, S. and Hoggett, B. 1984. *Women and the Law*. Oxford: Blackwell.

Atkinson, M. 2007. Playing with fire: Masculinity, health, and sports supplements. *Sociology of Sport Journal*, 24, 165–86.

Atkinson, M. 2008. Exploring male femininity in the 'crisis': Men and cosmetic surgery. *Body & Society*, 14, 67–87.

Bakhtin, M. M. 1984. *Rabelais and his World*, trans. H. Iswolsky. Bloomington, IN: Indiana University Press.

Ball, K. 2005. Organization, surveillance and the body: Towards a politics of resistance. *Organization*, 12, 89–108.

Balsamo, A. 1996. *Technologies of the Gendered Bodies: Reading Cyborg Women*. Durham, NC and London: Duke University Press.

Barber, K. 2008. The well-coiffed man: Class, race, and heterosexual masculinity in the hair salon. *Gender & Society*, 22, 455–76.

Barboza, D. 2006. China turns out mummified bodies for displays. *The New York Times*, 8 August.

Barthel, D. 1989. Modernism and marketing: The chocolate box revisited. *Theory, Culture and Society*, 6, 429–38.

Bartky, S. L. 1988. Foucault, femininity and the modernization of patriarchal power. In I. Quinby and L. Diamond (eds) *Feminism and Foucault: Reflections on Resistance*. Boston, MA: Northeastern University Press.

Bates, S. 2010. Body impolitic? Reading cadavers. *International Journal of Communication*, 4, 198–219.

Bauman, Z. 1992. Survival as a social construct. *Theory, Culture and Society*, 9, 1–36.

BBC/OU 1991. *Flesh and Blood*. Directed by Ex-S, 30 min., BBC2 [videocassette].

Beck, U. 1992. *Risk Society: Towards a New Modernity*. London: Sage.

Bell, K. and McNaughton, D. 2007. Feminism and the invisible fat man. *Body & Society*, 13 (1), 107–31.

Bennett, K. C. and Thompson, N. L. 1991. Accelerated aging and male homosexuality: Australian evidence in a continuing debate. *Journal of Homosexuality*, 20 (3–4), 65–75.

Benoist, J. and Catheras, C. 1993. The body: From an immateriality to another. *Social Science and Medicine*, 36, 857–66.

Berger, J. 1972. *Ways of Seeing*. Harmondsworth: Penguin.

Biggs, S. 1993. *Understanding Ageing: Images, Attitudes and Professional Practice*. Buckingham: Open University Press.

Birke, L. 1999. *Feminism and the Biological Body*. Edinburgh: Edinburgh University Press.

Blackwood, E. 2002. Sexuality and gender in certain native American tribes: The case of cross-gender females. In C. L. Williams and A. Stein (eds) *Sexuality and Gender*. Oxford: Blackwell.

Blaikie, A. 1999. *Ageing and Popular Culture*. Cambridge: Cambridge University Press.

Blaikie, A. and Hepworth, M. 1997. Representations of old age in painting and photography. In A. Jamieson, S. Harper and C. Victor (eds) *Critical Approaches to Ageing and Later Life*. Buckingham: Open University Press.

Blaikie, A., Sartan, S., Hepworth, M., Holmes, M., Howson, A. and Inglis, D. 2003. *The Body: Critical Concepts in Sociology*. London: Routledge.

Bland, L. 1982. 'Guardians of the race', or 'vampires upon the nation's health'?: Female sexuality and its regulation in early twentieth-century Britain. In E. Whitelegg et al. (eds) *The Changing Experience of Women*. Buckingham: Open University Press.

Blomberg, K., Forss, A., Ternestedt, B. M., Tishelman, C. 2008. From 'silent' to 'heard': Professional mediation, manipulation and women's experiences of their body after an abnormal Pap smear. *Social Science & Medicine*, 68, 479–86.

Bogart, L. M., Cowgill, B. O., Kennedy, D., Ryan, G., Murphy, D. A., Elijah, J. and Schuster, M. A. 2008. HIV-related stigma among people with HIV and their families: A qualitative analysis. *AIDS Behavior*, 12, 244–54.

Bologh, R. 1990. *Love or Greatness? Max Weber and Masculine Thinking: A Feminist Enquiry*. London: Unwin Hyman.

Bolton, S. C. 2005. Women's work, dirty work: The gynaecology nurse as 'Other'. *Gender, Work and Organization*, 12, 169–86.

Bordo, S. 1989. The body and the reproduction of femininity: A feminist appropriation of Foucault. In A. Jaggar and S. Bordo (eds) *Gender/Body/Knowledge*. New Brunswick, NJ: Rutgers University Press.

Bordo, S. 1992. Anorexia nervosa: Psychopathology as the crystallization of culture. In D. Curtin and L. Heldke (eds) *Cooking, Eating, Thinking: Transformative Philosophies of Food*. Bloomington, IN: Indiana University Press.

Bordo, S. 1993. *Unbearable Weight: Feminism, Western Culture and the Body*. Berkeley, CA and London: University of California Press.

Bourdieu, P. 1984. *Distinction: A Social Critique of the Judgement of Taste.* London: Routledge.

Bowlby, R. 1993. *Shopping with Freud.* London: Routledge.

Brace-Govan, J. 2004. Weighty matters: Control of women's access to physical strength. *The Sociological Review*, 52 (4), 503–31.

Brace-Govan, J. 2010. Representations of women's active embodiment and men's ritualized visibility in sport. *Marketing Theory*, 10, 369–96.

Braidotti, R. 1989. Organs without bodies. *Differences*, 1, 147–61.

Braverman, H. 1974. *Labor and Monopoly Capital: The Degradation of Work in the Twentieth Century.* New York: Monthly Review Press.

Bridgeman, J. 2002. The child's body. In M. Evans and E. Lee (eds) *Real Bodies: A Sociological Introduction.* Basingstoke: Palgrave.

Bridges, T. S. 2009. Gender capital and male bodybuilders. *Body & Society*, 15, 83–107.

Brittain, K. R. and Shaw, C. 2007. The social consequences of living with and dealing with incontinence – A carer's perspective. *Social Science & Medicine*, 65, 1274–83.

Brook, B. 1999. *Feminism and the Body.* London and New York: Longman.

Brooks, A. 2004. 'Under the knife and proud of it': An analysis of the normalization of cosmetic surgery. *Critical Sociology*, 30, 207–39.

Brownlie, J. 2001. The 'being-risky child': Governing childhood and sexual risk. *Sociology*, 35, 519–37.

Brownlie, J. 2006. 'The basic stuff of our memories': Embodying and embedding discipline. *Sociological Research Online*, 11.

Brownlie, J. and Sheach Leith, V. M. 2011. Social bundles: Thinking through the infant body. *Childhood*, 18 (2), 196–210.

Brumberg, J. J. 1997. *The Body Project: An Intimate History of American Girls.* New York: Random House.

Buckley, T. and Gottlieb, A. (eds) 1988. *Blood Magic.* Berkeley, CA: University of California Press.

Budgeon, S. 2003. Identity as an embodied event. *Body & Society*, 9, 35–55.

Burkitt, I. 1999. *Bodies of Thought: Embodiment, Identity and Modernity.* London: Sage.

Burnett, K. A. and Holmes, M. 2001. Bodies, battlefields and biographies: Scars and the construction of the body as heritage. In K. Backett-Milburn and S. Cunningham-Burley (eds) *Exploring the Body.* Basingstoke: Palgrave.

Burrows, R., Nettleton, S. and Bunton, R. 1995. Sociology and health promotion: Health, risk and consumption under later capitalism. In R. Bunton, S. Nettleton and R. Burrows (eds) *The Sociology of Health Promotion: Critical Analyses of Consumption, Lifestyle and Risk.* London: Routledge.

Bury, M. 1995. Ageing, gender and sociological theory. In S. Arber and J. Ginn (eds) *Connecting Gender and Ageing: A Sociological Approach.* Buckingham: Open University Press.

Bush, J. 2000. 'It's just part of being a woman': Cervical screening, the body and femininity. *Social Science and Medicine*, 50, 429–44.

Butler, J. 1990. *Gender Trouble: Feminism and the Subversion of Identity*. London and New York: Routledge.

Butler, J. 1993. *Body Matters: The Discursive Limits of Sex*. London: Routledge.

Bytheway, B. and Johnson, J. 1998. The sight of age. In S. Nettleton and J. Watson (eds) *The Body in Everyday Life*. London: Routledge.

Callaghan, K. A. (ed.) 1994. *Ideals of Feminine Beauty: Philosophical, Social and Cultural Dimensions*. Westport, CT: Greenwood Press.

Calnan, M., Badcott, D. and Woolhead, G. 2006. Dignity under threat? A study of the experiences of older people in the United Kingdom. *International Journal of Health Services*, 36 (2), 355–75.

Canto, M. 1985. The politics of women's bodies: Reflections on Plato. In S. Suleiman (ed.) *The Female Body in Western Culture: Contemporary Perspectives*. Cambridge, MA and London: Harvard University Press.

Carpenter, L. M. and Casper, M. J. 2009. A tale of two technologies: HPV vaccination, male circumcision, and sexual health. *Gender & Society*, 23, 790–816.

Carter, S. K. 2010. Beyond control: Body and self in women's childbearing narratives. *Sociology of Health & Illness*, 32, 993–1009.

Cartwright, L. 1995. *Screening the Body: Tracing Medicine's Visual Culture*. Minneapolis, MN: University of Minnesota Press.

Casper, M. J. and Moore, L. J. 2009. *Missing Bodies: the Politics of Visibility*. New York: New York University Press.

Ceyhan, A. 2008. Technologization of security: Management of uncertainty and risk in the age of biometrics. *Surveillance & Society*, 5, 102–23.

Charles, N. and Kerr, M. 1988. *Women, Food and Families*. Manchester: Manchester University Press.

Cheney, A. 2011. 'Most girls want to be skinny': Body (dis)satisfaction among ethnically diverse women. *Qualitative Health Research*, 21 (10), 1347–59.

Christensen, P. H. 2000. Childhood and the cultural construction of vulnerable bodies. In A. Prout (ed.) *The Body, Childhood and Society*. Basingstoke: Macmillan.

Clark, D. 2002. Between hope and acceptance: The medicalisation of dying. *British Medical Journal*, 324, 905–7.

Clarke, A. and Montini, T. 1993. The many faces of RU486: Tales of situated knowledges and technological constraints. *Science, Technology and Human Values*, 18, 42–78.

Clarke, A. E., Shim, J. K., Mamo, L., Fosket, J. R. and Fishman, J. R. 2003. Biomedicalization: Technoscientific transformations of health, illness, and US biomedicine. *American Sociological Review*, 68, 161–94.

Clifford, J. 1988. *The Predicament of Culture: Twentieth-Century Ethnography, Literature and Art*. Cambridge, MA: Harvard University Press.

Collinson, J. A. and Hockey, J. 2007. 'Working out' identity: Distance runners and the management of disrupted identity. *Leisure Studies*, 26, 381–98.

Connell, R. W. 1987. *Gender and Power*. Cambridge: Polity.

Connell, R. W. 1995. *Masculinities*. Cambridge: Polity.

Connell, R. W. 2005. *Masculinities*, 2nd edn. Cambridge: Polity.

Cooley, C. H. 1902. *Human Nature and the Social Order*. New York: Charles Scribner's Sons.

Corea, U. 1985. *The Mother Machine*. London: Women's Press.

Costello, L. 1993. New ways of seeing, new stories to tell: Homeless girls, feminism and postmodernity. Unpublished MS, Monash University, Victoria, Australia.

Coward, R. 1984. *Female Desire*. London: Paladin.

Crawford, R. 1980. Healthism and the medicalisation of everyday life. *International Journal of Health Services*, 10, 365–83.

Crawford, R. 1984. A cultural account of 'health': Control, release and the social body. In J. McKinley (ed.) *Issues in the Political Economy of Health*. London: Tavistock.

Crawford, R. 1994. The boundaries of self and the unhealthy other: Reflections on health, culture and Aids. *Social Science and Medicine*, 38, 1347–66.

Crimp, D. 1988. Aids: Cultural analysis/cultural activism. *October*, 43, 3–16.

Crossley, N. 1995a. Body techniques, agency and intercorporeality: On Goffman's *Relations in Public*. *Sociology*, 29, 133–50.

Crossley, N. 1995b. Merleau-Ponty, the elusive body and carnal sociology. *Body & Society*, 1, 43–63.

Crossley, N. 2004. Fat is a sociological issue: Obesity rates in late-modern, 'body-conscious' societies. *Social Theory and Health*, 2, 222–53.

Csordas, T. 1990. Embodiment as a paradigm for anthropology. *Ethos*, 18, 5–47.

Csordas, T. 1994. *Embodiment and Experience*. Cambridge: Cambridge University Press.

Cunningham-Burley, S. and Backett-Milburn, K. 1998. The body, health and self in the middle years. In S. Nettleton and J. Watson (eds) *The Body in Everyday Life*. London: Routledge.

Dally, K. 1991. *Women under the Knife: A History of Surgery*. London: Hutchinson Radius.

Davidson, J. 2000a. A phenomenology of fear: Merleau-Ponty and agora-phobic life-worlds. *Sociology of Health & Illness*, 22, 640–60.

Davidson, J. 2000b. *Phobic Geographies: The Phenomenology and Spatiality of Identity*. Aldershot: Ashgate.

Davidson, J. 2000c. '...the world was getting smaller': Women, agoraphobia and bodily boundaries, *Area*, 32 (1), 31–40.

Davidson, J. and Smith, M. 2003. Bio-phobias/techno-philias: Virtual reality exposure as treatment for phobias of 'nature'. *Sociology of Health & Illness*, 25, 644–61.

Davidson, R. 1993. Measuring the 'social evil': The incidence of venereal diseases in interwar Scotland. *Medical History*, 37, 167–86.

Davis, F. 1994. *Fashion, Culture and Identity*. Chicago, IL: University of Chicago Press.

Davis, K. 1995. *Reshaping the Female Body: The Dilemma of Cosmetic Surgery*. New York: Routledge.

Davis, K. 1997. My body is my art: Cosmetic surgery as feminist utopia. *European Journal of Women's Studies*, 4, 168–81.

de Beauvoir, S. [1949] 1972. *The Second Sex*. Harmondsworth: Penguin.

Descartes, R. 1980. Discourse 5. In *Discourses on Method*. Harmondsworth: Penguin.

de Swaan, A. 1990. *The Management of Normality*. London: Routledge.

Diehl, M. K. and Wahl, H-W. 2010. Awareness of age-related change: Examination of a (mostly) unexplored concept. *Journal of Gerontology: Social Sciences*, 65B (3), 340–50.

Diprose, R. 1994. *The Bodies of Women: Ethics, Embodiment and Sexual Difference*. London: Routledge.

Doane, M. A. 1982. Film and the masquerade: Theorizing the female spectator. *Screen*, 23, 78–87.

Dolezal, L. 2010. The (in)visible body: Feminism, phenomenology, and the case of cosmetic surgery. *Hypatia*, 25, 357–75.

Donnisson, J. 1977. *Midwives and Medical Men: A History of Interprofessional Rivalries and Women's Rights*. London: Heinemann.

Donzelot, J. 1979. *The Policing of Families*. London: Hutchinson.

Dossa, P. 2009. *Racialized Bodies, Disabling Worlds: Storied Lives of Immigrant Muslim Women*. Toronto: University of Toronto Press.

Douglas, M. 1970. *Natural Symbols: Explorations in Cosmology*. New York: Pantheon.

Doyal, L. 1983. Women, health and the sexual division of labour: A case study of the women's health movement in Britain. *Critical Social Policy*, Summer, 21–33.

Duncombe, J. and Marsden, D. 1993. Love and intimacy: The gender division of emotion and 'emotion work'. *Sociology*, 27, 221–42.

Durkheim, E. 1976. *Elementary Forms of Religious Life*. London: Allen & Unwin.

Ebin, V. 1979. *The Decorated Body*. London: Harper & Row.

Edvardsson, D. and Street, A. 2007. Sense or no-sense: The nurse as embodied ethnographer. *International Journal of Nursing Practice*, 13, 24–32.

Edwards, J. and McKie, L. 1996. Women's public toilets: A serious issue for the body politic. *European Journal of Women's Studies*, 3, 215–32.

Ehrenreich, B. and English, D. 1973. *Witches, Midwives and Nurses: A History of Women Healers*. Old Westbury, NY: Feminist Press.

Ehrenreich, B. and English, D. 1974. *Complaints and Disorders: The Sexual Politics of Sickness*. London: Compendium.

Ehrenreich, B. and English, D. 1979. *For Her Own Good: 150 Years of the Experts' Advice to Women*. London: Pluto Press.

Ekins, R. and King, D. 2001. Telling body transgendering stories. In K. Backett-Milburn and L. McKie (eds) *Constructing Gendered Bodies*. Basingstoke: Palgrave/BSA.

Elias, N. 1983. *The Court Society*. Oxford: Blackwell.

Elias, N. 1985. *The Loneliness of Dying*. Oxford: Blackwell.

Elias, N. 1991. Human beings and their emotions. In M. Featherstone, M. Hepworth and B. S. Turner (eds) *The Body: Social Process and Cultural Theory*. London: Sage.

Elias, N. [1978, 1982] 1994. *The Civilizing Process, Vols. 1 and 2*, trans. E. Jephcott. Oxford: Blackwell.

Eribon, D. 1992. *Michel Foucault*. London: Faber & Faber.

Ertman, M. M. and Williams, J. C. (eds) 2005. *Rethinking Commodification: Cases and Readings in Law and Culture*. New York: New York University Press.

Erwin, K., Adams, V. and Le, P. 2009. Glorious deeds. Work unit blood donation and postsocialist desires in urban China. *Body & Society*, 15 (2), 51–70.

Eubanks, V. 1996. Zones of dither: Writing the postmodern body. *Body & Society*, 2, 73–88.

Everett, M. 2003. The social life of genes: Privacy, property and the new genetics. *Social Science & Medicine*, 56, 53–65.

Ewan, S. 1976. *Captains of Consciousness: Advertising and the Roots of Consumer Culture*. London: McGraw-Hill.

Exley, C. 2004. Review article: The sociology of dying, death and bereavement. *Sociology of Health & Illness*, 26, 110–22.

Fairhurst, E. 1998. 'Growing old gracefully' as opposed to 'mutton dressed as lamb': The social construction of recognising older women. In S. Nettleton and J. Watson (eds) *The Body in Everyday Life*. London: Routledge.

Falk, P. 1994. *The Consuming Body*. London: Sage.

Falk, P. 1995. Written in the flesh. *Body & Society*, 1 (1), 95–106.

Featherstone, M. 1982. The body in consumer culture. *Theory, Culture and Society*, 1, 18–33.

Featherstone, M. 2006. Body image/body without image. *Theory, Culture and Society*, 23 (2–3), 233–6.

Featherstone, M. 2010. Body, image and affect in consumer culture. *Body & Society*, 16, 193–221.

Featherstone, M. and Hepworth, M. 1984. Changing images of retirement: An analysis of representations of ageing in the popular magazine. In D. B. Bromley (ed.) *Gerontology: Social and Behavioural Perspectives*. London: BSG/Croom Helm.

Featherstone, M. and Hepworth, M. 1991. The mask of ageing and the postmodern life course. In M. Featherstone, M. Hepworth and B. S. Turner (eds) *The Body: Social Process and Cultural Theory*. London: Sage.

Fee, E. and Porter, D. 1992. Public health, preventive medicine and professionalisation: England and America in the 19th century. In A. Wear (ed.) *Medicine in Society*. Cambridge: Cambridge University Press.

Ferguson, M. 1983. *Forever Feminine: Women's Magazines and the Cult of Femininity*. London: Heinemann Education.

Ferreira, V. S. 2009. Youth scenes, body marks and bio-sociabilities. *Young*, 17, 285–306.

Finkelstein, J. 1989. *Dining Out: A Sociology of Modern Manners*. Cambridge: Polity.

Foucault, M. 1972. *The Archaeology of Knowledge and the Discourse on Language*. London: Pantheon.

Foucault, M. 1973. *The Birth of the Clinic*. London: Routledge.

Foucault, M. 1979. *Discipline and Punish*. London: Peregrine.

Foucault, M. 1980. *Power/Knowledge*, ed. C. Gordon. Brighton: Harvester.

Foucault, M. 1988. *The Care of the Self*. Vol. 3 of *The History of Sexuality*. New York: Vintage Books.

Foucault, M. 1990. *The History of Sexuality: An Introduction*. New York: Vintage Books.

Fox, D. 1986. Aids and the American health polity: The history and prospects of a crisis of authority. *Millbank Quarterly*, 64 (1), 7–33.

Fox, N. 1993. *Postmodernism, Sociology and Health*. Buckingham: Open University Press.

Fox, R. and Swazey, J. 1992. *Spare Parts*. New York: Oxford University Press.

Franckenstein, F. 1997. Making up Cher: A media analysis of the politics of the female body. *European Journal of Women's Studies*, 4, 7–22.

Frank, A. 1990. Bringing bodies back in: A decade review. *Theory, Culture and Society*, 7, 131–62.

Frank, A. 1991. For a sociology of the body: An analytical review. In M. Featherstone, M. Hepworth and B. S. Turner (eds) *The Body: Social Process and Cultural Theory*. London: Sage.

Frankfort, E. 1972. *Vaginal Politics*. New York: Quadrangle Press.

Franko, D. L., Thompson-Brenner, H., Thompson, D. R. et al. 2012. Racial/ethnic differences in adults in randomized clinical trials of binge eating disorder. *Journal of Consulting & Clinical Psychology*, 80 (2), 186–95.

Freund, P. A. 1982. *The Civilized Body: Social Domination, Control and Health*. Philadelphia, PA: Temple University Press.

Freund, P. A. 1988. Bringing society into the body: Understanding socialised human nature. *Theory, Culture and Society*, 17, 839–64.

Freund, P. A. 1998. Social performances and their discontents: Reflections on the biosocial psychology of role playing. In G. Bendelow and S.

Williams (eds) *Emotions in Social Life: Critical Themes and Contemporary Issues*. London: Routledge.

Freund, P. and McGuire, M. 1999. *Health, Illness and the Social Body*, 3rd edn. Upper Saddle River, NJ: Prentice-Hall.

Frew, M. and McGillivray, D. 2005. Health clubs and body politics: Aesthetics and the quest for physical capital. *Leisure Studies*, 24 (2), 161–75.

Friedan, B. 1963. *The Feminine Mystique*. New York: W. W. Norton.

Frisby, D. and Featherstone, M. 1997. *Simmel on Culture*. London: Sage.

Furman, F. K. 1997. *Facing the Mirror: Older Women and Beauty Shop Culture*. New York: Routledge.

Gamarnikow, E. 1978. Sexual division of labour: The case of nursing. In A. Kuhn and A. Wolpe (eds) *Feminism and Materialism: Women and Modes of Production*. London: Routledge & Kegan Paul.

Garber, M. 1992. *Vested Interests: Cross-Dressing and Cultural Anxiety*. London: Routledge.

Gardner, K. 1982. Well woman clinics: A positive approach to women's health. In H. Roberts (ed.) *Women, Health and Reproduction*. London: Routledge & Kegan Paul.

Garfinkel, H. 1967. Passing and the managed achievement of sex status in an inter-sexed person. *Studies in Ethnomethodology*. Englewood Cliffs, NJ: Prentice-Hall, pp. 116–85.

Garland, D. 1990. *Punishment and Modern Society: A Social Analysis*. London: Heinemann.

Gatens, M. 1988. Towards a feminist philosophy of the body. In B. Caine, E. A. Grosz and M. de Lepervanche (eds) *Crossing Boundaries: Feminisms and the Critique of Knowledges*. Sydney: Allen & Unwin.

George, A. and Murcott, A. 1992. Research note: Monthly strategies for discretion: Shopping for sanitary towels and tampons. *Sociological Review*, 40, 146–62.

George, M. 2005. Making sense of muscle: The body experiences of collegiate women athletes. *Sociological Inquiry*, 75, 317–45.

Getz, L. and Kirkengen, A. L. 2003. Ultrasound screening in pregnancy: Advancing technology, soft markers for fetal chromosomal aberrations, and unacknowledged ethical dilemmas. *Social Science and Medicine*, 56, 2045–57.

Giacomini, M. 1997. A change of heart and a change of mind? Technology and the re-definition of death in 1968. *Social Science and Medicine*, 44, 1465–82.

Giddens, A. 1991. *Modernity and Self-Identity: Self and Society in the Late Modern Age*. Cambridge: Polity.

Gill, R., Henwood, K. and McLean, C. 2005. Body projects and the regulation of normative masculinity. *Body & Society*, 11, 37–62.

Gilman, S. 2002. Black bodies, white bodies: Toward an iconography of female sexuality in the late nineteenth century. In S. Jackson and S. Scott (eds) *Gender: A Sociological Reader*. London: Routledge, pp. 392–400.

Gimlin, D. 2002. *Body-work: Beauty and Self-Image in American Culture*. Berkeley, CA. University of California Press

Gimlin, D. 2007. Accounting for cosmetic surgery in the USA and Great Britain: A cross-cultural analysis of women's narratives. *Body & Society*, 13, 41–60.

Glaser, B. and Strauss, A. 1965. *Awareness of Dying*. Chicago, IL: Aldine.

Glassner, B. 1995. In the name of health. In R. Bunton, S. Nettleton and R. Burrows (eds) *The Sociology of Health Promotion: Critical Analyses of Consumption, Lifestyle and Risk*. London: Routledge.

Glenn, E. N. 2008. Yearning for lightness: Transnational circuits in the marketing and consumption of skin lighteners. *Gender & Society*, 22 (3), 281–302.

Goffman, E. 1956. Embarrassment and social organization. *American Journal of Sociology*, 62 (3), 264–71.

Goffman, E. 1963. *Behaviour in Public Places*. London: Allen Lane.

Goffman, E. 1968. *Stigma: Notes on the Management of Spoiled Identity*. Harmondsworth: Penguin.

Goffman, E. [1959] 1971. *The Presentation of Self in Everyday Life*. Harmondsworth: Penguin.

Goffman, E. 1972. *Interaction Ritual: Essays on Face-to-Face Behaviour*. London: Allen Lane.

Goffman, E. 1979. *Gender Advertisements*. London: Macmillan.

Gordon, L. 1978. The politics of birth control, 1920–1940: The impact of professionals. In J. Ehrenreich (ed.) *The Cultural Crisis of Modern Medicine*. New York: Monthly Review Press.

Grabham, E. 2009. 'Flagging' the skin: Corporeal nationalism and the properties of belonging. *Body & Society*, 15, 63–82.

Graham, H. 1979. Prevention and health: Every mother's business. In C. Harris (ed.) *The Sociology of the Family: New Directions for Britain*. Keele: University of Keele Press.

Graham, H. and Oakley, A. 1981. Competing ideologies of reproduction: Medical and maternal perspectives on pregnancy. In H. Roberts (ed.) *Women, Health and Reproduction*. London: Routledge & Kegan Paul.

Greco, M. 1993. Psychosomatic subjects and the 'duty to be well': Personal agency within medical rationality. *Economy and Society*, 22, 357–72.

Green, J. M., Hewison, J., Bekker, H. L., Bryant, L. D. and Cuckle, H. S. 2004. Psychosocial aspects of genetic screening of pregnant women and newborns: A systematic review. *Health Technology Assessment*, 8 (33).

Greer, G. 1991. *The Change: Women, Ageing and the Menopause*. London: Penguin.

Griffiths, F., Bendelow, G., Green, E. and Palmer, J. 2010. Screening for breast cancer: Medicalization, visualization and the embodied experience. *Health*, 14 (6), 653–68.

Grogan, S. 2010. Promoting positive body image in males and females: Contemporary issues and future directions. *Sex Roles*, 63, 757–65.

Grosz, E. 1990. The body of signification. In J. Fletcher and A. Benjamin (eds) *Abjection, Melancholia and Love*. London: Routledge, pp. 80–104.

Grosz, E. 1994. *Volatile Bodies: Toward a Corporeal Feminism*. Bloomington, IN: University of Indiana Press.

Gullette, M. M. 1997. *Declining to Decline: Cultural Combat and the Politics of the Midlife*. Charlottesville, VA: University Press of Virginia.

Gupta, J. A. and Richters, A. 2008. Embodied subjects and fragmented objects: Women's bodies, assisted reproduction technologies and the right to self-determination. *Bioethical Inquiry*, 5 (4), 239–49.

Gurney, C. M. 2000. Accommodating bodies: The organization of corporeal dirt in the embodied home. In L. McKie and N. Watson (eds) *Organizing Bodies: Policy, Institutions and Work*. London: BSA/Macmillan.

Hacking, I. 1990. *The Taming of Chance*. Cambridge: Cambridge University Press.

Haddow, G. 2005. The phenomenology of death, embodiment and organ transplantation. *Sociology of Health and Illness*, 27 (1), 92–113.

Hall, A. 1991. *Hidden Anxieties: Male Sexuality, 1900–1950*. Cambridge: Polity.

Hall, A., Hockey, J. and Robinson, V. 2007. Occupational cultures and the embodiment of masculinity: Hairdressing, estate agency and firefighting. *Gender, Work and Organization*, 14 (6), 534–51.

Hallam, E., Hockey, J. and Howarth, G. 1999. *Beyond the Body: Death and Social Identity*. London: Routledge.

Hans, M. L., Selvidge, B. D., Tinker, K. A. and Webb, L. M. 2011. Online performances of gender: Blogs, gender-bending, and cybersex as relational exemplars. In K. B. Wright and L. M. Webb (eds) *Computer-Mediated Communication in Personal Relationships*. New York: Peter Lang.

Haraway, D. 1985. A manifesto for cyborgs: Science, technology and socialist feminism. *Socialist Review*, 80, 65–108.

Hardey, M. 2002. Life beyond the screen: Embodiment and identity through the internet. *Sociological Review*, 50 (4), 570–85.

Harré, R. 1991. *Physical Being: A Theory for a Corporeal Psychology*. Oxford: Blackwell.

Harwood, K. 2009. Egg freezing: A breakthrough for reproductive autonomy? *Bioethics*, 23, 39–46.

Hastie, S., Porch, S. and Brown, L. 1995. Doing it ourselves: Promoting women's health as feminist action. In G. Giffin (ed.) *Feminist Activism in the 1990s*. London: Taylor & Francis.

Healy, K. 2006. *Last Best Gifts: Altruism and the Market for Human Blood and Organs*. Chicago, IL: University of Chicago Press.

Hearn, J. 1995. Imaging the aging of men. In M. Featherstone and A. Wernick (eds) *Images of Aging: Cultural Representations of Later Life*. London: Routledge.

Helman, C. 1991. *Body Myths*. London: Chatto & Windus.

Hepworth, M. 1987. The mid-life phase. In G. Cohen (ed.) *Social Change and the Life Course*. London: Tavistock.

Hepworth, M. 1995a. Wrinkles of vice and wrinkles of virtue: The moral interpretation of the ageing body. In C. Hummel and J. Lalive d'Epinay (eds) *Images of Ageing in Western Societies*. Geneva: University of Geneva, Centre for Interdisciplinary Gerontology.

Hepworth, M. 1995b. Change and crisis in midlife. In B. Davey (ed.) *Birth to Old Age: Health in Transition*. Buckingham: Open University Press.

Hepworth, M. 1995c. Positive ageing: What is the message? In R. Bunton, S. Nettleton and R. Burrows (eds) *The Sociology of Health Promotion: Critical Analyses of Consumption, Lifestyle and Risk*. London: Routledge.

Hepworth, M. 2000. *Stories of Ageing*. Buckingham: Open University Press.

Hepworth, M. and Featherstone, M. 1998. The male menopause: Lay accounts and the cultural reconstruction of midlife. In S. Nettleton and J. Watson (eds) *The Body in Everyday Life*. London: Routledge.

Hermes, J. 1995. *Reading Women's Magazines: An Analysis of Everyday Media Use*. Cambridge: Polity.

Herzlich, C. and Pierret, J. 1987. *Illness and Self in Society*. Baltimore, MD: Johns Hopkins University Press.

Hevey, D. 1992. *The Creatures Time Forgot: Photography and Disability Imagery*. London: Routledge.

Hewitt, M. 1983. Biopolitics and social policy: Foucault's account of welfare. *Theory, Culture and Society*, 2, 67–84.

Hewitt, M. 1991. Biopolitics and social policy: Foucault's account of welfare. In M. Featherstone, M. Hepworth and B. S. Turner (eds) *The Body: Social Process and Cultural Theory*. London: Sage, pp. 225–55.

Higgonet, A. 1998. *Pictures of Innocence: The History and Crisis of Ideal Childhood*. London: Thames & Hudson.

Higgs, P. 1998. Risk, governmentality and the reconceptualisation of citizenship. In G. Scambler and P. Higgs (eds) *Modernity, Medicine and Health*. London: Routledge.

Hill-Collins, P. 1990. *Black Feminist Thought: Knowledge, Consciousness and the Politics of Empowerment*. Boston, MA: Unwin Hyman.

Hines, S. 2007. *Transforming Gender: Transgender Practices of Gender, Intimacy and Care*. Bristol: The Policy Press.

Hochschild, A. R. 1983. *The Managed Heart: The Commercialization of Human Feeling*. Berkeley, CA: University of California Press.

Hochschild, A. R. 1998. The sociology of emotion as a way of seeing. In G. Bendelow and S. Williams (eds) *Emotions in Social Life: Critical Themes and Contemporary Issues*. London: Routledge.

Hockey, E. and James, A. 1993. *Growing Up and Growing Old: Ageing and Dependency in the Life Course*. London: Sage.

Hockey, J. 2009. 'Switch on': Sensory work in the infantry. *Work, Employment, and Society*, 23, 477–93.

Høeg, P. 1995. *Borderliners*, trans. B. Haveland. London: Harvill.

Hogle, L. F. 1995. Tales from the cryptic: Technology meets organism in the living cadaver. In C. H. Gray (ed.) *The Cyborg Handbook*. New York: Routledge.

Hogle, L. F. 2005. Enhancement technologies and the body. *Annual Review of Anthropology*, 34, 695–716.

Hollis, M. 1997. *Invitation to Philosophy*. Oxford: Blackwell.

Holmes, M. 2009. *Gender and Everyday Life*. London: Routledge.

Holmwood, J. 1993. Welfare and citizenship. In R. Bellamy (ed.) *Theories and Concepts of Politics*. Manchester: University of Manchester Press.

Hood-Williams, J. 1996. Good-bye to sex and gender. *Sociological Review*, 44, 1–16.

hooks, b. 1981. *Ain't I a Woman: Black Women and Feminism*. Boston, MA: South End Press.

hooks, b. 1992. *Black Looks: Race and Representation*. Boston, MA: South End Press.

Horsley, L. and Horsley, K. 2006. Body language: Reading the corpse in forensic crime fiction. *Paradoxa: Terrain Vagues*, 20, 7–32.

Howson, A. 1998. Surveillance, knowledge and risk: The embodied experience of cervical screening. *Health*, 2, 195–215.

Howson, A. 1999. Cervical screening, compliance and moral obligation. *Sociology of Health and Illness*, 21, 401–25.

Howson, A. 2001. 'Watching you – watching me': Visualising techniques and the cervix. *Women's Studies International Forum*, 24, 97–110.

Howson, A. and Inglis, D. 2001. The body in sociology: Tensions inside and outside sociological thought. *Sociological Review*, 49, 297–317.

Hoeyer, K., Nexoe, S., Hartlev, M., Koch, L. 2009. Embryonic entitlements: Stem cell patenting and the co-production of commodities and personhood. *Body & Society*, 15, 1–24.

Hubbard, R. 1984. Personal courage is not enough: Some hazards of child-bearing in the 1980s. In R. Arditti, R. D. Klein and S. Minden (eds) *Test-Tube Women: What Future for Motherhood?* London: Pandora.

Hughes, A. and Witz, A. 1997. Feminism and the matter of bodies: From de Beauvoir to Butler. *Body & Society*, 3, 47–60.

Hunter, M. L. 2011. Buying racial capital: Skin-bleaching and cosmetic surgery in a globalized world. *The Journal of Pan African Studies*, 4 (4), 142–64.

Iantaffi, A. and Bockting, W. O. 2011. Views from both sides of the bridge? Gender, sexual legitimacy and transgender people's experiences of relationships. *Culture, Health and Sexuality*, 13 (3), 355–70.

Ihde, D. 2002. *Bodies in Technology*. Minneapolis, MN: University of Minnesota Press.

Illich, I. 1976. *Medical Nemesis: The Expropriation of Health*. Harmondsworth: Penguin.

Illich, I. 1986. Body history. *The Lancet*, 11, 1325–7.

Inglis, D. 2000. *A Sociological History of Excretory Experience: Defecatory Manners and Toiletry Techniques*. Lampeter: Edwin Mellen Press.

Inglis, D. and Holmes, M. 2000. Toiletry time: Defecation, temporal strategies and the dilemmas of modernity. *Time and Society*, 9, 223–45.

Inhorn, M. C. 2007. Masturbation, semen collection and men's IVF experiences: Anxieties in the Muslim world. *Body & Society*, 13, 37–53.

Inwood, J. F. and Yarborough, R. A. 2010. Racialized places, racialized bodies: The impact of racialization on individual and place identities. *GeoJournal*, 75, 299–301.

Isaacson, N. 2002. Preterm babies in the 'mother-machine': Metaphoric reasoning and bureaucratic rituals that finish the 'unfinished infant'. In K. A. Cerulo (ed.) *Culture in Mind: Toward a Sociology of Culture and Cognition*. New York: Routledge, pp. 89–100.

Jackson, M. 1983. Thinking through the body: An essay on understanding metaphor. *Social Analysis*, 14, 127–49.

James, A. 1992. *Childhood Identities: Self and Social Relationships in the Experience of the Child*. Edinburgh: Edinburgh University Press.

James, A., Jenks, C. and Prout, A. 1998. *Theorizing Childhood*. Cambridge: Polity.

James, N. 1989. Emotional labour: Skill and work in the social regulation of feelings. *Sociological Review*, 37, 15–42.

Jeffords, S. 1994. *Hard Bodies: Hollywood Masculinity in the Reagan Era*. New Brunswick, NJ: Rutgers University Press.

Jenks, C. 1996. *Childhood*. London: Routledge.

Jewson, N. D. 1976. The disappearance of the sick man from medical cosmologies, 1770–1870. *Sociology*, 10, 225–44.

Johnson, T. 1987. Pre-menstrual syndrome as a Western culture-specific disorder. *Culture, Medicine and Society*, 11, 337–56.

Jones, I. R. and Higgs, P. F. 2010. The natural, the normal and the normative: Contested terrains in ageing and old age. *Social Science & Medicine*, 71 (8), 1513–19.

Jordanova, L. 1989. *Sexual Visions: Images of Gender in Science and Medicine between the 18th and 20th Centuries*. London: Harvester Wheatsheaf.

Kai-Cheong Chan, N. and Gillick, A. 2009. Fatness as disability: Questions of personal and group identity. *Disability and Society*, 24, 231–43.

Kang, M. 2003. The managed hand: The commercialization of bodies and emotions in Korean immigrant-owned nail salons. *Gender and Society*, 17 (6), 820–39.

Kang, S. 2007. Disembodiment in online social interaction: Impact of online chat on social support and psychological well-being. *Cyberpsychology and Behavior*, 10 (3), 475–7.

Kaplan, J. 1989. Public pregnancy. *Self*, April, 155–7.

Kay, L. 2002. Frills and thrills – pleasurable dissections and responses to the abject: Female pathology and anthropology in *Déjà Dead* and *Silent Witness*. *Mortality*, 7, 155–70.

Kessler, S. J. and McKenna, W. 1978. *Gender: An Ethnomethodological Approach*. New York: Wiley.

King, C. 2004. Race and cultural identity: Playing the race game inside football. *Leisure Studies*, 23 (1), 19–30.

Kirk, S. 2010. How children and young people construct and negotiate living with medical technology. *Social Science & Medicine*, 71, 1796–803.

Kitzinger, S. 1992. Birth violence against women: Generating hypotheses from women's accounts of unhappiness after childbirth. In H. Roberts (ed.) *Women's Health Matters*. London: Routledge.

Klein, R. 2008. From test-tube women to bodies without women. *Women's Studies International Forum*, 31, 157–75.

Kolnai, A. 2004. *On Disgust*. Chicago and La Salle, IL: Open Court.

Kroker, A. and Kroker, M. 1988. *Body Invaders: Sexuality and the Postmodern Condition*. Basingstoke: Macmillan.

Kruger, E., Magnet, S. and Van Loon, J. 2008. Biometric revisions of the 'body' in airports and US welfare reform. *Body & Society*, 14, 99–121.

Kunzru, H. 1996. Interview with Donna Haraway. *Wired*, December, 84–7, 114.

Kuzmics, H. 1988. The civilizing process, trans. H. G. Zilian. In J. Keane (ed.) *Civil Society and the State: New European Perspectives*. London: Verso.

Kvigne, K. and Kirkevold, M. 2003. Living with bodily strangeness: Women's experiences of their changing and unpredictable body following a stroke. *Qualitative Health Research*, 13, 1291–310.

Kwan, S. and Trautner, M. N. 2009. Beauty work: Individual and institutional rewards, the reproduction of gender, and questions of agency. *Sociology Compass*, 3 (1), 49–71.

Laermans, R. 1993. Learning to consume: Early department stores and the shaping of the modern consumer culture (1860–1914). *Theory, Culture and Society*, 10 (4), 79–102.

Lakoff, G. and Johnson, M. 1980. *Metaphors We Live By*. Chicago, IL: University of Chicago Press.

Lambert, J., Laslett, P. and Clay, M. 1984. *The Image of the Elderly on TV*. Cambridge: University of the Third Age.

Lane, K. 1995. The medical model of the body as a site of risk: A case study of childbirth. In J. Gabe (ed.) *Medicine, Health and Risk*. Oxford: Blackwell.

Langman, L. 2008. Punk, porn and resistance: Carnivalization and the body in popular culture. *Current Sociology*, 56, 657–77.

Laqueur, T. 1990. *Making Sex: Body and Gender from the Greeks to Freud*. Cambridge, MA: Harvard University Press.

Lasch, C. 1979. *The Culture of Narcissism: American Life in an Age of Diminishing Expectations*. New York: W. W. Norton.

Lash, S. and Urry, J. 1994. *Economics of Sign and Space*. London: Sage.

Lawler, J. 1991. *Behind the Screens: Nursing, Somology and the Problem of the Body*. Melbourne and Edinburgh: Churchill Livingstone.

Lawrence, S. C. and Bendixen, K. 1992. His and hers: Male and female anatomy in anatomy texts for US medical students 1890–1989. *Social Science and Medicine*, 35, 925–34.

Laws, S. 1990. *Issues of Blood*. London: Macmillan.

Lawton, J. 1998. Contemporary hospice care: The sequestration of the unbounded body and 'dirty' dying. *Sociology of Health and Illness*, 20, 121–43.

Le Breton, D. 2004. Genetic fundamentalism or the cult of the gene. *Body & Society*, 10, 1–20.

Leder, D. 1990. *The Absent Body*. Chicago, IL: University of Chicago Press.

Lee, D. and Newby, H. 1989. *The Problem of Sociology*. London: Unwin Hyman.

Lee, J. 2008. Bodies at menarche: Stories of shame, concealment, and sexual maturation. *Sex Roles*, 60 (9–10), 615–27.

Lee, J. 2009. Escaping embarrassment: Face-work in the rap cipher. *Social Psychology Quarterly*, 72 (4), 306–24.

Lewin, E. and Olesen, V. (eds) 1985. *Women, Health and Healing: Toward a New Perspective*. New York: Methuen/Tavistock.

Lewis, J. 1993. Feminism, the menopause and hormone replacement therapy. *Feminist Studies*, 43, 38–56.

Lock, M. 1991. Contested meanings of the menopause. *The Lancet*, 337, 1270–2.

Loland, N. W. 2000. The art of concealment in a culture of display: Aerobicizing women's and men's experience and use of their own bodies. *Sociology of Sport Journal*, 17, 111–29.

Lonsdale, S. 1990. *Women and Disability: The Experiences of Women and Physical Disability*. London: Macmillan.

Lorentzen, J. M. 2008. 'I know my own body': Power and resistance in women's experiences of medical interactions. *Body & Society*, 14, 49–79.

Lowe, D. M. 1995. *The Body in Late Capitalist USA*. Durham, NC: Duke University Press.

Lupton, D. 1993. Risk as moral danger: The social and political functions of risk discourse in public health. *International Journal of Health Services*, 23, 425–35.

Lupton, D. 1994. *Medicine as Culture*. London: Sage.

Lupton, D. 1995. *The Imperative of Health: Public Health and the Regulated Body*. London: Sage.

Lupton, D. 1996. *Food, the Body and the Self*. London: Sage.

Lupton, D. 1997. Foucault and the medicalisation critique. In R. Bunton and A. Petersen (eds) *Foucault, Health and Medicine*. London: Routledge.

Lupton, D. and Seymour, W. 2000. Technology, selfhood and physical disability. *Social Science & Medicine*, 50 (12), 1851–62.

Lurie, A. 1992. *The Language of Clothes*, rev. edn. London: Bloomsbury.

MacDonald, H. 2006. *Human Remains: Dissection and its Histories*. New Haven, CT: Yale University Press.

Macfarlane, A. and Mugford, M. (eds) 2002. *Birth Counts: Statistics of Pregnancy and Childbirth*. London: HMSO.

McGillivray, A. 1997. 'He'll learn it on his body': Disciplining childhood in Canadian law. *International Journal of Children's Rights*, 5, 193–242.

McGrath, S. A. and Chananie-Hill, R. A. 2009. 'Big freaky-looking women': Normalizing gender transgression through bodybuilding. *Sociology of Sport Journal*, 26 (2), 235–54.

McKechnie, R. and MacLeod, R. 2007. Facing uncertainty: The lived experience of palliative care. *Palliative and Supportive Care*, 5, 255–64.

Mcleod, M. 1986. The role of science and technology in the process of medical specialisation. Unpublished PhD thesis, University of Edinburgh.

McRobbie, A. 1990. Women in the arts into the 1990s. *Alba*, September, 4–12.

McRobbie, A. 1991. *Feminism and Youth Culture: From 'Jackie' to 'Just Seventeen'*. Basingstoke: Macmillan.

Macsween, M. 1993. *Anorexic Bodies: A Feminist and Sociological Perspective on Anorexia Nervosa*. London and New York: Routledge.

McVeigh, R. and Rolston, B. 2009. Civilising the Irish. *Race and Class*, 51, 2–28.

Maffesoli, M. 1995. *The Time of Tribes: The Decline of Individualism in Mass Society*. London: Sage.

Maguire, J. and Mansfield, L. 1998. 'No-body's perfect': Women, aerobics, and the body beautiful. *Sociology of Sport Journal*, 15, 109–37.

Mansfield, A. and McGinn, B. 1993. Pumping irony: The muscular and the feminine. In S. Scott and D. Morgan (eds) *Body Matters*. London: Taylor & Francis.

Markson, E. W. and Taylor, C. A. 1993. Real world versus reel world: Older women and the Academy Awards. In N. D. Davis, E. Cole and E. D. Rothblum (eds) *Faces of Women and Aging*. New York: Haworth Press.

Marshall, B. 1994. *Engendering Modernity: Feminism, Social Theory and Social Change*. Cambridge: Polity.

Marshall, G. (ed.) 1994. *The Concise Oxford Dictionary of Sociology*. Oxford: Oxford University Press.

Marshall, H. 1996. Our bodies ourselves: Why we should add old fashioned empirical phenomenology to the new theories of the body. *Women's Studies International Forum*, 19, 253–66.

Martin, E. 1989. *The Woman in the Body*. Buckingham: Open University Press.

Martin, E. 1990. Toward an anthropology of immunology: The body as a nation-state. *Medical Anthropology Quarterly*, 4, 410–26.

Martin, L. J. 2010. Anticipating infertility: Egg freezing, genetic preservation, and risk. *Gender & Society*, 24, 526–45.

Mauss, M. [1934] 1973. Techniques of the body. *Economy and Society*, 2, 70–88.

Mauss, M. 1990. *The Gift: The Form and Reasons for Exchange in Archaic Societies*, trans. W. D. Hall. London: Routledge.

Mayall, B. 1998. Children, emotions and daily life at home and school. In G. Bendelow and S. Williams (eds) *Emotions in Social Life: Critical Themes and Contemporary Issues*. London: Routledge.

Mead, G. H. 1934. *Mind, Self and Society*. Chicago, IL: University of Chicago Press.

Mead, G. H. 1938. *The Philosophy of the Act*. Chicago, IL: University of Chicago Press.

Mead, G. H. 1949. *Male and Female: A Study of the Sexes in a Changing World*. Chicago, IL: University of Chicago Press.

Mellor, D., Fuller-Tyszkiewicz, M., McCabe, M. P. and Ricciardelli, L. A. 2010. Body image and self-esteem across age and gender: A short-term longitudinal study. *Sex Roles*, 63, 672–81.

Mellor, J. and Shilling, C. 1993. Modernity, self-identity and the sequestration of death. *Sociology*, 27, 411–31.

Mellor, J. and Shilling, C. 1997. *Re-forming the Body: Religion, Community and Modernity*. London: Sage.

Mennell, S. 1991. On the civilizing of appetite. In M. Featherstone, M. Hepworth and B. S. Turner (eds) *The Body: Social Process and Cultural Theory*. London: Sage.

Merleau-Ponty, M. [1962] 2001. *Phenomenology of Perception*, trans. C. Smith. London: Routledge.

Mishkind, M. E., Rodin, J., Silberstein, L. R. and Striegel-Moore, R. H. 1987. The embodiment of masculinity: Cultural, psychological and behavioural dimensions. In M. S. Kimmel (ed.) *Changing Men: New Directions in Research on Men and Masculinity*. London: Sage.

Moore, S. E. H. 2010. Is the healthy body gendered? Toward a feminist critique of the new paradigm of health. *Body & Society*, 16, 95–118.

Morgan, D. 1986. Doing gender. In R. Burgess (ed.) *Key Variables in Social Investigation*. London: Routledge.

Morgan, D. 1993. You too can have a body like mine: Reflections on the male body and masculinities. In S. Scott and D. Morgan (eds) *Body Matters*. London: Taylor & Francis.

Morgan, D. and Scott, S. 1993. Bodies in a social landscape. In S. Scott and D. Morgan (eds) *Body Matters*. London: Taylor & Francis.

Morris, J. 1993. *Independent Lives: Community Care and Disabled People*. London: Macmillan.

Mort, F. 1988. Boys' own? Masculinity, style and popular culture. In R. Rutherford and J. Chapman (eds) *Male Order: Unwrapping Masculinity*. London: Lawrence & Wishart.

Moscucci, O. 1990. *The Science of Woman: Gynaecology and Gender in England 1800–1929*. Cambridge: Cambridge University Press.

Mulkay, M. and Ernst, J. 1991. The changing position of social death. *European Journal of Sociology*, 32, 172–96.

Mulvey, L. 1975. Visual pleasure and narrative cinema. *Screen*, 16 (3), 6–18.

Murcott, A. 1993. Purity and pollution: Body management and the social place of infancy. In S. Scott and D. Morgan (eds) *Body Matters*. London: Taylor & Francis.

Nettleton, S. 1992. *Power, Pain and Dentistry*. Buckingham: Open University Press.

Nettleton, S. 1995. *The Sociology of Health and Illness*. Cambridge: Polity.

Nettleton, S. 1997. Governing the risky self: How to become healthy, wealthy and wise. In R. Bunton and A. Petersen (eds) *Foucault, Health and Medicine*. London: Routledge.

Nettleton, S. and Watson, J. (eds) 1998. *The Body in Everyday Life*. London: Routledge.

Nettleton, S., Burrows, R. and Watt, I. 2008. Regulating medical bodies? The consequences of the 'modernisation' of the NHS and the disembodiment of clinical knowledge. *Sociology of Health & Illness*, 30, 333–48.

Nicolson, L. 1994. Interpreting gender. *Signs*, 20, 79–103.

Nixon, S. 1996. *Hard Looks: Masculinities, Spectatorship and Contemporary Consumption*. New York: St Martin's Press.

Nixon, S. 1997. Exhibiting masculinity. In S. Hall (ed.) *Representation: Cultural Representations and Signifying Practices*. London: Sage.

Nussbaum, M. C. 2004. *Hiding from Humanity: Disgust, Shame, and the Law*. Princeton, NJ: Princeton University Press.

Oakley, A. 1980. *Woman Confined: Towards a Sociology of Childbirth*. Oxford: Martin Robertson.

Oakley, A. 1984. *The Captured Womb*. Oxford: Blackwell.

Oakley, A. [1972] 1985. *Sex, Gender and Society*, 2nd edn. London: Gower.

Oakley, A. 1998. Science, gender and women's liberation: An argument against postmodernism. *Women's Studies International Forum*, 21, 133–46.

Oates, T. P. and Durham, M. G. 2004. The mismeasure of masculinity: The male body, 'race' and power in the enumerative discourses of the NFL Draft. *Patterns of Prejudice*, 38 (3), 301–20.

Oberg, P. and Tornstam, L. 2001. Youthfulness and fitness – Identity ideals for all ages? *Journal of Aging and Identity*, 6 (1), 15–29.

Oetterman, S. 1984. *Tecken phuden*. Stockholm: Symposion Bokförlag.

Oliver, M. 1996. *Understanding Disability*. London: Macmillan.

O'Neill, J. 1985. *Five Bodies: The Human Shape of Modern Society*. Ithaca, NY: Cornell University Press.

O'Neill, J. 1986. Bio-technology empire, communications and bio-power. *Canadian Journal of Political and Social Theory*, 10, 66–78.

Orbach, S. 1988. *Fat is a Feminist Issue*. London: Arrow Books.

Ostrander, N. R. 2008. When identities collide: Masculinity, disability and race. *Disability and Society*, 6, 585–97.

Oudshoorn, N. 1994. *Beyond the Natural Body: The Archaeology of Sex Hormones*. New York and London: Routledge.

Ozawa de-Silva, C. 2002. Beyond the body/mind? Japanese contemporary thinkers on alternative sociologies of the body. *Body & Society*, 8 (2), 21–38.

Paterson, K. and Hughes, B. 2000. Disabled bodies. In P. Hancock, B. Hughes, E. Jagger, K. Paterson, R. Russell, E. Tulle-Winton and M. Tyler, *The Body, Culture and Society*. Buckingham: Open University Press.

Patterson, J. and Schroeder, J. 2010. Borderlines: Skin, tattoos and consumer culture theory. *Marketing Theory*, 10 (3), 253–67.

Patton, C. 1986. *Sex and Germs: The Politics of AIDS*. Boston, MA: South End Press.

Paulson, S. 2006. 'Beauty is more than skin deep.' An ethnographic study of beauty therapists and older women. *Journal of Aging Studies*, 22, 256–65.

Peletz, M. G. 2009. *Gender Pluralism: Southeast Asia since early Modern Times*. New York and London: Routledge.

Pellegrino, E. D. 1986. Rationing health care: The ethics of medical gatekeeping. *Journal of Contemporary Health Law and Policy*, 2, 23–44.

Phillips, A. and Rakusen, J. (eds) 1978. *Our Bodies Ourselves: A Health Book by Women for Women*. Harmondsworth: Penguin.

Phillipson, C. 1982. *Capitalism and the Construction of Old Age*. London: Methuen.

Pitts, V. 2005. Feminism, technology and body projects. *Women's Studies*, 34, 229–47.

Pointon, M. 1993. *The Body Imaged: The Human Form and Visual Culture since the Renaissance*. Cambridge: Cambridge University Press.

Pollock, L. 1983. *Forgotten Children: Parent–Child Relations from 1500–1900*. Cambridge: Cambridge University Press.

Poovey, M. 1987. Scenes of an indelicate character: The medical 'treatment' of Victorian women. In C. Gallagher and T. Laqueur (eds) *The Making of the Body: Science and Sexuality in the Nineteenth Century*. Berkeley, CA: University of California Press.

Poran, M. A. 2006. The politics of protection: Body image, social pressures, and the misrepresentation of young black women. *Sex Roles*, 55 (11–12), 739–55.

Prior, L. 1989. *The Social Organization of Death: Medical Discourse and Social Practices in Belfast*. London: Macmillan.

Prior, L. and Bloor, M. 1993. Why people die: Social representations of death and its causes. *Science as Culture*, 3, 346–75.

Probyn, E. 1995. Lesbians in space: Gender, sex, and the structure of missing. *Gender, Place and Culture*, 2 (1), 77–84.

Radley, A. 1995. *The Body and Social Psychology*. New York: Springer Verlag.

Rail, G., Holmes, D. and Murray, S. J. 2010. The politics of evidence on 'domestic terrorists': Obesity discourses and their effects. *Social Theory and Health*, 8, 259–79.

Rao, D., Pryor, J. B., Gaddist, B. W. and Myer, R. 2008. Stigma, secrecy, and discrimination: Ethnic/racial differences in the concerns of people living with HIV/AIDS. *AIDS Behavior*, 12, 265–71.

Rapp, R. 1999. *Testing Women, Testing the Fetus: The Social Impact of Amniocentesis in America*. New York: Routledge.

Reed, K. 2009. 'It's them faulty genes again': Women, men and the gendered nature of genetic responsibility in prenatal blood screening. *Sociology of Health & Illness*, 31, 343–59.

Rich, A. 1977. *Of Woman Born: Motherhood as Experience and Institution*. London: Virago.

Richardson, R. 1998. *Death, Dissection and the Destitute*. London: Routledge.

Riessman, C. K. 1992. Women and medicalisation: a new perspective. In G. Kirkupp and L. S. Keller (eds) *Inventing Women: Science, Technology and Gender*. Cambridge: Polity.

Ritzer, G. 1993. *The McDonaldization of Society*. London: Sage.

Roberts, D. E. 2009. Race, gender, and genetic technologies: A new reproductive dystopia? *Journal of Women in Culture and Society*, 34, 783–804.

Rodin, M. 1992. The social construction of premenstrual syndrome. *Social Science and Medicine*, 35, 49–56.

Rose, G. 1993. *Feminism and Geography: The Limits of Geographical Knowledge*. Cambridge: Polity.

Rose, N. 1990. *Governing the Soul: The Shaping of the Private Self*. London: Routledge.

Rose, N. 1996. The death of the social?: Re-figuring the territory of government. *Economy and Society*, 25, 327–56.

Rose, N. 2007. *The Politics of Life Itself: Biomedicine, Power, and Subjectivity in the Twenty-first Century*. Princeton, NJ: Princeton University Press.

Rothfield, P. 1997. Menopausal embodiment. In P. Komesaroff, P. Rothfield and J. Daly (eds) *Menopause: Cultural and Philosophical Issues*. London: Routledge.

Rowland, R. 1992. *Living Laboratories: Women and Reproductive Technologies*. Sydney: Pan Macmillan.

Russell, R. and Tyler, M. 2002. Thank heaven for little girls: 'Girl Heaven' and the commercial context of contemporary childhood. *Sociology*, 36, 619–38.

Ruzek, S. 1978. *The Women's Health Movement*. New York: Praeger.

Rysst, M. 2010. 'Healthism' and looking good: Body ideals and body practices in Norway. *Scandinavian Journal of Public Health*, 38, 71–80.

Sachs, A. and Wilson, J. H. 1978. *Sexism and the Law*. Oxford: Martin Robertson.

Salzman, M., Matathia, I. and O'Reilly, A. 2005. *The Future of Men*. New York: Palgrave Macmillan.

Sanders, T. 2004. Controllable laughter: Managing sex work through humour. *Sociology*, 38 (2), 273–91.

Savage, M., Barlow, J., Dickens, P. and Fielding, T. 1992. *Property, Bureaucracy and Culture: Middle Class Formation in Contemporary Britain*. London: Routledge.

Sawday, J. 1995. *The Body Emblazoned: Dissection and the Human Body in Renaissance Culture*. London: Routledge.

Scheper-Hughes, N. 2000. The global traffic in human organs. *Current Anthropology*, 41, 191–224.

Scheper-Hughes, N. and Lock, M. 1987. The mindful body: A prolegomenon to future work in medical anthropology. *Medical Anthropology Quarterly*, 1 (1), 6–14.

Schiebinger, L. 1993. *Nature's Body: Sexual Politics and the Making of Modern Science*. Boston, MA: Beacon Press.

Scott, S., Jackson, S. and Backett-Milburn, K. 1998. Swings and roundabouts: Risk anxiety and the everyday worlds of children. *Sociology*, 32, 689–706.

Scully, D. and Bart, P. 1978. A funny thing happened on the way to the orifice. In J. Ehrenreich (ed.) *The Cultural Crisis of Modern Medicine*. New York: Monthly Review Press.

Seale, C. 1998. *Constructing Death*. Cambridge: Cambridge University Press.

Seidler, V. J. 1994. *Unreasonable Men: Masculinity and Social Theory*. London: Routledge.

Seymour, J., Gott, M., Bellamy, G., Ahmedzai, S. H. and Clark, D. 2004. Planning for the end of life: The views of older people about advance care statements. *Social Science and Medicine*, 59 (1), 57–68.

Seymour, W. 1998. *Remaking the Body*. London: Routledge.

Shakespeare, T. 1994. Cultural representations of disabled people: Dustbins for disavowal? *Disability and Society*, 9, 283–301.

Shaw, R. 2010. Organ donation in Aotearoa/New Zealand: Cultural phenomenology and moral humility. *Body & Society*, 16, 127–47.

Sheach Leith, V. M. 2007. Consent and nothing but consent? The organ retention scandal. *Social Health & Illness*, 29, 1023–42.

Sheach Leith, V. M. 2008. Restoring trust? Trust and informed consent in the aftermath of the organ retention scandal. In J. Brownlie, A. Greene and A. Howson (eds) *Researching Trust and Health*. London and New York: Routledge.

Shildrick, M. 2008. Corporeal cuts: Surgery and the psycho-social. *Body & Society*, 14, 31–46.

Shildrick, M. and Price, J. 1994. Splitting the difference: Adventures in the anatomy and embodiment of women. In G. Griffin, M. Hester, S. Rai and S. Roseneil (eds) *Stirring it: Challenges for Feminism*. London: Taylor & Francis.

Shilling, C. 1993. *The Body and Social Theory*. London: Sage.

Shilling, C. 2003. *The Body and Social Theory*, 2nd edn. London: Sage.

Shilling, C. (ed.) 2007. *Embodying Sociology: Retrospect, Progress and Prospects*. Oxford: Blackwell.

Shilts, R. 1988. *And the Band Played On*. Harmondsworth: Penguin.

Silverman, D. (ed.) 1989. *The Impossible Dreams of Reformism and Romanticism*. London: Sage.

Simmel, G. 1908. *Soziologie: Untersuchungen über die Formen der Vergesellschaftung*. Berlin: Duncker and Humblot.

Simmel, G. 1971. *On Individuality and Social Forms: Selected Writings*, ed. D. Levine. Chicago, IL: University of Chicago Press.

Slevin, K. F. 2010. 'If I had lots of money . . . I'd have a body makeover': Managing the aging body. *Social Forces*, 88 (3), 1003–20.

Smith, D. E. 1990. *Texts, Facts and Femininity*. London: Routledge.

Sondheim, A. 2007. Gender, embodiment and ontology. *Transforming Cultures eJournal*, 2 (2), 201–25.

Sontag, S. 1991. *Aids and its Metaphors*. Harmondsworth: Penguin.

Sque, M. and Payne, S. A. 1996. Dissonant loss: The experiences of donor relatives. *Social Science and Medicine*, 43, 1359–70.

Stabile, C. 1994. *Feminism and the Technological Fix*. Manchester: Manchester University Press.

Stacey, M. 1977. *Health and the Division of Labour*. London: Croom Helm.

Stacey, M. 1988. *The Sociology of Health and Healing*. London: Unwin Hyman.

Stafford, B. 1991. *Body Criticism: Imaging the Unseen in Enlightenment Art and Medicine*. Cambridge, MA: MIT Press.

Stelarc. 1998. From psycho-body to cyber-systems: Images as post-human entities. In J. Broadhurst-Dixon and E. J. Cassidy (eds) *Virtual Futures: Cyberotics, Technology and Post-Human Pragmatism*. New York: Routledge, pp. 116–23.

Strathern, M. 1992. *Reproducing the Future: Anthropology, Kinship and the New Reproductive Technologies*. Cambridge: Cambridge University Press.

Sturdy, S. 1992. The political economy of scientific medicine: Science, education and the transformation of medical practice in Sheffield 1890–1922. *Medical History*, 36, 125–59.

Sudnow, D. 1967. *Passing On: The Social Organization of Dying*. Englewood Cliffs, NJ: Prentice-Hall.

Susman, J. 1993. Disability, stigma and deviance. *Social Science and Medicine*, 38, 15–22.

Sydie, R. A. 1987. *Natural Women/Cultured Men: A Feminist Perspective on Sociological Theory*. Milton Keynes: Open University Press.

Synott, A. 1993. *The Body Social: Symbolism, Self and Society*. London: Routledge.

Tamari, T. 2006. Rise of the department store and the aestheticization of everyday life in early 20th century Japan. *International Journal of Japanese Sociology*, 15, 99–118.

Taylor, S. and Tyler, M. 2000. Emotional labour and sexual difference in the airline industry. *Work, Employment and Society*, 14, 77–95.

Terada, S. 2007. Happy Buttocks: Toto ads take aim at America's great unwashed. *The Japan Times*, 15 November.

Tester, K. 1995. *The Flâneur*. London: Routledge.

Thomas, C. 1999. *Female Forms: Experiencing and Understanding Disability*. Buckingham: Open University Press.

Thomas, H. 1992. Time and the cervix. In R. Frankenberg (ed.) *Time, Health and Medicine*. London: Sage.

Thomas, L. 2009. Skin lighteners in South Africa: Transnational entanglements and technologies of the self. In E. N. Glenn (ed.) *Shades of Difference: Why Skin Color Matters*. Palo Alto, CA: Stanford University Press.

Thompson, E. P. 1967. Time, work-discipline and industrial capitalism. *Past and Present*, 36, 57–97.

Thomson, R. (ed.) 1996. *Freakery: Cultural Spectacles of the Extraordinary Body*. New York: New York University Press.

Throsby, K. 2008. Happy re-birthday: Weight loss surgery and the 'new me'. *Body & Society*, 14 (1), 117–33.

Thurren, B. 1994. Opening doors and getting rid of shame. *Women's Studies International Forum*, 17, 217–27.

Tiefer, L. 2010. Female genital cosmetic surgery: Freakish or inevitable? Analysis from medical marketing, bioethics, and feminist theory. *Feminism & Psychology*, 18, 466–79.

Timmermans, S. 2005. Death brokering: Constructing culturally appropriate deaths. *Sociology of Health & Illness*, 27, 993–1013.

Titmuss, R. 1970. *The Gift Relationship: From Human Blood to Social Policy*. London: Allen Lane.

Tober, D. M. 2007. Kidneys and controversies in the Islamic Republic of Iran: The case of organ sale. *Body & Society*, 13, 151–70.

Toerien, M. and Kitzinger, C. 2007. Emotional labour in action: Navigating multiple involvements in the beauty salon. *Sociology*, 41, 645–62.

Toffoletti, K. 2007. *Cyborgs and Barbie Dolls: Feminism, Popular Culture and the Posthuman Body*. London: I.B. Tauris.

Treneman, A. 1988. Cashing in on the curse. In L. Gamman and M. Marshment (eds) *The Female Gaze: Women as Viewers of Popular Culture*. London: Women's Press.

Tseelon, E. 1995. *The Masque of Femininity: The Representation of Woman in Everyday Life*. London: Sage.

Tulle-Winton, E. 2000. Old bodies. In P. Hancock, B. Hughes, E. Jagger, K. Paterson, R. Russell, E. Tulle-Winton and M. Tyler, *The Body, Culture and Society*. Buckingham: Open University Press.

Turner, B. S. 1984. *The Body and Society*. Oxford: Blackwell.

Turner, B. S. 1987. *Medical Power and Social Knowledge*. London: Sage.

Turner, B. S. 1992. *Regulating Bodies: Essays in Medical Sociology*. London: Sage.

Turner, B. S. 1996. *The Body and Society*, 2nd edn. London: Sage.

Turner, B. S. 1997. Foreword: From governmentality to risk, some reflections on Foucault's contribution to medical sociology. In R. Bunton and A. Petersen (eds) *Foucault, Health and Medicine*. London: Routledge.

Twigg, J. 2004. The body, gender, and age: Feminist insights in social gerontology. *Journal of Aging Studies*, 18, 59–73.

Tyler, M. and Abbott, P. 1998. Chocs away: Weight watching in the contemporary airline industry. *Sociology*, 32, 433–50.

Urla, J. and Swedlund, A. C. 2000. The anthropometry of Barbie: Unsettling ideals of the feminine body in popular culture. In L. Schiebinger (ed.) *Feminism and the Body*. Oxford: Oxford University Press.

USAID 2011. United States Agency for International Development HIV/AIDS Statistics. http://www.usaid.gov/our_work/global_health/aids/News/aidsfaq.html (accessed December 2011).

Valentine, K. 2005. Citizenship, identity, blood donation. *Body & Society*, 11, 113–28.

Van Doorn, N. 2010. The ties that bind: The networked performance of gender, sexuality and friendship on MySpace. *New Media and Society*, 12 (4), 583–602.

Van Doorn, N., Wyatt, S., Van Zoonen, L. 2008. A body of text. *Feminist Media Studies*, 8, 357–74.

Vigarello, G. 1988. *Concepts of Cleanliness: Changing Attitudes in France since the Middle Ages*. Cambridge: Cambridge University Press.

Wacquant, L. 1995. Pugs at work: Bodily capital and bodily labour among professional boxers. *Body & Society*, 1, 65–93.

Wainwright, S. and Turner, B. S. 2006. 'Just crumbling to bits?': An exploration of the body, ageing, injury and career in classical ballet dancers. *Sociology*, 40 (2), 237–55.

Wajcman, J. 1991. *Feminism Confronts Technology*. Cambridge: Polity.

Waldby, C., Rosengarten, M., Treloar, C. and Fraser, S. 2004. Blood and bioidentity: Ideas about self, boundaries and risk among blood donors and people living with Hepatitis C. *Social Science & Medicine*, 59, 1461–71.

Walkowitz, J. 1980. *Prostitution and Victorian Society: Women, Class and the State*. Cambridge: Cambridge University Press.

Walter, T., Littlewood, J. and Pickering, M. 1995. Death in the news: The public invigilation of private emotion. *Sociology*, 29, 574–96.

Wang, C. 1992. Culture, meaning and disability: Injury prevention campaigns and the production of stigma. *Social Science and Medicine*, 35, 1093–102.

Warner, M. (ed.) 1993. *Fear of Queer Planet: Queer Politics and Social Theory*. Minneapolis, MN: University of Minnesota Press.

Warner, M. 2000. The slipped chiton. In L. Schiebinger (ed.) *Feminism and the Body*. Oxford: Oxford University Press.

Waskul, D. and Vannini, P. 2008. Smell, odor and somatic work: Sensemaking and sensory management. *Social Psychological Quarterly*, 71, 53–71.

Waters, M. 1994. *Modern Sociological Theory*. London: Sage.

Watney, S. 1988. *Policing Desire: Aids, Pornography and the Media*. Minneapolis, MN: University of Minnesota Press.

Watson, J. 2000. *Male Bodies: Health, Culture and Identity*. Milton Keynes: Open University Press.

Wear, A. (ed.) 1992. *Medicine in Society*. Cambridge: Cambridge University Press.

Webb, L., McCaughtry, N. and MacDonald, D. 2010. Surveillance as a technique of power in physical education. *Sport, Education, and Society*, 9, 207–22.

Weeks, J. 1985. *Sexuality and its Discontents: Meanings, Myths and Modern Sexualities*. London: Routledge.

Weeks, J. 1986. *Sexuality*. London: Routledge.

Weeks, J. 1988. Aids: The intellectual agenda. In P. Davies, G. Hart and P. Aggleton (eds) *Aids: Social Representations – Social Practices*. London: Falmer Press.

Weitz, R. 2003. Women and their hair: Seeking power through resistance. In R. Weitz (ed.) *The Politics of Women's Bodies*, 2nd edn. Oxford: Oxford University Press.

Wellington, C. A. and Bryson, J. A. 2001. At face value? Image consultancy, emotional labour and professional work. *Sociology*, 35, 933–46.

Wernick, A. L. 1991. *Promotional Culture: Advertising, Ideology and Symbolic Expression*. London: Sage.

West, C. and Zimmerman, D. 1987. Doing gender. *Gender and Society*, 1, 125–51.

Whitehead, H. 1981. The bow and the burden strap: A new look at institutionalized homosexuality in native North America. In S. Ortner and H. Whitehead (eds) *Sexual Meanings: The Cultural Construction of Gender and Sexuality*. Cambridge: Cambridge University Press.

Williams, R. 1990. *A Protestant Legacy: Attitudes to Death and Illness among Older Aberdonians*. Oxford: Clarendon Press.

Williams, S. 1987. Goffman, interactionism and the management of stigma. In G. Scambler (ed.) *Sociological Theory and Medical Sociology*. London: Tavistock.

Williams, S. 1997. Modern medicine and the 'uncertain body': From corporeality to hyperreality? *Social Science and Medicine*, 45, 1041–9.

Williams, S. 1999. Is anybody there? Critical realism, chronic illness and the disability debate. *Sociology of Health and Illness*, 21, 797–819.

Williams, S. and Bendelow, G. 1996. Emotions, health and illness: The missing link in medical sociology? In V. James and J. Gabe (eds) *Health and the Sociology of Emotions*. Oxford: Blackwell.

Williams, S. and Bendelow, G. 1998. *The Lived Body: Sociological Themes, Embodied Issues*. London: Routledge.

Williams, S. J. and Bendelow, G. A. 2003. Childhood bodies: Constructionism and beyond. In S. J. Williams, L. Birke and G. A. Bendelow (eds) *Debating Biology: Sociological Reflections on Health, Medicine and Society*. New York: Routledge.

Williamson, J. 1978. *Decoding Advertisements: Ideology and Meaning in Advertising*. London: Boyars.

Willis, P. E. 1993. *Learning to Labour: How Working Class Kids Get Working Class Jobs*. Aldershot: Ashgate.

Wilson, J. 2002. Body work. <http://www.bbc.co.uk/arts/news_comment/weekinfocus/bodies.shtml> (accessed 12 March 2002).

Witz, A. 1992. *Professions and Patriarchy*. London: Routledge.

Witz, A. 2000. Whose body matters? Feminist sociology and the corporeal turn in sociology and feminism. *Body & Society*, 6 (2), 1–24.

Wolf, N. 1990. *The Beauty Myth*. London: Vintage.

Woodward, K. 1991. *Ageing and its Discontents: Freud and Other Fictions*. Bloomington, IN: Indiana University Press.

Woodward, K. 2009. Bodies on the margins: Regulating bodies, regulatory bodies. *Leisure Studies*, 28, 143–56.

Work, H. 2002. Big bellies and bad language: Carnivalesque in *The Sopranos*. *Media Education Journal*, 32 (Easter), 29–31.

Wrentling, T., Windsor, E., Schilt, K. and Lucal, B. 2010. Walk like a man, talk like a woman: Teaching the social construction of gender. *Teaching Sociology*, 38, 132–43.

Young, I. M. 1990. *Throwing Like a Girl and Other Essays in Feminist Philosophy and Social Theory*. Bloomington, IN: Indiana University Press.

Young, J. 1971. *Drugtakers: The Social Meaning of Drug Use*. London: Paladin.

Zimmermann, C. 2007. Death denial: Obstacle or instrument for palliative care? An analysis of clinical literature. *Sociology of Health & Illness*, 29, 297–314.

Zola, I. K. 1972. Medicine as an institution of social control. *Sociological Review*, 20, 487–504.

Zola, I. K. 1982. *Missing Pieces: A Chronicle of Living with a Disability*. Philadelphia, PA: Temple University Press.

Zola, I. K. 1993. Self, identity and the naming question: Reflections on the language of disability. *Social Science and Medicine*, 36, 167–73.

Index